More Than Friends, Less Than Lovers

More Than Friends, Less Than Lovers

Managing Sexual Attraction in the Workplace

David R. Eyler
Andrea P. Baridon

JEREMY P. TARCHER, INC.
Los Angeles

Lyric excerpt from "Unanswered Prayers" (Pat Alger/Garth Brooks/Larry Bastian) Copyright © 1990 Bait And Beer Music/Forerunner Music, Inc./ Major Bob Music Co., Inc./Mid-Summer Music Co., Inc. Reprinted by permission of CPP/Belwin, Inc.

Library of Congress Cataloging-in-Publication Data

Eyler, David R.
  More than friends, less than lovers: managing sexual attraction in the workplace/David R. Eyler, Andrea P. Baridon.—1st ed.
    p. cm.
  Includes bibliographical references.
  ISBN 0-87477-651-1: $18.95
  1. Sex in the workplace. I. Baridon, Andrea P. II. Title.
  HF5549.5.S45B95   1991   91-23853
  306.7—dc20   CIP

Jeremy P. Tarcher, Inc.
5858 Wilshire Blvd., Suite 200
Los Angeles, CA 90036

Distributed by St. Martin's Press, New York

Design by Lee Fukui

Manufactured in the United States of America
10 9 8 7 6 5 4 3 2 1

First Edition

Contents

To our many friends, our only lovers,
and the pleasant reality that we are neither
to each other.

Acknowledgments

WE WANT TO thank a few of the people who made this book possible. To our agent, Bert Holtje, we owe the magic title that set the stage for introducing a new model of how the sexes can work together enjoyably and productively. To Hank Stine, our editor, we owe our thanks for the structure of the book, the clarity of its ideas, and for seeing its potential before it was very well revealed. To those who shared their experiences and enthusiasm for the concept, we also say thank you. And finally, deep gratitude to Jeremy Tarcher, our publisher, without whose faith and determined management the idea may never have reached a bookshelf.

Introduction

IF YOU ARE attracted to someone with whom you are close, but know the feelings won't lead to love, you may want to consider a new relationship model—more than friends, less than lovers. If, in addition, the circumstances of your lives cast you together frequently and intimately, your chances for becoming more than friends increase. And if, in the course of your work, study, or other activities, you find yourselves pursuing the same goals, solving problems and overcoming obstacles together, trusting each other's instincts while making critical choices, and sharing the euphoria of successful teamwork, you may become a new kind of couple—strongly attracted but not attached—a more-than-friends-less-than-lovers couple.

The ideas for this book began with our own closely shared work and travel. Unburdened by an attraction that demanded an affair, we developed an "on the road," intermittent life together that had clear boundaries in time, place, and degree of intimacy. At the office and in our personal lives we remained quite naturally what we always had been—trusting, friendly colleagues. Away from the routine, however, usually on extended business trips, we enjoyed a deeper communication and sensitivity that arises only between a man and woman.

Among personal acquaintances, business associates, corporate executives, and peers in a business-travel culture that provided uninhibited cross-country-flight conversations on the subject, we met men and women in vastly different circumstances who told us about their own situations, where work or other shared interests produced an inexplicable but compelling bond. They defined the connection as a tremendous *something*, partially rooted in their sexual energies, but without the commitments, limitations, or guilt of illicit loving. They variously described their payoffs as an unexpected capacity for creative productivity, extra excitement in their work, and the thorough enjoyment of a relationship suspended harmlessly between friendship and romance.

These men and women, their feelings and experiences, formed the basis for this book, which is in three parts. First, we describe our view of what the new relationship is and is not, its characteristics and potential pitfalls. We tell you how the modern workplace can be a sexually tempting environment, but how you, with the knowledge and the will to do so, can turn temptation into a positive force in your lives and careers. Next you explore with us the stages of a full more-than-friends-less-than-lovers relationship from its unintended beginnings, through its sometimes awkward establishment, and into the productive and fulfilling pleasures of its advanced stage. Finally, we answer the inevitable questions of how the relationship affects and is perceived by others in the workplace and at home. In this section, we offer cautions and guidance to those of you who aspire to be more than friends and less than lovers, and reassurances for (1) employers who fear the disruption caused by office affairs and (2) spouses who struggle to understand how deep intimacy between their mates and another can spell anything but disaster for their marriages.

Whether you share business travel that at times provides opportunities for intimacy in exciting places or have discovered your attraction in the routine of office life, you can identify directly with the challenges and rewards described in this book. We introduce a new relationship model—more than friends, less than lovers—and we provide guidance for developing the skills to make it a positive experience, filled with personal and professional growth—for you, your significant others, friends, colleagues, and employers. We offer you techniques for managing your frankly acknowledged, but deliberately private and limited, sexual attraction. We provide procedures by which you define, assess, and nurture the relationship, and we explore potential pleasures and pitfalls and make suggestions for achieving an artful balance.

While the world of business, increasingly populated by both men and women, offers an obvious arena for confronting this challenge, there are many others. You might also discover such an attraction among teams of medical professionals, entertainers, professors and students, clergy and parishioners, athletes, therapists and clients, government officials, attorneys, and police officers to name just a few. The more-than-friends-less-than-lovers model is for men and women who share an intimate attraction and, for any of a multitude of reasons, decide not to resolve it romantically.

I

A New Relationship Model for the Workplace

1

1. Sexual Attraction in the Workplace

Y OU ARE A married woman working with an attractive, engaged man as administrative assistants in a large corporate headquarters. The two of you have to spend many frantic overtime weekends together assembling materials for critical Monday-morning meetings. The task is bearable because you and he find each other attractive and stimulating. You tackle assignments together with an enthusiasm that just wouldn't be there if it were a work-only situation. But as the relationship deepens, you have begun to wonder if you might not be tempting fate. Is it really possible to keep the excitement that fuels your working relationship without one or both of you becoming romantically tempted?

You are a male social psychologist, and often make your calls with a female caseworker. You and she share great empathy for those you serve—*and* an increasing attraction for each other. You are both involved in serious relationships with others. You'd like to tell her that while you're not interested in romance, you'd like to be more than casual friends. But you worry that she will misunderstand and become embarrassed or uncomfortable if you bring it up.

You are breaking through the so-called glass ceiling that stops many women from advancing beyond a certain level in the banking industry. In the process, you often find yourself paired with an attractive male colleague who accompanies you on out-of-town presentations. You are married; he has a girl-friend. Neither of you wants an affair, but you feel an attraction that you can't deny. It supplies a large measure of your business motivation and sparkle. You would like to keep the relationship growing, but only if it isn't going to wreck your careers and home lives. Can you maintain a sexy but sexless relationship?

You are a divorced man enrolled at a group counseling session for parents without partners, where you meet a widow whose husband recently died in an accident. As you come to sympathize with each other's predicament in the group, you expand your association to include spending time alone dis-cussing your lives and what lies ahead for each of you. You grow quite close and share a deep intimacy with each other. Still, you are not ready to become involved in a loving relation-ship again, and you worry that she may be looking for more. Is there a way to keep what you have, expressing the affection and caring without scaring the other person off or giving the message that you want to escalate the relationship?

You are a single woman who owns a unisex hairstyling salon. One of your operators, an attractive male, has helped you establish a clientele, and often accompanies you to eve-ning and weekend workshops where industry leaders teach the latest techniques. He is in an established relationship, and you aren't interested in becoming part of a triangle. In fact, there has never been any pressure to do so. Still, there's something sexy about doing business together that is positive for both of you, and the attraction between you adds tremendously to your creative energy. You want to keep it just that way—no more, no less. But is that asking too much of both of you?

You are a married man who is very involved in church work, and you cochair a statewide committee with a woman from a town about an hour away from your home. Many tele-phone calls and hasty business lunches at a point halfway be-tween your two homes find you growing quite close. But the occasional sexual feelings you have for her make you a little uneasy: married church workers aren't supposed to stimulate "those feelings" in each other. Might you find a way to manage the stimulation rather than run from it, one that gives you both satisfaction and discomfort?

In all of these cases the core elements are the same. The circumstances of your lives—your job, church, charitable work, therapy group, recreational activities, or whatever—have brought you together, without any deliberate initiative on your part, with someone of the opposite sex who ignites a special spark of interest. Although a sexual relationship is out of the question because at least one of you is happily married, committed to another lover, or otherwise not interested in an affair, you share a compelling personal attraction that includes an unmistakable sexual component. Like falling in love, this attraction is not something you anticipate or arrange. It simply occurs as the result of a chance pairing of chemistry and personality.

You are most likely to encounter the makings of such a relationship at a place where you stand an excellent chance of being thrown together with someone in your age group who has a similar socioeconomic and educational background, similar patterns of living, a similar set of values, and similar general aspirations.

The workplace is often where you unexpectedly find a member of the opposite sex to whom you are attracted, but it isn't the only setting where this might occur. Instead of work, you may share a common interest that becomes your focus. A school or social setting, a volunteer working arrangement, church work, a political campaign, a community-based lobbying group, an adult continuing-education class, a community cultural series, an aerobics class, a local theater group, tennis lessons—any of these situations could provide you with the circumstances in which to develop a deep attraction, which you must keep limited because of other commitments.

Your early encounters are pleasant but uneventful. You don't try to impress each other; the attraction develops slowly and naturally. It is not something you deliberately cultivate. It doesn't sweep you off your feet. Because events dictate your time together, the fact that you find each other interesting is almost incidental at the beginning.

For a while, the attraction remains subtly in the background, and you may not recognize how strong it has become for some time. Eventually, you spend enough time working together that you begin to realize there is *something* special developing between you. The two of you *connect* in a way that suggests something stronger than conventional friendship, and you enjoy each other's company beyond just the pleasure you take in the work you share.

You may even greet the emergence of this attraction with surprise. You are the same two people as you were before. Why would sexual attraction enter the picture now? How could it be that you hardly noticed each other before being assigned to the same project?

Your success in dealing with physical attraction to a co-worker is critical because each of you, with careers and other relationships to nurture, has much to lose if you fail. If you value your marriage, the respect of your associates, and the integrity of your work, you will not wish to risk the consequences of an affair. Yet circumstances may eventually place you across the table from someone of the opposite sex with whom you share the potential for far more than ordinary friendship.

Consequently, you are left with a whole new area of potentially problematic, and painfully confusing, personal relations. You face the difficult task of handling a relationship that has no place among people's traditional expectations: it is neither completely romantic nor completely platonic. It has an initial similiarity to a budding affair, and you need special skills to make the distinctions for yourself, your partner, and those upon whom your relationship impacts at work and home.

We have not yet created rules or social structures for dealing with today's unfamiliar intermixture of men and women working together who meet and develop personal attraction—and the old rules are obsolete. Traditionally we have lived in societies in which opportunities for relationships and interaction between the sexes have been severely limited, and have taken place within clearly drawn boundaries. Unmarried men and women who were attracted to each other could date, court, or marry, raising no eyebrows unless romance interfered with work. But the only options for attracted couples who were already married or committed to someone else were either to studiously avoid each other and possible temptation, or to have an affair that they attempted to keep secret.

Traditional advice would have you avoid or downplay man/woman attractions at work—or have one of you, usually the woman, find a new job. This approach was fundamentally unfair because it was usually based on assuming the worst about human character and not allowing for the possibility of controlling the attraction rather than actually giving in to it.

"Each person has to work out his or her own resolution. Some resolve it by working hard to make sure feelings never develop," writes David L. Bradford and his colleagues in their article "The Executive Man and Woman: The Issue of Sexuality." "However, although such a solution prevents the problem from arising, it may have a hidden cost, for to be so concerned and guarded against ever developing attractions can produce a greater than necessary distance and formality. . . . Another resolution distinguishes between feelings and behavior. The former need not dictate the latter. People have much more control over their actions than over their emotions. A person can have strong feelings of attraction, and these can continue to exist without leading either to an affair or to disruption of the work relationship."

Further complicating matters is the likely possibility of disappointment in an affair that does not progress fully to the satisfaction of one or both participants. Feelings of exploitation or rejection may lead to recriminations on the part of one or both participants and all the hurt feelings, damaged relationships, and disrupted working routines that go with them. In *The Third Sex,* Patricia McBroom writes that former lovers may "begin slugging through professional channels. But even if the two hide their feelings and conduct themselves with polite discretion, there is an emotional price to be paid every day they walk into the office and have to face the person with whom they once shared a dream."

Even when a sexual attraction in the workplace does not result in an affair, the very nature of the friendship, which would be wholly unsuspect if it were between two heterosexual members of the same sex, may be laden with (1) personal confusion, (2) harassment, either actual or perceived, and (3) misunderstanding. This can make life in both the workplace and the home difficult. Your supervisors may perceive a loss of morale among those who are close to you, a decline in your professional objectivity and productivity, unpleasant gossip and factions among the office staff, and bad publicity in the business world. Your spouse might imagine an affair that doesn't exist and attempt to defend against or attack it, resulting in estrangement—even divorce and the breakup of the family.

Either option—an affair or avoidance—can make working together difficult and uncomfortable for the two of you at best, and impossible at worst.

More important, the intimacy, sexual energy, and enthusiasm generated by your attraction, properly and creatively channeled, can yield tremendous productivity when you harness and direct it toward business objectives. As Bradford and associates write, "Friendship and liking are important facilitators in work, be they between the sexes or with the same sex." The attraction generates creativity and motivation to do your best for the company, and creates positive morale for both of you, who are able to enjoy each other's company while heightening your productivity as a team.

Studies of workplace behavior endorse the legitimacy of controlled attraction and cite it as being good for productivity.

According to Leola Furman's research at the University of North Dakota, work teams composed of men and women were more productive than those made up of same-sex colleagues. This makes the sexual chemistry between professional colleagues a force to be reckoned with—and positively. Thus when you and a coworker find yourselves attracted to each other, you can turn your work into a passion—a creative endeavor that generates energy unknown in ordinary relationships. This makes your relationship a net plus on a personal dimension as well as for the organization that employs the team. Focused and managed, your attraction can motivate you to do more, with greater energy and enthusiasm, than your ordinary business associates.

Psychologist Lillian Rubin observes that the sexual element provides "a certain zest, a special excitement," not present in same-sex pairings. It contains "a flirtatious quality" that creates vitality and excitement. Work just would not be the same without it. The energy that transfers to the work comes from your sexual attraction, and the motivation for extended effort together is partially sexual. Rubin continues: "Sex, whether acted on or not, both gives the relationship a special charge and also creates difficulties that are not easily overcome." Unlike traditional sexual pursuit, there are no written rules for such a relationship. It can be confusing and puzzling as well as exciting.

This all suggests a new option, a third possibility: the more-than-friends-less-than-lovers relationship. You make use of sexual attraction to deepen your relationship and become more successful and productive together than either of you could be separately, while focusing and channeling the sexual aspects in such a way that you avoid becoming involved in an affair. It is a far more realistic and productive approach to dealing with personal attraction between coworkers, one that allows you to manage and redirect the attraction toward productive ends that benefit everyone involved. In making your relationship clearly understood as personally intimate and professionally ambitious, yet romantically limited, you consciously choose to become more than friends and less than lovers.

The story of Jason and Nancy, who formed such a workplace relationship when they found themselves alone at their place of work during a severe snowstorm, illustrates the way safely limited nonsexual intimacy heightens and energizes shared work.

Jason, a technician at a downtown medical laboratory, and Nancy, an attractive woman ten years his junior who had joined the staff only a few months before as an administrative assistant, shared no regular work assignments. If it hadn't been an unusually bad winter, they most likely would not have become anything more than coworkers.

Jason, whose family had not yet relocated to follow his work, heard on the radio the weather-related closings that entitled him to roll over and not make the trek to the lab, although it was just a few blocks away from his small studio apartment. However, the prospect of spending the day in his apartment was so unappealing that he opted to shave, shower, and head for the lab.

Once there, he made coffee, answered the calls of suburban colleagues looking for reassurance that they should stay home, and proceeded to tackle long-neglected tasks. An hour later, Nancy, who also lived only a short walk away, arrived at the laboratory. Jason had not been involved in her hiring and knew little about her except her name and the fact that she was waiting for her husband to join her after completing a remote unaccompanied tour of duty with the military.

Jason and Nancy exchanged pleasantries about the weather and the coffee and went their separate ways. It felt good to have another warm body in the quiet, empty space, and, as the day passed, they nonchalantly acknowledged this to each other. Early afternoon arrived. Nancy stayed to finish a project; Jason left early; and the day ended uneventfully.

A few weeks later, Nancy and Jason again were the only staff in the lab when snows once more virtually closed the city for two days. On the foundation of their previous experience, they talked over morning coffee and bagels in the lunchroom, and this time their conversation was more protracted and personal. Nancy pitched in and helped him unravel a drug-testing report for a client company that he couldn't have finished alone. Jason appreciated it, and she enjoyed making the contribution. The afternoon ended. They departed seperately, both thinking the day had been more interesting and productive due to the other's company.

That winter was the worst in the city's history. Other storms came and went. Nancy and Jason continued to work on snowy days and looked forward to their private time in the empty laboratory. They came to know each other well as they shared comfortable, uncomplicated intimacy, confined to these hours and these days. Their coworkers were aware that they had manned the facility during the snows, but had no inkling that they shared a special relationship. In fact, during the regular working day they had only occasional project overlaps and, therefore, minimal contact.

However, as winter turned to spring, Jason and Nancy realized that they had begun a new kind of relationship. They were two people with narrow but complementary voids in their lives. Both had marriages that were of great importance to them but were temporarily out of reach. Jason and Nancy didn't discuss their personal situations in depth, but each developed an unspoken appreciation of the feelings of the other that brought them close.

Jason and Nancy's association had its sexual dimension; that the laboratory was empty and their two apartment were within short walks was lost on neither of them. They were tempted by the human urge to reach out to each other physically more than once, but for reasons they considered obvious, they instead cultivated a private and intimate friendship that meant a lot to both of them and never would have occurred had it not been for their work situation and the repeated exposure to each other that it provided. Jason and Nancy discovered:

- Work has a powerful socializing influence on those who share it. People we find at work are prescreened to be of potential interest to us personally—similar career paths, socioeconomic backgrounds, educations, social agenda, and so on.
- We open personal doors more readily to those we already know as members of the company family.
- Work provides some of us with a home away from home. For Jason and Nancy, during snowstorms that comfined them to activities within walking distance, spending the day in the laboratory with another human being was more desirable than spending it alone at their respective apartments.
- Work provides us with natural opportunities to communicate without anxiety. An attraction we might not pursue outside the business environment takes root in the time and privacy of shared work, and in it finds a comfortable environment in which to be nurtured in an unobtrusive way until it is established.

A NEW KIND OF WORKPLACE, A NEW KIND OF DILEMMA

You work in a world where the roles of professional women and men have changed in important ways—a world in which you find countless opportunities for working friendships to develop into even more intimate relationships. Today, the other half of a team may constitute not only a colleague with complementary skills and similar interests, but an attractive member of the opposite sex as well. As a result, men and women who share similar training, career objectives, and ambitions might spend long hours together, but not as siblings, spouses, or lovers. You interact as professional peers in settings that create the potential for sexual attraction—overtime spent completing special projects alone together or assignments that place you together inside the office, working in close collaboration.

Historically, there were few women working outside the home until the late 1800s, so men and women rarely mixed socially after marriage. The women went off to one room (usually the kitchen or nursery) together, doing and talking *women things,* while the men gathered on the porch, and later around sports events on TV, talking *men things.* So they lacked opportunities for the kind of interaction that could lead to involvement with someone besides their spouses.

Then in the 1890s women began to move into the workplace, but in clearly subordinate roles. Only "twenty years ago women with chemical engineering degrees often started as secretaries," writes Janice Castro in a special issue of *Time.* Attraction and sometimes affairs between the superior (male boss) and the subordinate (female secretary) took place.

Today, Castro notes, not only the number of women in the workplace has changed but the *role* they play as well. No longer are they automatically subordinate: "Nearly 18 percent of doctors are now women, as are 22 percent of lawyers, 32 percent of computer systems analysts, and nearly half of accountants and auditors." James Martin and Sheila Murphy agree: "The demography of the American labor force has changed significantly over the past twenty-five years, so that far more men now spend their days working next to women—women who are their equals, not their secretaries. In 1960, the work force was composed of 34 percent women [in mostly subordinate positions] and 66 percent men; by 1980, it was 42 percent women and 58 percent men. Looked at it in another way, work-force participation among women rose from 34 percent to 51 percent in only twenty years."

Today, statutes and protocols have given women an equal place, and "in medicine, law and management, [women] have increased their participation by 300 percent to 400 percent since the early '70s," writes Barbara Ehrenreich. And the office is not the only workplace coworkers share today. "Business travel, once . . . the domain of salespersons, sports and entertainment figures, pilots, and the military, is now exploding across the globe. As technology develops and the world shrinks . . . , people with backgrounds as divergent as banking, communications, fashion, manufacturing, health, foodstuffs, and education are hitting the road . . . and the airways," writes Denise V. Lang in *The Phantom Spouse*.

Fewer than twenty years ago, when a relative handful of women were working side by side with their male counterparts as professionals, and ninety-nine out of one hundred business travelers were men, sexual attraction at work was rarely an issue. With men and women suddenly making up nearly equal proportions of the work force, often in positions of relative equality, the opportunity for attraction, sexual temptation, and the emergence of confusing relationships between them has increased enormously. Thus the odds of your developing personal attraction at work or on the road with a coworker of the opposite sex have also increased enormously.

Sexual Attraction at Work

No matter how we try to avoid it, women and men today spend a lot of time with each other during the working day, and perhaps in the after hours of evening obligations or business travel. In the extended workplace, we find all the ingredients for personal attraction:

- attractive physical and intellectual traits
- levels of energy that complement your own
- conversations that suggest larger questions; she or he might hold the key to professional insights you feel you lack or self-knowledge you feel is incomplete
- confirmation that you're desirable in the eyes of a worthy companion

- something that is situationally forbidden and more intoxicating because it is forbidden
- satisfaction of accomplishment and success together that comes from the above qualities and justifies further development

Physical attraction. Simpler species, lacking the complex emotions of humans, are attracted by shapes, colors, movement, and smells that trigger reproductive responses. Their territory is a mating ground on which a prescreened cadre of potential breeding partners examine one another in a protracted way. In much the same way, we are stimulated by the appearance, scents, and movements of our coworkers and involuntarily react to signals that nature designed to be alluring long before we developed language to express our desires or discovered the connection between sexual activity and the reproduction of our species. In the grand scheme of things, the workplace, for all its restraint, is indeed part mating ground. We inevitably find sexual stimulation there despite all the reasons we might feel we should not.

Intellectual attraction. A coworker may be a near-perfect complement to our interests and abilities. Years of similar preparation on similar career tracks have given us both similar knowledge. To utter an idea and have it not only instantly grasped but also rapidly developed in challenging new directions is exciting. Such moments of understanding create a sense of intellectual kinship and intimacy.

Shared energy levels. In any setting, we are attracted to those who share our pace and our energy level. None of us enjoys being held back, or being dragged reluctantly into activities in which we find no value. Those who share our pace and way of doing things are those with whom we would normally spend more time, grow closer, and seek greater personal intimacy if the opportunity presented itself. We are drawn to those among our colleagues whose approaches to accomplishing the task at hand are compatible with our own.

Positive self-image. No matter how many good qualities we might actually have—looks, brains, compassion, or whatever—we are all insecure about ourselves to some degree and never tire of positive feedback. To find the source of such feedback in an attractive peer is all the more gratifying. Author Peter Marsh believes that "we become interested in people who . . . support our self-esteem—people who will confirm our worldview and tell us that we have worth as individuals."

This is not unlike the primitive competition to be perceived as the most attractive breeding stock on the tundra—or in the jungle. Men and women in the modern workplace retain the drive to sort and be sorted on the basis of desirability in one another's eyes. Only someone to whom we are attracted can comfirm our status as attractive. Positive reinforcement makes us look forward to future encounters, as mutual attraction is fed by appreciation for one another.

Forbidden attraction. Few things are as enticing as that which we know we can't have. And the workplace may offer us someone we can't have. We may not even wish we could, but this doesn't diminish the attraction. In the case of a forbidden romance with a work partner, we establish the perfect bewitching contradiction. All the risks of the forbidden are there—our careers, marriages, reputations, even the threat of rejection and disappointment. Array this set of dangerous consequences against constant exposure to the temptation (the attractive coworker), throw in intimate working situations— perhaps even travel away from home—and we have a protracted struggle with the forbidden in the midst of our working lives.

Accomplishments. Sexiest of all the attractions in the workplace is success itself—winning as a team of two. It is easy to see this as prima facie evidence that we belong together—that we are well-matched peers with a mandate to share our lives more completely.

Working Together and Courtship

Compounding natural attraction in the workplace is the fact that work can create courtshiplike conditions that subliminally and subconsciously reinforce our perceptions of ourselves as a couple, and our expectations that sex will naturally accompany this involvement.

Privacy. Like courtship, work brings us together in intimate privacy. Our time spent working together in private becomes, by practical reality, intimate time. When that happens, we see and learn things about each other that were never apparent before. As in courtship, personal pluses that were overlooked become apparent, and a relationship grows as two people have the time to become comfortable and exchange intimate communication in the privacy of the modern workplace. As Marilyn Moats Kennedy points out in *Office Warfare,* "People get involved in the workplace because . . . the relationship has time to develop a solid base of shared experience before anyone does anything overt. They become friends first."

A dating situation. Like courtship, work creates a dating situation. We find ourselves making what amount to dates for meals. We touch glasses in toasts to common interests, spend periodic weekends doing things we mutually enjoy, and sometimes end our evenings with the reluctant good nights of people growing interested in knowing each other better. We are two coworkers whose pattern of working together places us in a swiftly moving stream of natural behavior that parallels what dating couples do—a working dinner at a favorite eating place near the office, or the emptiness of an unpopulated office on a weekend or evening, where we turn on the radio to music we both enjoy, order pizza for dinner, and replace our formal business clothing with jeans and sneakers. We have come together for a common business purpose, but soon it is colored with the pleasure of time spent together.

Work is exciting. Working together to the successful conclusion of a team effort can be euphoric. Just observe the winners of the World Series in their locker room. They laugh and cry and hug and pour champagne on one another, rejoicing and exalting in the success of their common effort.

"Shared work brings shared emotions," James Martin and Sheila Murphy commented in the *Washington Post*, "and occasionally in moments of success or failure, physical gestures of affection. Professional athletes often embrace after a big win; so do trial attorneys. When a work project brings with it a high degree of tension, stress, and competition, the response to 'winning'—whether it is the contract, the design concept, the political strategy, or the sales goal—naturally and effortlessly yields the social-sexual release of touching, holding, and hugging. Winning is exciting. Physical connection in response to both [is] natural and charged."

In *Corporate Wives—Corporate Casualties,* Robert Seidenberg recognized the sexual magic of shared working excitement: "As people who have interesting careers have always known, work is very sexy, and the people with whom one is working are the people who excite. A day spent launching a project or writing a paper or running a seminar is . . . likely to stimulate—intellectually and sexually."

Similar people with time to share. Like courtship, work brings together people with many things in common. When we spend long hours together, whether at the office or on the road, we may come to know someone intimately with whom we share many similar interests. Coworkers of the opposite sex spend a lot of time together pursuing the same goals and sharing the same successes and disappointments. "People in the same workplace tend to be drawn in the same mold," writes Dr. Carl Eisdorfer, psychiatrist and president of Mount

Sinai Medical Center. "You are probably more like the people you work with than in many instances you are like members of your family. The things you read, the things you talk about, the social events you attend in connection with work—all these give the opportunity for warmth and intimacy."

According to Marilyn Kennedy, coworkers may "have months, even years, to learn about each other under many different conditions." In working together many hours a week we learn to know each other's "wants, anxieties, vulnerabilities and prejudices."

Long periods together. Like courtship, work creates long periods of shared activity. During hectic business cycles, we may spend more time with our colleagues than with our spouses, and the circumstances might be far more conducive to intimate communication than those of a harried domestic setting. There are things that only people who have "lived" their work together can share, according to Michael McGill: "The time we spend with others, and the variety of things we know about them, bond us together, creating the interpersonal exchanges that lead to intimacy."

OLD OPTIONS AND NEW HOPE

At some time or other in our careers, most of us probably will be sexually attracted to a coworker. But until recently, most men and women who felt a strong attraction for a coworker thought their choices were limited to either becoming involved in an affair or avoiding the temptation completely. Because they believed that their feelings were taboo, they were unable to candidly discuss their attraction and how they might deal with it without guilt.

Despite today's somewhat relaxed social standards, this dilemma is still a common one. Most professional men and women, when asked, will say that sex with coworkers is taboo, that there is just too much to lose. According to Patricia A. McBroom, many in the work world view love affairs as dangerous because they make us "vulnerable to double doses of trouble when things go bad. A man or woman who, for whatever reasons, has trouble with a sexual or romantic union in a career setting runs the risk of being hurt professionally and personally."

Affairs

Like most people in the workplace, you probably have imagined having a sexual relationship with a coworker, especially if you've spent a lot of time together, find each other attractive, and share common interests. But often, one or both of you have family commitments or career concerns that keep a love affair from being a real-life option.

For most of us, a workplace affair is one of the most destructive acts that we can engage in. Two dominant underpinnings of our lives are put at risk: (1) the love of our spouses, and (2) the trust and confidence of our employers. In actuality, the ripples of a failed affair reach out into even broader life interests that exist in the shadows of marriage and work, such as:

- our image in the community and among professional colleagues and friends, and ostracism by some or all of them
- our own self-image as we continue to discover the negative impacts of the affair on the lives of others
- loss of trust with our spouses, accompanied by loneliness as they withdraw emotionally from us
- the economic impact on our careers and lives; we may even end up providing support to a family that we are no longer part of

Faced with a powerful sexual attraction and ample opportunity to act on it, you may not pause long enough to consider the odds against remaining unscathed. Seduced by the siren song of passion, your minds may conspire to convince you that a physical relationship is the only way to go. Without a workable alternative to expressing your feelings, you make the decision to deepen your intimacy the only way you know—by entering into a love affair.

According to anthropologists, the mating behavior of hundreds of generations remains imprinted on us while we now have to function within a workplace that places demands for restraint on us undreamed of in more primitive times. The powerful sexual urges that have brought men and women together for millennia endure, and in spite of our increased social sophistication they surface abruptly, triggering natural responses that, without conscious management, may lead to a workplace affair.

Swept up by overpowering impulses they do not know how to control, most people begin to look for reasons to justify or rationalize their actions rather than admit the truth. Over the years, people drawn toward affairs they knew would prove destructive have rationalized:

- that the affair can be conducted secretly and simultaneously with their marriages because the relationships take place in different locales
- that they can devote time, money, and personal energy to an affair and not have them missed at home or at work
- that the impact of guilt will be small
- that they can tolerate living with important parts of their lives concealed
- that the impact on their work will be minimal
- that the responses of company management and coworkers to their affair will be neutral or indifferent
- that the affair will have no effect on their reputations among family, friends, supervisors, coworkers, and clients
- that their physical relationship will forever be thrilling and unaffected by discovery, routine, or a status change in the relationship

- that their lover shares the same time frame for the relationship's progress
- that both participants will remain content with the status of clandestine lover
- that neither will want to escalate the relationship into a life-changing event, or if so, the other's wishes will be compatible

Even when the attraction is less compelling and you remain ambivalent, in the absence of any other reasonable alternative, you may in time drift unconsciously into an affair. You start out hoping the attraction will just go away on its own, and instead, nature takes it course—with the two of you eventually falling into each other's arms.

Or, one of you may feel the attraction more strongly than the other and pressure the other into reluctant acquiescence. This is seldom a happy situation for either of you for very long. For the one who initiates the affair, the excitement of acting out the sexual desire subsides, while the reluctant partner begins to resent being pressured into an association more contrived to meet the other's needs than his or her own, and the relationship disintegrates as recrimination overrides attraction.

Although women today take an active role in initiating sex and asserting themselves sexually, the male is still the most frequent initiator—and likely to be the most insistent partner when it comes to the subject of having an affair. As Michael McGill noted in his study of male intimacy, "Nearly every woman who befriends a man and becomes intimate with him must sooner or later deal with his sexual desires. When the time comes, the woman holds the fate of the relationship in her hands." Whether it is the male or female partner who pressures the other to deepen the relationship through sex, the result is always disastrous.

Having an affair may provide a fleeting release for desire that we think we are unable to repress. Weighed objectively,

though, the benefits are all short-lived, the negative consequences all long-term.

For example, at the beginning you enjoy a stimulating
physical relationship with someone attractive, who, at this
point, appears to be an undemanding and self-sufficient person. But as the newness of the physical relationship yields to
predictable familiarity, or one or both of you may begin to feel
insecure (especially since you are not officially committed to
each other), jealous, and possessive. Like a marriage or any relationship that has lost its newness, you question things that
should be taken in stride—wondering about your partner's
loyalty, stretching to be something you feel you must be—
instead of enjoying the relaxed confidence of mutual time
spent with each other.

Your once-sexy relationship has become complicated.
You seem to be continually making secret arrangements to
meet; you are always concerned about not being seen; you lie
to your spouse and feel guilty about it. The excitement is gone,
and you wish you hadn't given in to your hormones.

As the initial glow fades into the reality of two people
coping with their lives together, there is even an excellent
chance that you will eventually face the same problems in your
affair that you do in your marriage—familiarity, routine, control, and incompatible expectations. In every relationship,
even with close friends of the same sex, you grow weary of
certain personal traits and activities you share too often. The
newness you initially thrive on becomes the familiarity from
which you seek flight.

Up till now, coworkers had few guidelines to help them
manage their sexual feelings, so when the right circumstances
were presented, many began a destructive clandestine romance, as the story of Dana and Kevin illustrates.

*Kevin's marriage was a utilitarian one in which both spouses
worked too hard and took too little time for themselves. Their
children were the focus of all their energy and attention. Dana*

was a bit older, divorced, with a grown son, and known for her independence when it came to life after working hours. They met in a job-training program for workers displaced by the closing of a local manufacturing plant and were surprised to find themselves hired as a team of troubleshooting technicians for a network of office-equipment service contractors.

After several months of day trips together in the region, Kevin and Dana found themselves spending several days outside their region in Louisville to resolve an especially trying series of problems in the headquarters of a national hospital-management company. As yet, they didn't know each other well, and gave little thought to each other as anything more than a team member with complementary skills.

Dana's knack for electronics matched Kevin's for mechanical things; they worked efficiently and quickly. They had built a reputation as the best team in the region, the major reason they had been brought to Louisville in lieu of a local team. At home, they often made long drives between service calls, and they took advantage of the time and privacy to get to know each other well. Eventually, Kevin saw in Dana what he no longer had at home—a woman who excited him, shared his interests, and enjoyed being with him. She had no romantic entanglements and seemed as attracted to him as he was to her. He was sure they could be the exception: become physically as well as emotionally intimate with no complications and no one hurt.

After a late dinner in the hotel in Louisville, following an exhilarating day on the job, Kevin and Dana found returning to separate rooms particularly difficult. Yet they had so thoroughly dissected the topic of physical intimacy that there was nothing left to argue. The answer for both of them was still a resounding no.

As she lay in her bed, Dana asked herself why she was being so prudish at the midpoint of a life that was good, but unadorned with any great sense of romantic satisfaction. She thought that maybe she was foolishly denying herself deserved joy.

Turning in bed, she remembered a fantasy that Kevin had

described once. They had endured their usual parting, but as he drifted into sleep alone, she came to his room. Without words, they embraced and with slow-motion deliberateness basked in a passion long denied.

Impulsively, Dana decided to fulfill Kevin's fantasy. He didn't say no. They were passionate and joyful that night, but they were faced by grim reality in the following days and months. Kevin still had a wife and family to whom Dana did not want to cause pain, and try as they might, they couldn't keep their liaison secret from the office or from their clients around the region. A splendidly simple fascination with boundless promise became a fantasy fulfilled that irreparably damaged their lives and careers.

For Dana and Kevin, the focus rapidly changed from their professional to their personal relationship. The unconsummated attraction that had energized their work was gone. Their ability to find creative solutions to their clients' problems faded as their enthusiasm for each other dwindled. Kevin and Dana were wracked with guilt, romantic jealousy, and possessiveness, and were no longer productive as a team.

Kevin's wife and children felt hurt and betrayed. The personal warmth that was ebbing from the marriage when the affair began now quickly disappeared. Routine and overwork might have been fixable; broken trust and infidelity were not. An integral unit consisting of a mother, father, and children had been fractured, with the father split off from the others and reestablished in their minds as someone hurtful, deceitful, and never to be taken into their full confidence again.

The company management and their coworkers felt angry and embarrassed by their indiscretion. Clients no longer explicitly requested their services; their professional reputations were damaged. Their professional value was greatly diminished in the eyes of their employer. Where once they were seen as essential staff who contributed mightily to the enterprise, they now detracted from its energy and even its image as a disciplined and positive entity whose workers constituted a welcome presence in the community—role models in other people's daily lives.

They no longer looked forward to long rides to work sites, and out-of-town travel became a ritual to endure—mechanical passion, even more guilt, and finally, the weighty fatigue of a spent affair. This was not the objective of the intimacy they sought with each other, and when the reality failed to match the dream, their relationship dissolved. Like most people who engage in office affairs, they were both left alone, with heavy losses in their professional and personal lives.

Withdrawal

Faced with a powerful personal attraction, most people who do not wish to mar their lives with an affair become frightened and decide that the safest thing to do is withdraw emotionally, and perhaps physically as well. Avoiding the other person and the situation this way at first may seem safer than confronting the attraction, but it tends to make your workplace communication with each other uncomfortable, unsettled, and awkward. This can have only a negative impact on your work together, its quality and success, and both of your self-images.

You feel unable to revert to your former state of comfortable intimacy, but are equally at a loss as to how you might deal with a sexual attraction that you acknowledge to yourself but are reluctant to discuss with your partner. What if it's one-sided and you are rejected? Or worse, what if it's mutual? If you both admit it and talk about it, aren't you admitting something that is considered wrong? Afraid to move either backward or forward, you compensate with distancing that doesn't work: the caring still shows, but it isn't permitted to add the sparkle it should to your lives and careers. You are safely away from feelings that make you feel guilty about something that hasn't even happened, but incapable of grasping the possibility of exploiting the energy of those feelings and using them productively—as more than friends. The story of Roberta and Andrew offers an example of this type of confusion and withdrawal.

Andrew and Roberta shared a longstanding friendship. They and their spouses had an excellent social rapport. Roberta held a senior marketing position in a crosstown division of the Atlanta investment firm where Andrew was a partner. Roberta's husband, Tom, managed a successful health club.

When they got together, it was Andrew's wife, Ginny, and Roberta's husband, Tom, who dominated the conversation. Andrew and Roberta were quieter people who found themselves on the other side of the room talking together. There were unarticulated feelings of attraction between them, along with expectations that there were much deeper things for them to share— intimate, exciting things. And, given that they were husbands and wives of others, potentially frightening things.

Their firm was about to introduce an initiative marketing the stock of a joint venture by several Silicon Valley companies. Andrew was designated to spend a few weeks on-site examining their management. Quite independently, Roberta was chosen to make the trip to devise a marketing strategy. They were booked in the same hotel in the Silicon Valley. Andrew and Roberta looked forward to the trip.

Their first days were busy, and each had seperate evening obligations. But on Friday, they decided to have dinner together in the hotel and discuss work events.

As the evening wore on, their conversation drifted from business to personal matters, as it usually did when they were together for any length of time. But this time it was different. The environment had changed. They were in a position to act on what had never really been a convenient possibility before. Their once-effortless friendship was taking on new and surprisingly uncomfortable dimensions.

As appealing as the whole situation was to their egos— each had the pleasure of comfirming that he or she could

*seriously tempt the other—they were no longer comfortably inti-
mate. They said awkward good nights that left them both filled
with unresolved, ambivalent feelings and questions. They both
wondered if an affectionate touch would have been misunderstood and sent the other running away, or encouraged him or
her to move too close.*

*And just exactly what was the attraction they felt for each
other—mind? body? sense of humor? intellect? forbidden fruit?
all or none of the above? And did the other feel it as strongly?
What would the next day, week, or year bring if they shared a
bed that night? Would they ever be comfortable together again?*

Why did they feel so guilty? After all, nothing happened.

*Over Saturday-morning coffee, both Roberta and Andrew
were at a loss to give their relationship an acceptable direction,
and after all their years of chattering away together, they were
silent. Something had happened between them, but they didn't
have the courage to discuss it.*

*After another busy week, Roberta and Andrew caught a
plane back to Atlanta. The former easy intimacy and comfort
were gone. At work, they lapsed into a guarded communication,
both hesitating to encourage anything, and their potential for inspired work together on the Silicon Valley project was lost. In the
company of their spouses, their former effortless communication
was constrained because of doors that had opened only far
enough to let them see danger, and because neither was sure if he
or she would walk away from the other the next time they were
alone. Their solution was to avoid spending time alone together.*

Roberta and Andrew's relationship was ultimately a
failure because they failed to talk about how they really felt
about each other and what they could and could not expect
to share. They had established and successfully tested sexual
boundaries, but instead of communicating directly and providing feedback to each other, they retreated and individually
decided that they had no options other than having an affair or
running from feelings that made them feel guilty.

A New Option: The More-Than-Friends-Less-Than-Lovers Relationship

The two options we've discussed—romantic involvement and flight—deny us the sustainable spark of excitement that can bring a great deal of energy and enthusiasm to our work. But there is another option—one that has grown from the trial-and-error experiences of men and women who not only have sidestepped the trauma of an affair but actually have found a way to continue to channel the excitement that flows from their sexual energy into productive work.

In "The Executive Man and Woman: The Issue of Sexuality," David L. Bradford and his colleagues write, "One of the most consistent findings of social psychological research is that contact leads to liking, which in turn leads to more interaction. Two people who work together for some time learn to trust, rely on, and respect each other with a corresponding increase in liking. . . . Knowing a man and woman as an equal may remove the mystique and could lead to a rich friendship without sexual involvement."

For reasonable people, attraction can and does stop short of destructive romantic commitment many times a day. According to Leola Furman, a social worker at the University of North Dakota who studied man-and-woman colleagues, most opposite-sex associations remain platonic: "Many recognized that there was a sexual undercurrent to their friendship but kept it under control. Just as they didn't go around bopping someone every time they felt angry, they didn't say, 'Let's hit the couch,' every time they had a sexual feeling."

This is basis of the more-than-friends-less-than-lovers model, in which a man and a woman determine that they will not have a romantic relationship, but keep the sexual feelings and deliberately sublimate them into their work together. By doing so, they grow to know each other intimately, inspire each other creatively, and spare themselves the inevitable disruption of careers and personal lives that are the consequences of affairs.

Rather than withdrawing or engaging in an affair, you can learn to consciously channel the power of the sexual attraction you feel into new heights of creativity and productivity—at work and in your personal lives. You can learn to consciously and safely manage, even deepen, the attraction and intimacy, turning your relationship into something that is far more than mere friendship, yet remains significantly less than romance.

A well-executed more-than-friends–less-than-lovers relationship offers you a creative outlet for your sexual attraction while preserving the excitement. You acknowledge the attraction, even nurture it, but avoid the problems associated with acting on it, while sharing a deep nonphysical intimacy free of the complications of love.

In a more-than-friends–less-than-lovers relationship, your work and your personal interaction have a positive synergy—each contributing constructively to the other. You aren't deceiving anyone or stealing time from work, so you don't waste energy on feeling guilty. Instead, you can work consciously together to develop the basis for a unique relationship that harnesses your personal attraction to heighten production and creativity while remaining compatible with your existing lifestyle and obligations. Such a relationship allows you to capture much of the charm and enthusiasm of an affair, but without the guilt and anguish that come from living a lie.

The more-than-friends–less-than-lovers model thus offers you a way to avoid affairs or painful misunderstandings while maximizing the productive aspects of your especially well-matched male-female team. You can use this energy as you consciously control its direction with mutually established and maintained restraint. There are rewards for both of you personally and professionally:

- You find a satisfying, intimate way of interacting with the opposite sex that frees you from having to choose between a passionate affair and withdrawal from each other.

- You bring the inevitability of sexual attraction among coworkers out of the office closet and let it find its motivational and creative application in broad aspects of your professional lives.
- You sublimate sexual tension and focus the resulting energies on sharing each other's company in a non-destructive, controlled way that makes you a more productive team.

You can accept the good parts of being a business couple together, enjoy your simulated courtship in the work setting, find the whole process sexually stimulating, and still draw boundaries where you must. If you consciously manage your behavior from the beginning, you can enjoy an exciting relationship without threatening either your marriage or your career. Doug and Janet are typical of many who have done so.

Janet and Doug worked as computer-systems trainers/troubleshooters in a firm that assigned them to specific regions within their home state. Their relationship at the office had been pleasantly superficial. Neither registered with the other as anything remotely more than another member of the staff. Normally assigned to different territory, they were asked to conduct a joint training session at a large corporation that had just installed a new system in Minneapolis. After coordinating their schedules, they proceeded to make their travel arrangements independently. Doug give his wife a copy of his itinerary and left a few days before Janet because he had additional business to conduct prior to the training exercise.

On the road, Doug tidied up his business and hurried to the concourse to meet his colleague's arriving flight. When Janet mentioned that the corporate travel agent had put her in an airport motel, Doug suggested changing to his quieter one nearby since they had only one car. She agreed and secured a room of her own.

After unpacking, Doug called to tell Janet he'd be at the

pool. As she approached from a distance a little while later, they saw each other differently for the first time. She had a surprisingly well-proportioned body and hair that bounced naturally just off bare shoulders. Doug's hair was wet and disheveled, unlike his usual ultragroomed look. Suddenly, the two coworkers saw each other as a woman and man instead of as perfectly appointed business associates. No alarms sounded, but they found the relaxed setting very appealing, and each noticed that the other was really quite attractive.

Their work as joint trainers was fruitful. They were sent out regularly as a team, and their unanticipated attraction blossomed. No specific event or time marked the occasion, but each of them realized that a deep trust amd warmth had grown between them. Janet and Doug found themselves looking forward to their next assignment.

As the job grew more complex, they developed an intimacy that at times rivaled the depth—if not the breadth—of their marriages. At first, they talked about how they perceived other people's feelings; later they talked about their own.

Janet emphatically dismissed an affair as an option for her. Having seen Janet in her swimsuit, Doug was less vehement, but he ultimately agreed that an affair would be counterproductive to their business success and credibility and would betray the trust of their spouses. While there was a slight imbalance—Janet was more deeply attached to her spouse than Doug was to his—he respected her feelings and never attempted to breach this barrier, inspiring even deeper trust on her part, leading to increased intimacy. They acknowledged their attraction to each other, discussed its frustrations, and arrived at behavior boundaries that were acceptable to both of them. Janet and Doug promised to warn each other whenever one or the other felt the relationship was getting off track.

Through it all, they shared not so much as one kiss, nor was a hand ever held too long. Quite by accident at first, but with constant communication and careful management later, they had become far more than friends, but comfortably less than lovers.

The following elements made Doug and Janet's relationship a workable one.

- They were able to develop sufficient trust to discover their potential together.
- They agreed to communicate openly and honestly.
- They set limits to their intimacy at the very beginning, promised to respect them, and agreed to steady the course if one or the other was out of line.
- They attached great value to their work together so that its preservation became a primary focus for the relationship, with their attraction seen as supporting, not dominant.
- Both were willing to extend sufficient nonphysical intimacy for the relationship to be worthy of valuing and perpetuating.

The difference between their successful example and the unsuccessful ones described earlier was conscious management. Doug and Janet made choices instead of allowing their attraction either to drive them blindly into short-term pleasures or to frighten them away from its potential. They took control of the path of their association, directing their sexual attraction toward a sustainable more-than-friends-less-than-lovers relationship.

The balance of this book is devoted to showing you techniques and approaches for channeling the sexual energies generated by your workplace attraction to benefit you, your employer, and your loved ones. You will find out how you can:

- discover a previously unrecognized path of controlled, marvelously uninhibited self-exploration and sharing without traditional commitments or obligations
- constructively focus the excitement generated by your attraction on your professional effort—channeling it into your work rather than consummating it sexually
- reaffirm your primary relationship as you take sexual desire home to your lover.

2. *The More-Than-Friends-Less-Than-Lovers Relationship*

AS MORE THAN friends and less than lovers, you and a coworker with whom you share a strong attraction can move to an intense level of intimacy and caring that is beyond everyday friendship but stops short of romantic love. While friends can surely experience a kind of love and lovers can indeed be friends, as more than friends and less than lovers, the two of you develop a relationship that is different in intensity from either of these alternatives. As more than friends, you add a dimension of increased intimacy to your friendship, and as less than lovers, you remove the sexual aspect of your love.

The more-than-friends-less-than-lovers relationship can certainly have its sexual moments and overtones. The important distinction is that they do not carry with them the expectation of physical love. During the course of your association, the two of you may share moments of great personal revelation and intimacy, but unlike lovers, you do not expect to share your bodies and souls with each other. You divulge only those thoughts that you choose to; others may be totally off-limits.

This is a limited relationship. You do not need to know or tell all. You will and can give a great deal—and yet not give all.

Intimacy need not be synonymous with sex. On the contrary, as more than friends and less than lovers, the two of you can focus the positive energy of sexual attraction on your work from the safety of a consciously managed relationship founded on mutual trust, respect, and acceptable boundaries. With these boundaries in place, consciously agreed on, and monitored by both of you, a relationship of remarkable intimacy and power can blossom and grow.

The more-than-friends-less-than-lovers relationship provides the structure for successfully enjoying the experience—without hurt and without guilt. Your relationship might unfold like this:

1. You and an attractive colleague of the opposite sex are assigned professional duties that require working together as a team.

2. The assignment brings you into periods of prolonged intimate contact where you find new energy and creativity in your combined effort.

3. You find yourselves spending extended hours side by side, working with intense energy and closely sharing a wide range of emotional experiences—from rock-bottom lows to exhilarating highs. And you discover, a step at a time, that you enjoy not only what you do but also the person with whom you do it.

4. From shared efforts and emotions, you develop an unspoken connection and relate as two people who know each other very well, cultivating a deep non-physical, nonloving intimacy and mutual trust.

5. You become pleasantly aware of sexual overtones, and one or both of you rules out a sexual relationship due to prior commitments, concern for professional integrity, or other reasons. Instead of becoming sexually involved, you discuss the sexual attraction, recognize the contribution of its energy to your ability to work

well together, and agree to channel it into enhancing your productivity instead of gratifying the underlying physical aspects of the attraction.

6. You set boundaries for the relationship and agree to respect them, periodically adjust and expand them to accommodate the dynamics of the growing relationship, and give up some of the original spontaneity of your attraction in order to operate within those boundaries.

7. You realize that you are going to have to consciously manage the relationship if the attraction is to stay within the allowable boundaries of your professional and personal lives. You agree to practice restraint in the face of inevitable sexual temptation and to share the obligation of monitoring and resolving unacceptable departures from the relationship's boundaries.

8. You know that the attraction and intimacy are a direct outgrowth of work, and depend on the professional relationship. You don't spend evenings together during your leisure time, nor do you call each other at home just to chat. The relationship is a private one, limited to shared work time, and is not a conspicuous part of your everyday lives.

9. You mutually commit to the relationship and discover that you feel safe and trusting as you pursue increasingly intimate levels of knowing each other, realizing in the process that a man and woman can find each other professionally stimulating and personally attractive *and* successfully develop both of these aspects without sexual involvement.

This relationship has as its foundation the sexual attraction between men and women. This is what distinguishes it from ordinary friendship. Lillian Rubin, a psychologist and authority on friendship, explains that this sexual component is the distinguishing characteristic between friendship and more intimate relationships:

> *For most of us, the sexual encounter taps layers of feelings that, in adult life, are unique to it—feelings that are roused, at least in part, by the actual blurring of boundaries that takes place only in sex. Whether in a man or woman, this fusion seems to promise to fulfill our most archaic amd infantile fantasies, exposing in us a set of needs and longing for union with another that are anti-thetical to a friendship. For sex requires the merging of two people—not just physically but psychologically as well— where friendship rests on respect for their separateness.*

As more than friends and less than lovers, you can go beyond the separateness of friendship to substantial intimacy and closeness, but without crossing the boundaries to the complete merging of a physical relationship.

For the more-than-friends-less-than-lovers couple, at-traction is the magnet that tugs the participants toward each other—the focus that draws them together in a manner that normally might have paired them as lovers. It is a multifaceted attraction that includes elements of sex, love, romance, friend-ship, work, and intimacy, each in a deliberately limited way. In the right doses, these elements combine and pull men and women into the process of discovery, creativity, and produc-tivity that constitutes both the means and the end for a relationship.

THE FIVE KEYS TO THE MORE-THAN-FRIENDS-LESS-THAN-LOVERS RELATIONSHIP

By applying the following five keys to your relationship, you can achieve a stability and self-assurance that lets you enjoy the attraction you feel as more than friends and less than lovers

while you focus it to stimulate creativity, inspiration, and productivity neither of you would ever have achieved alone.

Setting Boundaries

Our personal boundaries are the psychological barriers that
define us as individuals. These boundaries vary in purpose and
intensity throughout our lives. Establishing, accepting, and
maintaining personal boundaries are central to succeeding as
more than friends and less than lovers. You need a strong sense
of your own values and purposes to risk sharing them intimately with someone else—even more so when you rely on
your boundaries to permit tremendous personal intimacy yet
prevent its becoming physical.

As more than friends and less than lovers, you and your
partner establish boundaries and expectations for the relationship at the *outset* as a means for defining and consciously managing it. You determine what sort of boundaries will allow
you to enjoy the pleasure of each other's company in a way that
respects the realities of your lives and yet allows you to thrive
on your sexual attraction.

You agree that your relationship will not be allowed to
become a love affair. Some boundaries, such as the sexual one,
are lines that you agree are not to be crossed, and remain forever out of bounds. Related boundaries may include physical
contact and using the language of lovers. Neither has a place in
your relationship and will send only misunderstood signals.

Other boundaries are dynamic and expand as you trust
and grow together. You might feel safe in expanding the kinds
of situations in which you allow yourselves to be alone, be
willing to discuss certain facets of your personal lives, comfortably give and accept compliments, allow your partner to
see you when you're not at your best, be willing to share the
company condominium, admit the high value you place on the
relationship without fear of being misunderstood, and so on.

You may also have internal boundaries with which to

deal—very personal ones that you maintain without the knowledge of your partner. These are the lines you draw for monitoring your own thoughts and behavior. For example, coping with near-love feelings is a personal matter that each of you must handle in your own way. Some people do this by determining which emotions they consider acceptable and deliberately stopping short of those they feel are not. Others accomplish it by denying the forbidden feelings, keeping an internal boundary that, while imperfectly maintained, says, in effect, "I can't feel that way; therefore I don't."

As more than friends and less than lovers, you respect each other's privacy and do not use the relationship to satisfy invasive curiosity. Part of the contract between you is an agreement to respect personal boundaries and individual identities. However, as time passes and you establish confidence in each other, you will expand the boundaries to include many areas that were initially off-limits. When you feel you must reinforce a boundary, you can do so indirectly, by altering the direction of a conversation, or directly, by discussing the unwelcome inquiry openly as a part of the process of consciously managing your relationship.

Conscious Management

There are no sure paths to ideal relationships between mutually attracted men and women in any circumstances, much less for those romantically committed to others and destined to face each other every business day. Without conscious relationship management, personal attraction can lead to destructive consequences—from ruined marriages to tainted professional reputations.

Conscious management is the key to successful more-than-friends-less-than-lovers relationships. Consciously managing your behavior will prevent your relationship from crossing the boundary into an affair. You consciously make your association a series of purposeful, directed events rather than

random ones that could drift into unplanned physical intimacy. You expect to have differences that you will resolve together openly. Instead of dancing around issues and leaving
yourself open to risk, through discussion you create a volun-
tary contract in which you both:

- agree that since a sexual relationship is not in the cards,
  you will divert your sexual energy from personal attraction between you to the working relationship supporting it
- agree that your attraction is a positive thing that makes
  your working relationship exciting and worthy of the
  extra effort you give it
- define ways to behave that will help you maintain your
  mutual boundaries
- analyze thoroughly the potential for what might develop as you combine your working and personal relationships
- communicate honestly with each other about your feelings and expectations
- make no attempt to keep your relationship secret from
  your spouse, lover, or company managers, though you
  maintain discretion
- expect to grow and change together, being open to expanding old boundaries and establishing new ones as
  your trust in each other increases

In short, you agree to consciously direct your relationship toward a specific and limited set of objectives that are
helpful in accomplishing your personal and professional goals
together. You do so in the context of much broader, separate
lives that include important events and people outside the
highly valuable but bounded relationship that the two of you
share as more than friends and less than lovers.

At first, you will probably find it difficult to discuss the
emotional issues involved in creating and consciously managing your relationship. Although you've made a contract with

each other that is intended to be as inviolable as if you had both signed on the dotted line, you are still at an unsettled stage where you don't want to convey more commitment than is appropriate, and you are not sure what constitutes the right measure. It takes experience and the kind of trust that comes later in the relationship to feel comfortable expressing caring that might be misconstrued early on in the relationship, before you have learned to trust each other more completely.

You build this trust by consciously following a six-step plan to manage problems before they start. You:

1. *sense when tension builds* and something needs to be brought into the open for discussion and resolution
2. *communicate honestly*, both verbally and nonverbally, about what you want and don't want
3. *monitor your own and your partner's behavior* for any signals of unbalanced expectations, breaching of boundaries, jealousy and possessiveness, or attempts to escalate the relationship
4. *provide and be ready to receive prompt feedback* as a result of the above monitoring
5. *deliberately redirect your sexual energies* to your work if you should be tempted to fall in love or become sexually involved
6. *remain receptive to maximum growth* and shared experience within the relationship's parameters

With conscious management, you can establish a mechanism to deal with the problems, misunderstandings, unbalanced expectations—to put things in perspective without hurt or misunderstanding. The means of control themselves require ongoing revision to suit the evolving relationship. As you develop trust and comfort with each other, you make any needed adjustments and keep your relationship as vital as it can be within the boundaries you have agreed to while moving it forward along a path that will enrich your work and your lives.

Monitoring Each Other

You share responsibility, along with increased productivity and personal growth, in the more-than-friends-less-than-lovers relationship. Part of your job is to keep your own behavior, expectations, and feelings in line with the established boundaries. Another part is helping your partner do the same. Monitoring each other will ensure that open communication indeed takes place when you sense your partner is about to infringe on a boundary or is losing the battle with temptation and wants to make the relationship more physical.

Two people seldom approach a relationship with perfectly matched expectations. As more than friends and less than lovers, you have defined a mutually acceptable middle ground that represents what you both want, are willing to tolerate, and hope to gain in the relationship. You can make it work only by communicating honestly with each other when you see signs that you have begun marching to different relationship drummers. When the beat one of you hears is substantially out of tune with that obviously being heard by the other, it's time to provide some feedback. Whatever the point of contention, monitoring each other in this way is the necessary first step leading to open communication and needed change.

Monitoring plays its most important role by setting the expectation of open communication as a standard. You come to your relationship with respect for each other's intellect, tastes, and working competencies. You look to each other to supplement what you individually bring to your work—to stimulate your thinking and enhance your creativity. This process requires interacting intimately, constantly monitoring your boundaries and your own and your partner's behavior. Your egos are secure, your feelings protected by the fact that you both know that adjustments in your behavior will sometimes be necessary to keep things on an even keel. Through monitoring, you help keep each other on the right track and within safe boundaries, enabling you and your partner to reason together, make the required changes, and proceed onward.

Open Discussion

Where conscious relationship management, along with monitoring, is the overarching technique you use to keep your behavior within its boundaries, open discussion is a primary tool used to achieve this goal. By openly discussing your feelings, you can help keep the relationship in its proper perspective by:

- clarifying areas of misunderstanding where individual interpretations of events have been wrong or incomplete
- raising concerns from the level of internalized one-person coping to the consciousness of two-person reasoning
- venting frustration to each other, as well as understanding and being understood—thus eliminating the need to reject and the pain of rejection

You gain tremendous staying power as a more-than-friends-less-than-lovers couple from your ability to bring your relationship's frustrations to full consciousness and deal with them together. Open communication short-circuits problems that tend to build with time—misperceptions that, left unresolved, feed dissension and ultimately bring your relationship crashing down, with neither of you certain as to just what triggered the fall.

Sometimes you find good cause for questioning the validity of continuing in your relationship. Open communication doesn't always bring the answer you want to hear, but it does put the issue on the table for exploration and possible resolution. At other times, once you've clarified your intentions

by direct communication, you laugh at a simple misunderstanding that could have become major; relationship ghosts
tend to fade in the light of honest inquiry. The secret is not in a
perfect progression through some ideal set of relationship-
building steps, but rather in the openness that says, "Ask me.
Let's talk about it. I'm sure we can work this out." Short of
fundamental differences that cannot be resolved, open communication will dispel the more innocuous suspicions and
misunderstandings that shouldn't be allowed to build unwanted walls between you. It gives you the feedback necessary
to use the other keys that make your assocation self-renewing
and viable.

Cooling-Off Periods

Unlike husbands and wives, as more than friends and less than
lovers you have the advantage of regular time-outs from each
other, away from a nonphysical but intimate, demanding association. You come together for purposeful periods of work
that you enjoy and do well. It ends there until the time comes
to do it again.

In permanent relationships, a large tolerance quotient is
both desirable and required. By contrast, in the limited more-
than-friends-less-than-lovers association, you are not obli-
gated to keep each other happy or take care of each other—or
tolerate different tastes in food, music, or television shows on a
daily and nightly basis. This can be critical for cooling down
work-frayed tempers or passions that seem to be getting out of
hand. While you deny yourselves some of the privileges of a
fully committed couple, you earn the right to avoid some of
their frictions.

Thus on those rare occasions when work isn't going well,
or your usual conscious management techniques aren't fully
handling the sexual aspects of your attraction, you can acknowledge that this is not going to be the right day to accom-

plish much together, and part company until you are again back in sync. Since you are both comfortable discussing problems, this is not an escape mechanism to avoid dealing with them, but a way of stepping back and gaining a renewed perspective from a comfortable distance.

Inspired work is intense, demanding, and fulfilling. And when it ends, there is ambivalence in your parting. Because you enjoy what you do so much, you are reluctant to stop, but at the same time you feel a sense of relief in getting away from each other for a time to relax with your family and friends. The creative juices stimulated by your hours together need to be complemented by a change of pace. Your expectations of each other in the working area are high: you view your partner as special, and you both expect a lot from your partnership. Down time spent apart allows you to keep your partner in that special niche. If you spend too much time together, the faults you easily tolerate for short periods of time may become extremely irritating, or you may lean toward sharing too much, causing your interaction to become routine and predictable. Then some of the magic ebbs away.

Instead, proper balance is a necessity for the more-than-friends-less-than-lovers work style. You find a rhythm that comes naturally out of your work—never too much time between sessions, never a continuous association that becomes counterproductive. You attack the task at hand by the numbers and with good form—helping each other in every way you can, motivating each other to make the extra effort. Then, pleasantly exhausted, you cool down as the intensity of your most productive hours lapses into refection, consolidation, and signals to each other that you're spent and it's time to go. You return to your marriages and family relationships, where you are able let the intensity of this special work relationship flow out of your minds for a while—until it's time to begin again.

You can see how all this works in the story of Jean, an

attractive middle-aged woman who got her law degree late in life and loves her work as an advocate for tenants in the city's rent-control wars, and Stan, who just turned thirty and is a federal civil servant with prestigious security clearances and a pretty wife who is even busier than he is.

As president of his building's tenants' association, Stan found himself spending long hours with Jean, reviewing strategy for foiling his landlord's moves to raise the rent.

One evening when his wife was out of town on business, Stan hosted a tenants'-association board meeting at his apartment. Not by design, he and Jean paused in a heated exchange of views to notice that they were looking out across the lights of the city from an empty apartment; the others had gone, one by one. It was the first opportunity they had to comfront what both had felt and not expressed openly: they found their work on behalf of others stimulating, and each other of more than mere professional interest.

Jean's husband had taken early retirement a year before and expected her to join him wintering in the sun. He was disappointed to learn that she was too attached to her work to spend months away from it. And her quitting was out of the question. Divorce was never discussed, but they had tacitly agreed to separate lives. He was gone during much of the winter, and she visited him periodically for a long weekend.

Stan and Jean continued to see each other at hearings and still met to work on certain issues. They tried denying the special feelings that accompanied their genuine professional relationship without much success. Finally, after a lot of private thinking on both their parts, they agreed to meet to sign some petition at a local restaurant, and both had other business in mind as well.

As compelling as he found the idea of a "Mrs. Robinson" attraction, neither did Stan want to cheat on his ambitious young wife, with whom he shared a lot of treasured aspirations, nor could he afford to risk security clearances with an affair that

*might cause an inappropriate bleep on his next polygraph test.
To his great relief, Jean wasn't any more interested in an affair
than he was. What they both wanted was to keep doing what
they were doing—stimulating the best in each other as they
worked on behalf of others, while enjoying a privately sexy attraction. More than client and attorney, and clearly more than
friends, they would remain less than lovers as well.*

*After they discussed it and informally established the first
boundaries of their relationship, Jean and Stan were more comfortable. It wasn't all natural and relaxed at first, but gradually
the uneven spots were leveled, and they settled into regular patterns of communication about their developing relationship.
They decided what they wanted from each other and monitored
their behavior carefully—consciously managing their way to a
safely intimate relationship that allowed them to spend very rewarding hours together in a mix of personally and professionally
stimulating effort.*

*It was not an everyday thing. Sometimes weeks, even
months passed as legal instruments wound their way through the
city's rent-control bureaucracy. Stan and his wife enjoyed their
usual social life and trips together; their plans for children and a
home in the suburbs moved forward without interruption. Jean
and her husband worked out a lifestyle that seemed to accommodate both of them, too.*

As more than friends and less than lovers, the young government careerist and the attractive middle-aged attorney who
found themselves uniquely drawn to each other found a safe,
constructive way to share each other's attention and focus their
enjoyment of its stimulation on their work together. Using
the five keys to building and maintaining a more-than-friends-
less-than-lovers relationship, they defined an arrangement
with limited purposes that could be consciously managed; discussed it openly from the point of inception through its awkward moments, all the time setting and adjusting boundaries

that kept them safely on their intended track; monitored each other for compliance; and found renewal instead of disappointment in the natural breaks that let them avoid becoming burned out with the relationship.

PUTTING THE RELATIONSHIP TO WORK

You are at work. You like what you do and the people you do it with. They are decent, competent coworkers with whom you willingly share your days, engage your thinking processes, and even experience some satisfaction in a job well done—nice, but hardly special.

You get an assignment. It is with an attractive peer you've known casually, but not well. The task is not a routine one; special effort will be required if it is to come out right. It requires intensive concentrated effort, and you need to find some space, go off alone, and work without interruption. You brainstorm for hours, exchanging ideas and information, becoming so enthusiastic about the project that you don't notice that the rest of the staff has gone home for the evening. Suddenly you realize you're alone in the conference room with the door closed, with still more ideas for the project. You don't want to break your train of thought, but you don't want to infringe on each other's private lives, either.

Phone calls home inform spouses that you're going to work for a few more hours, so you order a pizza, relax a bit, and continue working. You've not been so excited about a team project in years, and begin to realize that your partner is an extremely attractive package—both mind and body. You're downright inspired and can't wait to come to work tomorrow to begin again. What you thought was going to be just another project suddenly has the potential to be more fun than it seems work should be. Along with your stated professional thoughts come the unspoken parenthetical personal ones:

- I estimate that we're going to need from eight to ten weeks to actually pull this thing together. (And I'm really looking forward to doing it with you.)
- That's a great idea, and what do you say we also . . . (I've never worked with anyone so attractive *and* so creative. When we're together, ideas come faster than we can get them into the computer!)
- You've been great. You've brought incredible inspiration to our planning sessions. (There's something very special about working with you that really gets me going!)

In time, you just have to admit to yourself that the work is wonderful, but so is your partner. Work has never been sexy before, your peer is a member of the opposite gender with a great deal of appeal, and you're having a tough time sorting out just what that means and how to handle it. Your partner's bright mind and high level of both professional competency and motivation further enhance your image of the physically attractive person you find him or her to be. Or is it the physically attractive person who enhances your perceptions about the bright mind and professional competency?

The force of sexual attraction is basic and unparalleled in its power and energy. Consciously controlled and properly channeled into the task at hand, sexual attraction can bring extra vitality to your work, and add much to your ability to function as an inspired team. If you are both willing players who have agreed to consciously manage your relationship within a set of mutually acceptable boundaries, you can avoid the pitfalls of uncontrolled sexual attraction and tap an unprecedented vein of professional potential.

Benefits for Work

What sexual energy can accomplish at work is impressive. Two people who enjoyed their jobs before suddenly find them more exciting when work becomes the occasion for sharing each other's company. This may sound like an artificial situation, but in a properly managed more-than-friends-less-than-lovers relationship, both the attraction and the inspired work are genuine—as is the shared realization that one makes the other possible.

Something unique is brought to a task when a woman and a man tackle it together. In a special issue of *Time*, journalist Anastasia Toufexis discussed how differently women and men approach things: "The reality is that women experience life differently from men; consequently, they think differently. In the words of Harvard psychologist Carol Gilligan . . . they have 'a different voice.' Relationship colors every aspect of a woman's life, according to the researchers. Women use conversation to expand and understand relationships; men use talk to convey solutions, thereby ending conversation. Women tend to see people as mutually dependent; men view them as self-reliant. Women emphasize caring; men value freedom. Women consider actions within a context, linking one to the next; men tend to regard events as isolated and discrete."

With these contrasts representing only the tip of the iceberg, it is apparent that the sexes bring exciting different and complementary orientations to shared work. When they are allowed to keep their sexual identities, rather than suppress them to conform to safe, genderless workplace stereotypes, a tremendous amount of creative energy can flow from their differences, bringing benefits to the job at large as well as to the individuals.

Because they enjoy their work and each other, more than friends, less than lovers willingly spend long hours of focused effort and achieve the kind of results that lead to future projects together. Jointly sharing the glory of success increases the probability that the team will look forward to being reconstituted for still more work together. They value their identity as an effective working team with a positive, successful image. Indiscretion would threaten the relationship, and they carefully avoid behavior that would even hint at it.

What's good for the team is good for work, and vice versa. Look beyond the apparent superficiality of that statement and realize how very true it can be for a man and woman who have a more-than-friends-less-than-lovers relationship. It creates a win-win situation for the employer and the employees. From the perspective of everyone involved, the rewards are found in professional success, and you have a pair of uniquely motivated employees with every reason to do the right thing—personally and on the job.

General Rules

Every more-than-friends-less-than-lovers relationship is different. Each pair comes together under different circumstances. The type of work they do is different, making the way in which they spend their work time together distinctive. In addition, the level of attraction between men and women is highly variable, and each chooses to become involved in an intimate but nonsexual relationship for distinct personal reasons. However, even with these differences, there are still many general rules and guidelines you will find critical in forming and maintaining your own such relationship.

Let the relationship find you; don't go out looking for one. This is not to discourage you from applying what you are now learning to an existing situation that you determine to be a more-than-friends-less-than-lovers relationship in waiting.

Don't shrink from the task just because your feelings about each other are ambivalent. If they were otherwise, you would easily slip into being friends, lovers, or nothing and let it go at that.

Give the relationship time to develop. Don't try to force immediate intimacy. Trust and comfort grow over time, so as you begin, there really isn't a lot to do except be receptive to the idea and honest about your feelings and commitments.

Don't expect a relationship that never causes you moments of concern or embarrassing exchanges. Remember that you are dealing with some very basic human drives and emotions. Be willing to discuss them. If you're not, you won't be able to agree on boundaries or provide feedback as you monitor each other in the process of conscious relationship management.

Develop an appropriate identity in which you keep the work central to your relationship. Never yield to letting the relationship lead the work. It is inevitable that you will share some intense emotions, but don't let them lead you toward expectations that cannot be fulfilled. Your mind-set needs to be that the relationship is a pleasant and productive add-on to the work at hand, not vice versa.

Keep your behavior together stratified. The comfortable, intimate ways in which you relate when you are alone together are not appropriate in the formal workplace.

Give as much as you are willing to the relationship, but never feign interest. You may like the *concept* more than the *reality*. This isn't an affair of the heart, and only volunteers need participate.

Day-to-Day Guidelines

In addition to these general rules, here are some guidelines that may help you smooth out rough spots on a day-to-day basis.

Find a sustainable rhythm for your situation, and interact accordingly. The frequency and intensity of contact will depend partly on the demands of your work, but between working sessions in particular, it will be essential to strike a comfortable pattern that will include how you interact when not engaged in the project, and how you go about reestablishing necessary distance after periods of intense work.

Learn to enjoy even the routine interaction you share in the down times, and do not wish for more. Your relationship continues to exist even during dormant periods. Your coworkers view you as a tightly knit team, so don't feel you have to ignore each other just because you're outside an environment that promotes intimacy. As you participate in business meetings, sit in the lunchroom with the rest of the group, and partake in various other routine activities, you will find that these periods of lower intensity don't diminish your special relationship in any way. In fact, when it's time to get down to hard-core business again, you will feel refreshed, just as if you'd been on vacation.

Prepare yourself to enjoy the satisfactions and lack of accountability that come with the reasoned acceptance of a different kind of relationship. Unexplained absences, friction over children or household problems, and other common problems in marriages and romantic partnerships do not exist in this one.

Have fun together. What you bring to your working relationship as more than friends and less than lovers is a comfort and ease not felt by colleagues who know each other less well. As you progress in the relationship, you develop trust, and with it comes a feeling that you are a man and woman who have fun and find pleasure together—but, by your own choosing, within boundaries that preclude romance. You can experience the pleasure of your personal attraction without guilt. As long as you remain within the agreed-upon boundaries, you have license to enjoy your work *and* each other. The sexual element simply adds magic to your pursuit of the professional excellence you need to drive career success, and to the material and ego rewards you need for a satisfying life.

The following story shows how a pair of coworkers, Alfred and Katie, put these principles to work and created an enduring and productive professional team.

Alfred and Katie are a pair of technician-artists from the upper Midwest who began their relationship in a working environment and found that their inspired working chemistry gradually led them into a successful enterprise of their own. It all began with series of weekends and evenings at the studio of their firm's graphic-arts division. There were color separations to be done that had to be ready in a month.

To their surprise, drudgery ebbed from the task after the second week of overtime together. The quiet studio was such a contrast to the hustle and bustle of the business day. No ringing phones. No milling people to break their concentration. Katie and Alfred both liked it, quickly agreeing that this was really how a workplace should be. Another surprise was the way they seemed to anticipate and complement each other professionally. It seemed uncanny. And finally, these favorable events were all welded into an amalgam on their fourth evening, when their personal attraction became a primary element in the developing relationship. Exchanged glances marked the moment—no overt discussion at this point, just telling glances that said, "I know what you're thinking because I feel the same way."

Fortunately, their sexual feelings emerged against the established backdrop of valued marriages around which their own unique attraction would be shaped. As Alfred and Katie discussed the subject directly, both made it clear that they wanted to enjoy the pleasure of their attraction, but within clear parameters.

The project for their employer ended on time, with ample praise for Katie and Alfred, but a corporate decision had dictated that this would be the last project of the kind accepted by their division of the company. Partly lured by independence and potential extra income, and partly because they worked so well together and wanted to continue to do so, Katie and Alfred, with their employer's blessing, approached the clients their company was leaving behind and found them quite receptive to a private proposal. The next year was a frantic one—full-time jobs during day and after-hours burning of the midnight oil. Nothing could have been more exhausting—or more rewarding. Without the hindrance of company bidding and contracting, Katie and Alfred were free to propose and fulfill graphic enhancements that their clients were crazy about. They were developing a booming business as a team that neither could have created alone.

The projects and the money were one thing, but the joy they derived from filling in the blanks in each other's ambitions, competencies, and pleasures as a man and woman was what really made all the long hours worthwhile.

Thanks to secure and busy spouses, the extra effort caused hardly a ripple for either domestically. It wasn't as though they were spending long hours together. Their patterns actually paired them less frequently as free-lancers than it had when they were overtime employees. Whereas they had once worked in different corners of the same studio, coming together across the room for communication and inspiration, they now found that working separately in their own home studios, with lots of calls, faxes, and modem transmissions to connect them, worked even better for their highly individual styles.

The work was real; the challenge and growing rewards were tremendous. And it all comfortably embraced a maturing relationship that both understood to be quite valuable and unique. They had their times together, and the properly managed attraction that began their liaison never faded. Alfred and Katie were of particular interest to each other and they knew why. It was a healthy mix of personal attraction and common ambition that kept them both pushing hard to reach their goals together. As they eventually put together the commitments needed to comfortably start their own firm, they became business partners, and certainly friends—to their clients and soon-to-be former associates. But to each other they were more than friends and less than lovers—and still are.

INTERFACING AT HOME AND AT THE OFFICE

Your single acquaintances might well envy your situation: without paying a dating service, running a personals advertisement, or asking for the intervention of a common acquaintance, you have found someone of like mind, with common goals; you have neither an obligation nor a long-term commitment. But don't get carried away. If you and a coworker are to seize the opportunity to thrive on the creative energy of your sexual chemistry, you risk finding yourselves in a compromising position that could disrupt your professional and personal lives. You must carefully consider feelings and perceptions at home and at work and consciously manage the relationship so that its impact there is as positive as it is on you. If you don't, you shouldn't be surprised if your spouse, your boss, and your coworkers seem disapproving and misunderstand—with negative results.

"The accepted wisdom in the corporate world has long been that strong bonds between men and women can only lead to trouble—and result in messy sexual liaisons, distraction from the fast track, and destruction of marriages or other meaningful outside relationships. For decades, the only image that came to mind when you mentioned intimacy in the office was of a boss and his secretary sneaking off for a quickie in the supply closet or disappearing for a few hours at a lunchtime matinee," writes Maureen Dowd in an article entitled "Everything but Sex: The New Office Affair."

The dictionary definition of a couple includes the following: "two persons of opposite sex considered together, as a married or engaged pair, lovers, dance partners, etc.: They make a handsome couple." Most of the world outside your immediate office will perceive you as a couple and treat you as one. Vendors who support your activities have little basis for distinguishing you from ordinary couples, and your special relationship is reaffirmed at every turn—at car-rental and airline counters, by hotel clerks and waiters. When you appear for dinner, you are presumed to be a couple by the maitre d', who has no reason to evaluate you as business associates, to be treated differently than others he greets. You subtly acknowledge his perception of you as a man and woman intent on an enjoyable evening, and find yourselves comfortably meeting the expectations set.

An unknowing observer would agree that you look and act like any other couple. The courtesies you share in the course of doing business appear little different than those of romantic couples—doors are opened, chairs placed, cloaks held, appreciative acknowledgments made. It is apparent that you enjoy each other's company. Your dinner conversation is animated, eyes communicate, smiles flash, and few who see you know that the words exchanged largely concern business.

But take care—do not allow yourselves to be swept away by the complimentary misperceptions of strangers. You are not, and never will be, a real couple. You are two coworkers who share a special intimacy and rapport, but you are not headed for romance—by your own conscious choice. Your seeming togetherness may deceive others, and without conscious thought one or both of you could be drawn into a false sense of belonging together that might cause misunderstanding and lead to false expectations and a destructive imbalance between you. Be alert to the possibility that your special relationship may lead to situations that you cannot allow yourself or others to misread; enjoy your status as a mock couple, but carefully monitor your own actions and those of your partner for signs of behavior inappropriate to the boundaries you have established. Be prepared to remind each other if this happens, and take care that you behave in a manner that does not clash with your identity as a business team.

At the Office

When you choose to build an intimate relationship with a coworker of the opposite sex within the company family, you have to expect to deal with corporate dynamics, one aspect of which is an insatiable curiosity about company family members' personal lives. That alone is reason enough not to flaunt your special relationship too openly in the workplace. Your kinship and closeness will be apparent, and at first it might seem to you that the obvious solution would be to objectively explain your more-than-friends-less-than-lovers relationship to the group. But when you really think about what there is to say, you will reconsider. Granted, the following is a little exaggerated, to make a point, but it illustrates how awkward and inappropriate a thorough explanation might be.

> *"We realize you know we're very close, and we are concerned that you think we might be having an affair. We're not, but we are quite intimate in a nonromantic way. What we've done is take our sexual energies and channel them into our work. As you might imagine, that puts a lot of zing into our projects.*
>
> *"You see, we admit that we are attracted to each other, but we aren't sleeping together and don't plan to have an affair. I love my husband and Joe loves his girlfriend, and neither of us has any desire to end our relationships with them.*
>
> *"Now, everyone, please go back to your desks and don't give us another thought. We knew you'd be curious and just wanted you to understand."*

While this account might not be exactly how you would introduce your status to the office family, the essential elements are there, and with them the obvious potential for being misunderstood.

However, we do not advocate secrecy, for you have nothing that you should be ashamed to reveal. The more-than-friends-less-than-lovers relationship is a discreet one, not a secret one. You need not feel compelled either to announce it or to hide it. Behave professionally, and respond honestly to requests for elaboration.

At Home

To avoid potential problems at home, you need to focus attention on preserving deep reserves of respect, understanding, and trust in your marriage or other primary relationships.

Fortunately, most contemporary couples expect themselves and their mates to maintain close friendships with members of the opposite sex and are mature enough not to view them as subjects for jealousy or insecurity. In *Corporate*

Romance, Leslie Aldridge Westoff claims that "our social history and the myths we have digested have always made us believe there was one right person for each of us, when in fact there are many. If we are lucky enough to know two right people at the same time, we can express this caring in different ways and in different places without obliterating our marriages or careers. . . . You live with one of your lovers . . . and you can work with, and are simply very close to, the important friend in your life whom you care about quite separately."

You, as one-half of a more-than-friends-less-than-lovers pair, need to take time to discuss your relationship with your mate, explaining the way you monitor each other and use other techniques to prevent it from becoming anything more. You must make him or her understand that, while you and your colleague share common work interests, no one else can fill the shoes of your mate.

Consider the case of two coworkers, Molly and Hugo, who found their relationship foundering when Hugo failed to heed these principles.

> *Molly and Hugo were middle managers in a regional leasing organization whose growth made a new corporate headquarters an urgent matter. They were assigned the joint task of serving as day-to-day liaisons between senior management and the firm retained to design the new facilities.*
>
> *While the project seldom took Molly and Hugo farther than across town at midday, their intense private effort soon sparked an attraction that neither would have imagined, and that neither had room to act on in their already-full lives. Increasingly they thought and spoke with one voice as they enthusiastically represented their firm's interests to the architect and subcontractors at endless conferences and working luncheons that often left the two of them recounting events long after the others had left.*
>
> *At first, carryover thinking from the day's work prompted*

each of them to continue animated discussion of the day's challenges at their respective home dinner tables. That didn't last long, however, because they soon learned that their otherwise bright and involved spouses mirrored none of the intense appreciation for the problem being articulated that their colleague had shown on the way back to the office that afternoon. Soon a boundary arose that defined a small part of life more enjoyably shared with coworker than spouse. No one intended any deliberate distancing, but that was the result as, one at a time, more common interests were added to the working relationship, and simultaneously removed from the domestic one.

A quick stop to pick up a few groceries on the way back from a meeting that ran late, quiet advice on a spouse's anniversary gift, and a discussion of frustration about an MBA never apt to be completed all incrementally moved Molly and Hugo closer together personally. Add to that the excitement of enjoyable and productive professional accomplishment, and their interest in each other increased even more.

Molly eventually sensed that she was drifting away from her husband, and, with conscious effort, she was able to counter the flow with well-founded emphasis on topics that were of more general interest at home. She had plenty to talk about with both husband and coworker, and just needed to restore the balance that was being eroded in the course of a particularly interesting period of time at work—and she did.

In spite of her efforts to convince Hugo that he should be sensitive to the same problem, he just didn't get the point. He made matters even worse at home by adding talk of long, enjoyable lunches with Molly to his evening discourses. Wrapped up in his euphoria about working on a project that was going well with a professional peer who was becoming a companion in his eyes, Hugo began to convey the wrong impression to his wife—and to his attractive coworker.

Molly sensed that instead of enjoying their limited relationship for what it was, Hugo was turning it into an ill-conceived who-can-be-the-most-interesting competition between *his home and office relationships. She wanted no part of that and began to withdraw from the intimate side of the relationship. With not quite a strictly business tone, she reestablished profes-sional distance that clearly diminished the previous ease that she and Hugo had enjoyed. Hugo had made the mistake of interpret-ing the stimulation they found together at work as a sign that they should be seeking similar pleasures with each other in the personal arena.*

Sadly for both his home and working relationships, Hugo failed to settle for what was developing into a rich, quietly shared attraction that could have continued to stimulate good work at the office and good feelings at home. He read the situa-tion wrongly, failed to respond to Molly's warning with better-managed behavior, complicated the simple workplace relationship unnecessarily, and in the process disrupted both his career and marriage.

By mutually agreeing on the intended nature of their re-lationship, Hugo and Molly could have avoided this unhappy ending. The five keys to relationship management described earlier would have helped them see to it that the needed com-munication took place, that misperceptions were avoided, and that a potentially constructive relationship was fine-tuned suf-ficiently to survive, flourish, and pay well-earned dividends.

During hectic times at work, you will spend at least as much time with your attractive colleague as you do with your spouse. Even some of your interaction will be much like that of a married couple, particularly during lengthly periods of travel. However, there are major differences between marriage and the more-than-friends relationship, the most important of which are the depth of physical and emotional intimacy, the amount of obligation and responsibility, and the level of com-mitment.

Even in the course of a reasonably important project, you spend many evenings out of each other's company so that each new day brings you, refreshed and renewed, into intimate contact for another measured period of time. It isn't that way with a marriage, where your responsibilities, if not actual physical proximity, go on around the clock each calendar day. This represents a major difference in the degree of involvement and commitment associated with the two kinds of relationships.

Being highly situational and periodic in nature, your more-than-friends-less-than-lovers relationship can be complementary to your marriage. It is not demanding in the same ways. Because your association with your coworker is limited to specified periods of time, you tend to be more tolerant of things that would drive you crazy if you lived together. For the same reason, your working relationship doesn't reach into every part of your life as a marriage does—filled as it is with making love, planning vacations, caring for the kids, daily chores, bills to pay, lawns to mow, clothes to wash, and so on. Day-to-day intense interaction is not part of your tightly bounded, work-based association, except for those times when the job demands it. In fact, after a prolonged period of time together, you begin to notice things that really get on your nerves. Just as you begin to think, "Well, maybe this is an ideal relationship that would be better than my marriage," some small trait reaffirms what you already know: "This is not the 'perfect' person for me. And besides, I'm comparing apples with oranges. My coworker and spouse have totally different roles in my life."

Here are some comparisons between interaction in more-than-friends-less-than-lovers relationships and marriages that tend to illustrate how the two are similar, yet very different.

- Spouses share a personal attraction that leads to marriage and has unlimited potential. More than friends, less than lovers share an attraction that leads to a hybrid professional-personal relationship with fulfilling but limited potential.
- Spouses get to know each other, date, fall in love, and share private emotional and physical intimacy leading

to marriage. More than friends, less than lovers get to know each other at work, attend meetings and conferences, preclude love, and share selective emotional but no physical intimacy, leading to a solid personal and business relationship.

- Spouses establish total trust, baring their hearts, minds, and souls to each other. More than friends, less than lovers establish discretionary trust, baring selective parts of their souls and minds to each other.

- Spouses share total intimacy, including emotional, psychological, intellectual, and physical intimacy. More than friends, less than lovers share limited intimacy, including emotional, psychological, and intellectual intimacy. They specifically preclude physical intimacy.

- Spouses deal with sexual desire by making love. More than friends, less than lovers deal with sexual desire by channeling it into their work.

- Spouses deal with romantic love by acknowledging and fostering it. More than friends, less than lovers deal with romantic love by denying and sublimating it.

- Spouses develop security together based on a lifelong commitment to each other and their marriage. More than friends, less than lovers develop security together based on their limited commitment to each other and their work.

- Spouses regard jealousy and possessiveness as natural aspects of an exclusive relationship based on love and respect. More than friends, less than lovers regard jealousy and possessiveness as unacceptable aspects of an exclusive relationship based on situational attraction and respect.

- Spouses incur extensive obligations toward each other, including legal, financial, and emotional obligations and those of sexual fidelity. More than friends, less than lovers incur limited obligations toward each other professionally and personally.

- Spouses share routines at home—during mornings, noons, nights, weeks, months, years. More than friends, less than lovers share routines at work and during specific job-related times.
- Spouses are bound to enjoy and suffer all things together "for better or for worse." More than friends, less than lovers are bound to enjoy and suffer limited things together "for professional success or failure."
- Spouses remain together "till death [or divorce] do us part." More than friends, less than lovers remain together "till special work relationships do they end."

Within the limited obligations and privileges of the more-than-friends-less-than-lovers relationship, there is a wonderful potential for intimate sharing as a man and woman. In fact, you find some of the greatest joys as more than friends and less than lovers in experiences that test and reaffirm the boundaries of your relationship, where it borders on romantic love and sexual desire. Your biggest challenges come from keeping the relationship fully charged and still nonromantic, coping with issues of lust, sex, loving feelings, emotional intimacy, rejecting and being rejected, and loyalty and faithfulness.

II

Stages of the More-Than-Friends-Less-Than-Lovers Relationship

3. Getting to Know You: The Discovery Stage

THE MORE-THAN-FRIENDS-LESS-THAN-LOVERS relationship is a little bit like a marriage—always in flux, with a tendency to ebb and flow with the times and circumstances of the lives it occupies. A man and woman, with convergent needs in their lives, begin to relate. What they find in each other is a rewarding new source of creative energy professionally, and the exhilaration of a sexual attraction that is neither superficial flirtation nor the love of a lifetime. They quickly realize that there is a potentially constructive place for both of these pleasant finds in the existing structures of what are already two generally satisfying lives.

If a man and a woman are to grow from personally attracted coworkers to an inspired and balanced man-woman team in a more-than-friends-less-than-lovers relationship, they face the continuing challenge of nurturing and managing what they are about to create. Their task is to skirt traditional outcomes—to avoid risking an overindulgent affair or settling for an unproductive distancing—and find a way to accomplish their shared objective: building a relationship that steers clear of destructive outcomes that mean trouble for professional images and personal reputations. Men and women *can* become more than friends and remain less than lovers, but doing so takes deliberate, consciously managed effort.

Such a relationship has three stages: the getting-to-know-you-stage, the shakedown-cruise stage, and the reaping-the-benefits stage—that grossly separate different plateaus of understanding and interaction. The precise boundaries for the stages will vary for everyone. While our division may seem a bit arbitrary, it provides a framework in which the process of going safely from superficial to intimate involvement in a more-than-friends relationship can be understood.

While each such relationship is different, all have elements in common. You can use the stages as checklists for

- measuring your growth at various points along the way
- evaluating your reactions against reasonable expectations
- troubleshooting your own relationship

How to best approach managing feelings and actions at each stage varies considerably with the different understandings, trusts, and expectations in place at the time. With no two people likely to achieve perfect agreement in building even the most traditional of relationships, imagine how disparate people's views can be in a relationship as unconventional as the more-than-friends-less-than-lovers association.

We will focus on six areas that seem most critical in maintaining a successful more-than-friends-less-than-lovers relationship as we in turn discuss each of the three stages of interaction:

1. attraction and sexuality
2. commitment level and expectations
3. boundaries, intimacy, and trust
4. relationship-generated productivity
5. relating to colleagues
6. dealing with family

Though you won't proceed through a discrete set of stages in lockstep fashion for each and every area, you will be able to follow individual behavioral threads as they evolve separately. For example, your handling of sexual-attraction issues may move rapidly through the three stages of interaction while you still struggle with moving commitment issues from the beginning to the intermediate plateau. These issues and the behaviors associated with them have been chosen because of their universality: you will want to deal with each of these elements in building your relationship. You may breeze through certain ones and stall at others, but all must be handled in depth by any man and woman who choose to grow meaningfully intimate and stop short of falling in love.

As issues, these topics will be covered on three dimensions.

1. *Contracts:* bedrock understandings—verbal or implicit contracts—whose violation by one partner may well lead to termination of the relationship by the other

2. *Conversational gambits:* representative conversations the people we have interviewed used to approach the various topics and resolve the various issues, conflicts, and difficulties that arise from stage to stage (for example, sexual attraction may be discussed cautiously and indirectly in the discovery stage, openly but somewhat awkwardly in the establishment stage, and with relative ease and comfort during the consolidation stage)

3. *Conscious management:* agreements partners make consciously and verbally that assist them in monitoring each other and keeping the relationship safely within bounds and focused on work

Here is an overview of each of the three stages of the more-than-friends-less-than-lovers relationship.

The getting-to-know-you stage. A spontaneous attraction between a man and a woman occurs, deepens, and become significant enough to merit discussion; the emerging attraction and the excitement it adds to their work becomes an apparent part of dealing with each other; they agree to develop an intimate but limited relationship and begin defining boundaries.

This is the stage in which attracted coworkers begin discovering and building their relationship as they start the journey from mere workplace acquaintances to more than friends, less than lovers. Although the attraction has been admitted, it has not yet been handled in depth. Therefore, dealing with each other is simple and unencumbered. Actions are relatively extemporaneous; obligations and expectations are few.

The shakedown-cruise stage. The participants begin to see the need to consciously manage their interactions in order to steer their relationship deliberately toward the safety of being more than friends and less than lovers. It is a kind of shakedown cruise in which you watch for danger signs of weakened resolve or lost perspective and provide each other with feedback—avoiding slippage toward the unwanted outcome of romantic involvement or running away.

Spontaneity yields to a degree of routine, and your feelings about the attraction grow more complex and ambivalent. The defining and testing that are essential in firming boundaries become uncomfortable at times—but working productivity sustains the relationship while you work to resolve important questions regarding the appropriate place of personal attraction and privilege. This is the time during which mismatched expectations are likely to become evident, and when they must be resolved if the baggage of romantic relationships, such as possessiveness and jealousy—elements that have no place in the more-than-friends-less-than-lovers relationship—are to be left behind.

The reaping-the-benefits stage. The participants are comfortable with the kind of relationship they have crafted. Conscious management is easier as trust in self and each other replaces insecurity and the frustration of denied traditional pleasures. Sexual desire doesn't go away, but it is deliberately focused on work, which enables the participants to live with and actually benefit from what would have been a problem in a less firmly bounded relationship. With sexual energy openly acknowledged but controlled, you are in the unique position of enjoying an intimacy, based on sexual attraction, that you would have been unwilling to allow at earlier stages. Ease replaces tension as renegotiated boundaries are accepted; trust is complete and interaction natural within the parameters of the special relationship; working productivity based on team inspiration reaches exceptionally high levels, and the temptation to change a winning combination by reverting to sexual involvement subsides. The players become convinced that the relationship's rewards are worth tolerating its limitations as they begin to reap its benefits.

We will devote a chapter to the explanation and illustration of each of the stages. In these chapters, you will find some of the questions you might ask yourself, issues you might talk over with each other, things you might do together, and agreements you might make as you engage in the process of conscious relationship management.

While most of the examples will have relevance to your relationship, a few might not. Some may apply to your partner and not to you. Look for the message conveyed by the general sense of the item—the atmosphere in which the interaction takes place rather than exactly what is said or what happens to whom. As you read the illustrations, ask yourself if you could imagine this issue arising in your own relationship. If not, go on to the next point. If so, decide whether the problem applies to you, your partner, or both of you, and then view it in the appropriate context.

For example, the issue might deal with confusion or misunderstanding about a boundary issue that you aren't experiencing, but you think it's relevant to your relationship because you believe your partner is having a problem in that area. Instead of passing over the point because it refers to feelings that you don't *personally* have, remember that you and your partner are inseparable on these issues: when one of you has the problem, the other also must deal with it. You have an obligation to monitor each other's behavior and emotional states as you consciously manage the relationship and try to resolve troubling issues before they become serious problems that might jeopardize your personal and professional lives.

We will begin our discussion of the beginning, or discovery, stage with the circumstances surrounding the first realization of the attraction at a level where it warrants discussion. We will suggest ways for steering such an exchange toward the special ends we advocate for those who aspire to become more than friends and less than lovers. From there, we will illustrate encounters that you might have in the course of coping with discovery-stage elements that define this special relationship: attraction and the sexual component; commitment level and expectations; boundaries, intimacy, and trust; relationship-generated productivity; dealing with colleagues; and dealing with domestic relationship partners. Finally, we will tell you how the practice of monitoring each other's behavior at the discovery stage has special implications for successfully moving on to the next level of your more-than-friends-less-than-lovers relationship.

HOW TO BEGIN: THE INITIAL CONVERSATION

At first you and your coworker approach your attraction—which you didn't anticipate—and the questions that stem from it in the context of genuine, natural adult innocence. The attraction is magnetic, uncomplicated, and unquestioned; you find pleasure in each other's company. You share a brief window in time of uncomplicated relating—not unlike new love, where everything feels transparently *right*. You radiate a natural charm and make the good impressions that go with the mating dance you don't yet realize you're a part of—the smiles, the right things said, the unsolicited attention and unrivaled exclusivity in the limited working world you share.

As in the beginning of most new relationships, the two of you talk about a wide range of topics with the freedom of people who genuinely like each other and want to know each other better without getting terribly personal. There are no rules or expectations so far. You interact without artifice or pretense; work is done willingly, effortlessly, painlessly. Emotions or feelings of sexual tension have not surfaced to the extent that they require the building of noticeable boundaries. The relationship is stimulating, uncommitted—a blossoming friendship without a hint that it might ever become more.

You begin your work relationship expecting professional competence from your partner and hoping for compatible working styles, but you soon notice a spark that comes from a mixture of good working skills and special personal chemistry. You marvel at the charge it gives your mutual efforts as you find yourself persisting beyond the call of routine effort, and discover you are becoming unusually productive. Realizing that you have the promise of real professional gains as a team that you probably would not achieve separately, you look forward to future opportunities to work together.

At this early stage in your relationship, you are more aware of the outstanding results from your teamwork than you are of the growing attraction. And you think that if it weren't for the work, your attraction probably would have lain dormant. Although you like each other very much, when you've spent a lot of hours together over an extended period of time, you notice traits that might prove irritating if they were not overshadowed by professional satisfaction and success. Thus, at times, you feel ambivalent about the attraction itself but want to continue the relationship because you work so well together.

Maybe your partner feels the same way you do about the budding attraction, and maybe not, but you need to know. So you decide to talk it over. Extended work time and place might give you the opportunity to discuss your emerging personal attraction and the concerns it raises in your minds. Or you may want to arrange a lunch appointment to anyplace with a private setting and uninterrupted time together, where you can relax, be yourselves, and safely discuss the growing personal attraction and heightened productivity.

Although approaching your coworker on the issue of your apparent shared attraction is anything but a date, it activates enough similar underlying insecurities to bring out an adult version of the classic prom-invitation jitters. You wonder, "Is this person as interested in me as I assume he or she is? Am I about to bring on a very embarrassing moment for both of us? If we're going to be spending so much time alone together, shouldn't we have some basic rules? And what if my partner mistakes my opening this discussion as a come-on?"

No matter which of you opens the discussion, he or she probably will be apprehensive about how to begin and worried over possible misunderstandings or offending the partner. Some opening gambits might include: "You're not someone I expected to find myself interested in, but sometimes when we get all excited about an idea or suddenly come up with a solution to a problem, I have these feelings that I don't think are right." Or maybe, "I never realized that the thought would cross my mind—I'm already committed and certainly not looking for anything else. But since we've been working so closely, I feel drawn to you. You're a sexy person. But sometimes I feel guilty thinking so."

In order to extricate yourself from a potentially embarrassing situation, you may use third-party examples and generalize: "Do you think other people have such a good time working together?" At first, your partner may not get the idea. If that happens, press on. "What we do professionally is definitely first-rate and I like that, but I'm having a little trouble separating just what it is that attracts me to you—the working relationship for sure, but then I have to admit to a growing interest that's a more basic man/woman thing. Do you think that's a problem?" And at last it comes. The phrase that says he or she reads the situation like you do is uttered: "No, I think other people must feel the same way. Sometimes something just clicks. Frankly, I think we're lucky." This is one way you might articulate jointly and directly for the first time that you have something special building, and that it's okay.

You make it clear that you are not pressing any advances on the other person. However, you admit that your relationship has an extra sexual dimension that sets it apart from the typical friendship between coworkers—that there is an underlying attraction that neither of you is interested in either pursuing romantically or extinguishing.

You can reduce misunderstanding by emphasizing your interests in the professional payoff to come even as you admit the extra charge you've been enjoying, but not openly disclosing to each other: "I expected a capable, congenial worker, but this is really exciting. We're getting more done in a few days than I expected in ten." You welcome hearing your partner speak the very words you've thought so often in recent weeks: "We get going on a project and don't seem to know when to stop. We're putting in large blocks of extra time and effort, which isn't like either of us. I have to admit that part of the reason is because I enjoy working with you much more than I ever enjoyed working alone."

You are beginning to deal with the issue of whether or not an openly acknowledged sexual attraction is something you can deal with on the job, and whether it will make your interactions stilted or guarded: "Well, I don't want to offend you, but I find you attractive enough that sometimes I'm a little uncomfortable." Then your partner adds, "I feel the same way, and I think it's perfectly natural. After all, we *are* a man and a woman. I think we'll just have to find a way to deal with the occasional temptation and not feel guilty about it. We've decided that we're not interested in an affair, but that doesn't mean we won't be tempted now and then." You breathe a collective sigh of relief and head the attraction in the direction of willing sublimation into your work: "Okay, let's try putting the energy into the project instead of taking the traditional cold shower."

You begin to discuss the limitations that will need to be established if you are to develop the more-than-friends aspect of your relationship without it becoming an affair. Lillian Rubin, an authority on relationships, observed that "sex, whether acted on or not, both gives the friendship a special charge and also creates difficulties that are not easily overcome." To work effectively, this relationship, just like every other one you've shared, will need the unwritten objectives, rules, and understandings that structure protracted interactions between caring men and women.

You have begun to lay a firm foundation for your more-than-friends-less-than-lovers relationship. You have learned that the energy flowing between you might have useful applications in achieving your occupational goals together—if you can work out the hard parts. You will have much more to discuss as your attraction and interest in each other grow, and you will communicate at deeper levels, sharing personal insights and feelings as you build trust.

The following case history illustrates the discovery stage of a potential more-than-friends-less-than-lovers relationship, showing how a series of honest conversations put the relationship on the right track from the beginning.

Kelly and Eric work for the flagship hotel of a prestigious national chain. They are in-house support staff for the meeting coordinators of organizations that hold conventions at their hotel. Kelly is married, in her mid thirties, and attractive. She recently reentered the working world after her child began kindergarten; she is in convention sales. Eric, a few years older, is the concierge at the hotel. His irregular hours don't concern his airline-stewardess wife. Kelly and Eric often find themselves jointly coordinating special services requested by incoming groups.

They were recently asked to make city-tour and theater arrangements for a regional bankers' meeting. Calls and brochures only began to provide the kinds of information they would be expected to know, so they decided to take the tour themselves to be better prepared for clients' questions. With free tickets from the vendor, Kelly and Eric took the evening tour, complete with dinner and the theater. Kelly's husband understood and baby-sat. Eric's wife was returning from working a cross-country flight and didn't want to come along.

They joined the tour group for a ride through the city that ended with dinner at one of its prominent restaurants. Next came a thoroughly enjoyable theater performance. While they had worked several other conventions together, this was a new experience. Everything was strictly business, but with a decidedly enjoyable air and the opportunity to focus on each other personally for the first time. When the tour bus loaded up for a final stop at a nightclub, Kelly and Eric headed for their respective homes in separate cabs.

As they added their input at the next day's planning session, they felt closer than they had ever been. Part of it was no more than speaking from the common experience of the night before, but they felt much less formal as they huddled over seating arrangements, checked the hospitality packets, and secured parking space for the tour bus.

At lunch in the employee cafeteria, Eric mentioned how much he had enjoyed the tour. Kelly acknowledged that she had had a nice evening as well, but felt a little uneasy as she sensed a difference in how they were interacting: it was all a little more personal now. Eric wondered silently why Kelly's good looks hadn't been apparent to him earlier. In fact, he was noticing a number of interesting things he'd not seen in her previously, though he wasn't comfortable saying so. Kelly found Eric pleasant, but felt no romantic attraction; she was more concerned with the message he might be sending. A simple acknowledgment of a pleasant evening? Or the opening round of something she had no desire to deal with?

The bankers and other groups came and went. Kelly learned that Eric was not only a trustworthy colleague but also one she respected and enjoyed working with closely—not just with a free dinner sweetening the deal, but during long, grueling days of coping with demanding conventioneers. They were solving problems and soothing feelings with such effectiveness that management soon viewed them as an essential team and used them to good advantage. Their careers were on the rise, and they knew it was due to their joint efforts.

It became apparent to Kelly and Eric that their positive chemistry as a team was a salable commodity in the hospitality industry. Working as a couple had other advantages, like protection from awkward situations that sometimes arise when working with conventiongoers bent on having a good time. They laughed about such things, but took seriously their practical reliance on each other in an increasing number of important professional areas. Their feelings about each other gradually took on more personal overtones, and they eventually decided to talk about it.

What began as an awkward initial conversation lead to a series of discussions, held as opportunities presented themselves, in which they acknowledged that their relationship needed some structure if it was to remain comfortable and constructive. Neither had the slightest desire to have an affair, but each would come to admit a fantasy or two involving the other. Their sexual attraction was both fun and a boon to their work—and risky, because they weren't comfortable with where it might end up if left unmanaged. With personal and business incentives for keeping their attraction active but not letting it become a life-altering affair, they started searching for an option that would let them keep the best of both worlds.

Eric and Kelly would eventually become more than friends and remain less than lovers. Keep them in mind as this chapter unfolds.

ISSUES FOR DISCUSSION

Your initial conversation confirmed your mutual attraction, and your desire to pursue it to nonromantic ends. Now you need to start defining how to safely sustain the sexual magic that promises to make you an especially productive team.

While your first open discussion will break the ice, it does so only in the intellectual sense. The next steps require applying what you have resolved conceptually to your emotional life. You discover that it is one thing to state that falling in love is off the table, yet quite another to share trust, vulnerability, and empathy without sometimes reaching the fringes of forbidden emotion. It is easy to reason that your relationship should invoke no loyalties, but all the same you'll likely experience twinges of jealousy when you realize that someone you've allowed to become special has other loyalties.

You soon appreciate the crucial role of open discussion, for silence can be misunderstood in many ways. Without meaning to send a message, a silent partner can transmit inadvertent approval for an unwanted advance, or turn off a perfectly appropriate gesture that would be welcomed. Either of these outcomes is destructive to the delicate understandings you need to develop as more than friends and less than lovers.

Agreeing on the appropriate occasions for interacting as more than friends and less than lovers is something you need to settle early and naturally. It is essential to understand that your ease in the extended working environment is not the standard for relating in your lives at large. The personal intimacy you prize is confined to your workplace. As you come to understand your situational intimacy, you deal with the rest of the world as you always have—as two individuals with your own personas, circles of friends, and so forth. You make no real effort to stay away from each other at the office; distance is naturally maintained because the special conditions for your brand of intimacy do not exist there.

Your initial discussions need to cover the relationship fully enough that each of you can agree to its ground rules and appreciate its unique nature. You need to agree at a fundamental level on the objectives and limitations of what you are embarking on together. Such understanding forms the emotional bedrock that lets you develop an honest relationship that is special to you and threatening to no one.

Attraction and Sexuality

You begin your discussion with the obvious—that there is a sexual component to your working partnership that enhances it enormously while also disturbing you both. This component is perfectly natural, as David L. Bradford and his colleagues remind us in "The Executive Man and Woman: The Issue of Sexuality": "Being influenced and responding either consciously or unconsciously to the sexuality of the other is the primary way men and women have learned to relate to each other." Together you discuss these limits and discover that sexuality can play an important role in your relationship without ever having to become physical.

Discussing sexual attraction is crucial to the successful formation of your more-than-friends-less-than-lovers relationship. This is the point at which the two of you first consciously agree to deflect the temptation to have an affair and yet retain the sexual element. You underscore the essentials of your relationship—sexual energy with agreed limitations.

Contracts. As a fundamental basis for dealing with their attraction and its sexual component, discovery-stage candidates for becoming more than friends and less than lovers contract:
- that they will focus this sexual component on their work
- that the sexual dimension of their relationship adds spark to their work
- that neither will seek romance or an affair

- that each person is open to the possibility of pursuing a unique working relationship based on the special limited nature of the attraction

Conversational gambits. Bringing the issues of attraction and sexuality out of their private thoughts and into conversation intended to clarify their status, discovery-stage partners Ellen and Bob used the following gambits to initially approach the subject.

ELLEN: I really appreciated the help you volunteered at the last minute on the spring meeting. We got rave reviews for the first time. The summer one is only a few months away and is going to take a lot of work. Would you be interested in teaming up on that one, too?

BOB: Of course I would. The last one was really a lot of fun. Will we be able to keep the preparations pretty much to ourselves like last time?

ELLEN: Sure. I don't see anyone rushing in to take on the extra hours that this thing involves.

Ellen took the necessary conversational steps to confirm that Bob's spontaneous, last-minute offer of help wasn't just a fluke. He had enjoyed working with her, and wanted to do it again—long hours and all, as long as it's their show. Had Bob not wanted to continue the relationship, he would not have been embarrassed by her indirect approach.

BOB: It's a crazy world. My sister and her husband are breaking up after thirteen years and two beautiful kids. Turns out she's involved with a guy at work.

ELLEN: I guess we'll have to stop working evenings together. It might be a hereditary thing—in your genes or something.

BOB: Not a chance. I've been too close to those disasters over the years to ever be a part of one myself. Tell Jim you're safe with me.

While talking about the problem of a loved one, Bob was able to raise a question fundamental to all man/woman relationships: what are your intentions with me? By probing in the form of a joke, Ellen was able to clarify that their attraction held out no such possibilities, without directly talking about the two of them or embarrassing anyone.

BOB: So you agree that we make a pretty good team?

ELLEN: A pretty good *working* team.

BOB: And the fact that we enjoy that work together?

ELLEN: It's great—and I'd like to see it continue, but only if it stays simple.

BOB: Why wouldn't it?

ELLEN: I think we could both list reasons and cite examples of those who proved it couldn't—that's why.

BOB: But that's not the only direction to take.

Bob and Ellen went on to talk about the way they might be able to develop a disciplined, work-based relationship that could accommodate a measure of mutual attraction and not get out of hand.

Conscious management. When two people have a sexual attraction in common, safety requires them to consciously manage their behavior and thinking by monitoring each other and themselves. Here are six vital agreements you both need to make and keep if you are to be successful at managing your experience.

- Agree that the sexual attraction you are experiencing is natural, and not something to feel guilty about.
- Agree to preserve the vitality and special incentive that restrained sexual interest brings to your working relationship.
- Agree that you want to preserve life as you know it— including the relationships you already share with others professionally, with your spouses or lovers, and with each other as coworkers with a special ability to enjoy inspired work as a team.
- Agree that acting on your sexual attraction in a conventional way would alter your existing relationships undesirably and that you will avoid doing so.
- Agree that these initial conversations may not be the last you will need to have on the topic of your sexual attraction, but that you won't destroy its positive contribution to your working relationship by allowing sexuality to dominate it.
- Agree to work on defining a way of behaving together that can accommodate the sexual energy and not let it consume you.

Commitment Level and Expectations

As you begin your relationship, there is virtually no personal commitment to each other; the focus is your work. However, as the association deepens you find yourselves increasingly committed to and forming expectations about the relationship itself, if not each other personally. When that occurs, you begin sorting out just what it is you are looking for with each other. How much of a personal relationship will you allow within the overarching professional one? This question will be answered as each of you defines your own boundaries for a relationship in which the professional side dominates, while the personal side provides a source of carefully regulated energy for your work.

This focus on your work together gives you an excellent chance of finding areas of early satisfaction. You expect professional competence and find a desirable companion as well; polite company brings with it a stimulating attraction; an enthusiastic professional coworker ends up generating ideas related to doing business together and sharing common interests. What began as commitment only to your job evolves into something that has more personal overtones for both of you. With this comes the expectation that each of you will be honest about your feelings and intentions and will show respect for the feelings of your partner.

At this point, you've agreed that you expect to do more together professionally and will enjoy it personally, too. You have a natural place for your special relationship—at work and in the shared business hours after your regular workday, and sometimes on the road. Your relationship usually ends with the business day. Allowing yourselves to assume personal commitments beyond your work is a natural temptation, but one that can detract from the simplicity that keeps your relationship fresh and stimulating.

You don't rule out joint activities with spouses if such things were a previous part of your lives, or if spouses have met and enjoy the association, but you don't feel compelled to initiate them. While you are thoroughly entrenched as professional partners, you have no compelling need to share each other's total lives. Instead, you continue to maintain other independent relationships both professionally and personally. While you enjoy each other's professional contributions and personal company, you don't look for ways to draw each other into a broader sharing of lives.

Rewards of the more-than-friends-less-than-lovers relationship come most readily to those who define what to expect, and ask no more of each other. It is especially important to draw the lines clearly between professional and personal commitments as you begin, because those boundaries will be needed as intimacy grows. Failure to distinguish between the professional and personal opens the door to unbalanced expectations and unwanted emotions, such as jealousy and possessiveness. The most successful device for fending off inappropriate claims in this intimate but limited relationship is the presence of mutually defined commitments and expectations.

Contracts. In order to ensure that you both share appropriate commitments and expectations at the beginning, you contract:

- that working together offers rewards that make committing to a relationship worthwhile
- that your professional and personal fortunes are linked to each other to the extent of your common work
- that you will commit to certain obligations, including limited personal ones, in the interest of the working relationship
- that you recognize the possibility of your limited commitment growing relative to your joint working arrangement
- that your commitment is limited to your work-related activities and will not intrude into your broader lives

Conversational gambits. This is how Mark and Maria discussed questions of commitment and expectations in the discovery stage of becoming more than friends, less than lovers:

MARK: We seem to have everyone else convinced that we can deliver on this as a project team. What do you think?

MARIA: I think it's going to be an extraordinary effort, but we can do it.

MARK: We're being noticed you know—in a good way.

MARIA: You're right. I think it's starting to happen for us. I'm not so sure that would be true if we hadn't been asked to join forces.

MARK: And if we didn't click the way we have.

MARIA: That, too, but we need to understand each other on just what that means for us.

Mark used a discussion about a coming challenge to be sure that Maria wanted to go on together, that she, too, felt that a part of their success was owed to the character of their personal relationship. Maria, in her turn, made certain that the commitments and expectations each had were clear before they proceeded freely as a man/woman team.

MARIA: You've mentioned how much your wife loves to pilot her plane on regional trips. What if she and Kent flew over to meet us at the conference center next week?

MARK: I don't think so. We're there to sell our concept to a bunch of investors, and I'm afraid there wouldn't be much time to be with visiting spouses.

MARIA: But they'd have a chance to meet—see how we operate together.

MARK: And we wouldn't be ourselves.

MARIA: You're jealous?

MARK: Of the special something we'll do together over there to sell this project? You bet, I'm jealous of that. It's why we operate successfully. Remember?

A natural-enough discussion about the possibility of social interaction between their spouses provided Maria and Mark the opportunity to clarify that this relationship was really strictly business at this early stage. Maybe the right occasion would present itself, but a high-pressure presentation meeting wasn't the appropriate time. When pushed to examine the core of their relationship, Maria and Mark found that their commitment was to business first, while the desire to build a personal bond that included families was of secondary interest, if any at all.

Conscious management.   Maintaining the business focus as your relationship becomes more personal requires attention to what you define as its commitments and expectations. Here are the core agreements you need to make and keep in consciously managing your attraction.

- Agree to monitor each other for indications that too much is being expected of the relationship on the personal dimension, and to establish distance as necessary.
- Agree to maintain the personal aspects of the relationship in a position clearly secondary to the working aspects.
- Agree to verify periodically the existence of an overarching business purpose in the time you share.
- Agree to continue functioning separately as professionals when necessary.
- Agree to help each other make sure that comparable effort and enthusiasm for developing the relationship is coming from both of you.
- Agree that future relationship initiatives must be welcomed by both of you.
- Agree to periodically appraise the rewards coming from the relationship to judge the value of continuing it.

Boundaries, Intimacy, and Trust

At the beginning, as with a developing friendship, you trust that you are dealing with someone who will respect the boundaries you have agreed to draw. As with any relationship that grows and deepens, you soon discover whether your trust is well founded as you test and adjust some boundaries and re-affirm others. Such boundary testing and adjustment always involve risks on your part, but they must be taken if you are to develop a deeper work-related intimacy. Knowing that your trust was warranted is the reward of taking this risk.

With increased intimacy based on trust, you open doors normally kept closed between colleagues of the opposite sex. You exchange confidences in mutual safety and respect for what each of you views as essential boundaries. According to author Robin Norwood, closeness is bound to develop "between partners who share similar values, interests, and goals, and who each have a capacity for intimacy." It is a uniquely satisfying and secure closeness in which you accept restraints you normally wouldn't be able to tolerate in a relationship where someone you feel a physical attraction for lets you draw so near—no love, no sex, but a compensating intimacy and trust that lift it to a plane where your professional and personal connection as a team is tremendously enhanced. This restraint channels the attraction into enormous creative and productive potential in the relatively narrow sphere of interests you share.

Boundaries, intimacy, and trust are closely intertwined. None can exist in the absence of the others. Boundaries around sex and love leave you free to enjoy an otherwise inti-mate, caring relationship. This is achieved by establishing trust through observing each other's boundaries. This in turn creates the atmosphere of complete confidence necessary to yield the intimacy that allows two people to function as one—the source of your special productive power as an incompara-ble man/woman professional team.

Contracts. Boundaries, intimacy, and trust develop in the dis-covery stage when you both openly contract:
- that physical and romantic intimacy are outside the scope of your relationship
- that allowing the growth of mutually defined kinds of intimacy is desirable

- that you will change the degree of intimacy only by mutual consent
- to define boundaries by exploring anything relevant to your relationship
- to respect each other's boundaries
- that some boundaries may be subject to review and alteration in the interest of growth appropriate to the relationship
- that you are willing to assume your respective roles in the relationship
- that trust will warrant the confidential disclosure of personal matters relevant to your relationship
- that trust will include respecting each other's wishes to restrict any aspect of the relationship

Conversational gambits. Setting the boundaries, maintaining them, developing trust, and creating intimacy need not be difficult, tense, or overly serious, as the approach Roberto and Kim took proves.

ROBERTO: We probably will be the only two people in the lab tomorrow. Are you going to be comfortable with that?

KIM: Sure—why shouldn't I be?

ROBERTO: Just thought I should check and clear the air ahead of time in case it made you uncomfortable. I wouldn't want you to accuse me of setting you up [*spoken half in jest*].

KIM: Don't be silly. We've spent enough time together after everyone else has gone home, and I've never felt the least bit uneasy or threatened. But thanks for asking.

Here, Roberto subtly established that he recognized the possibility of discomfort in certain situations, while giving

Kim the opportunity to say either yes or no without awkwardness. Finally, by broaching the topic in this manner, he indirectly affirmed a contract for their behavior in the lab alone together, prior to actually being in the situation.

ROBERTO: That's a nice swimsuit, but I thought I heard you talking at the lab about a new bikini.

KIM: Yes, you did—the one Jeff helped me select on our trip to the islands last winter.

ROBERTO: These trunks are my old standbys. I've been buying them at the same shop for the past ten years or more.

KIM: Yeah, this one-piecer is in the same category. I thought it came as close to a business swimsuit as anything I had in my wardrobe.

Boundaries are not just verbal. In this case, Kim set a sexual limit by her conservative selection of swimwear on a business trip, where she and Roberto would have time to enjoy the conference-center pool for a few hours. Sartorial presentation is very much a part of body language and an effective way of communicating boundaries.

ROBERTO: While we're on the subject of quiet little places one or the other of us has enjoyed on special occasions around town, why don't we plan to have our wrap-up chat at the little French place you mentioned some evening next week?

KIM: There are a lot of more convenient and reasonably priced places that would do.

ROBERTO: Come on. We'd both enjoy it.

KIM: I appreciate the thought, but I'd be more comfortable with something a little more in the business line, if that's okay with you.

They had previously drifted into a personal discussion of romantic dinner spots they had individually enjoyed with others in the past. When the wrong linkage seemed to be emerging, Kim short-circuited it effectively, but not offensively—redirecting a conversation that was leading in a direction in which she was not ready to go by returning the tone to business.

Conscious management. For working partners to establish the boundaries and trust that lead to intimacy, you need to reach some understandings.

- Agree that the condition for gradually expanding boundaries is the continuation of past restraint in similar situations. For example, working alone in the conference room during business hours has brought no unpleasant advances, so you are comfortable with a weekend project at the office. After no problems in this area, you may agree to work at one or the other's apartment next time.
- Agree that concern about protecting your safety and reputations is shared.
- Agree to remain sensitive to when you are impinging on private areas not to be broached or probed.
- Agree to keep each other's confidences.
- Agree to get closer personally, but only as long as you feel you can control the situation.
- Agree that your partner's private behavior is not to deviate significantly from what you experienced with him or her in group settings.
- Agree not to presume liberties not granted.
- Agree to provide your partner a gracious way out of situations where you are not threatened but don't want to pursue the suggested activity.

- Agree to keep your boundaries in place until you are comfortable with relaxing them.
- Agree to avoid revelations that would make you unnecessarily vulnerable should the relationship fail at this early point.
- Agree to respect each other's independence personally and professionally, fitting into each other's lives only when justified by business necessity or the mutual interest of spouses or lovers.

Relationship-Generated Productivity

Recognizing that you have discovered an effective business partner comes early in the discovery stage of forging a more-than-friends-less-than-lovers relationship. The fact that you find your associate attractive is an inducement to develop the partnership, but is secondary, nonetheless. Creating space in your life for an attraction that you don't otherwise need requires justification; at least one of you probably has a domestic relationship and doesn't want romantic complications. The incentive for going ahead is provided by the promise of profitable professional interaction.

The initial business purpose is handed to you automatically by the working circumstances that brought you together as a team. The fact that you perform well together, mixed with emerging sexual attraction, leads you to recognize a sexual chemistry that can inspire enhanced productivity in your joint efforts. "There is no more compelling chemistry than this feeling of mysterious familiarity when a woman and man come together whose patterns of behavior fit like pieces of a jigsaw puzzle," writes Robin Norwood in *Women Who Love Too Much*.

The productive rewards must be real. If work is used only as an excuse to conduct your relationship, it won't develop fully or last for long. You will soon be left with no purposeful reason, except your sexual attraction, for dealing with each other and putting up with the discomforts that any sustained relationship brings. That won't do. The attraction might either be insufficient and you'll part, or too much and it will take an unwanted romantic turn. A genuine, ongoing business purpose will, on the other hand, give your relationship the substantive underpinnings it needs to endure and grow in the absence of what usually serves to cement caring man/woman relationships—romantic and sexual commitment.

Contracts. You start to create a solid basis for using the mutual excitement generated by your relationship to enhance your professional performance when you contract:

- that the sexual energy of your attraction contributes significantly to your ability to work productively as a team
- to direct your relationship's sexual energies into the attainment of professional excellence together
- that, in working together, each of you achieves more than you could separately
- to seek new applications for your relationship-generated working capabilities for as long as it is mutually advantageous to do so

Conversational gambits. Discussing that you have something special to give each other as a working team and that it is generated by sexual attraction needs to be approached gingerly at the beginning. This is how Sophy and William broached the subject:

WILLIAM: Would you be in here working on this project this weekend by yourself?

SOPHY: I doubt it.

WILLIAM: Neither would I. What are we doing here?

SOPHY: Well, I thought you expected it of me.

WILLIAM: Funny, I had the same impression from you.

William and Sophy established the fact that they had set indirect expectations of their team and each other that they wouldn't otherwise have done. There is a self-driving energy in the relationship that is not easy for them to define. It contains elements of subliminal sexual attraction and is filled with honest work-based motivation. William and Sophy are good at what they do together, and getting it done as a team produces the kind of results that earn both personal and career satisfaction.

SOPHY: You are very good at what you do.

WILLIAM: Thanks. I can honestly return the compliment.

SOPHY: It's fun watching things turn out right and the two of us having a good time in the process.

WILLIAM: Yeah. It helps to like the person you have to work with, too.

SOPHY: Especially when you keep the hours we do.

WILLIAM: I have to admit that work is more pleasant with you.

Without ever bringing the sexual connection directly into the conversation, Sophy and William let it be known that it is there, drawing them willingly together and contributing energy to the focus of their relationship—their work.

SOPHY: Under the reorganization, the department is forming a team to coordinate the kinds of things we do at the other branches around the city. No one else has the combination of skills that we'd bring to the task.

WILLIAM: We should volunteer. It would be a promotion, and riding around and working out of different offices wouldn't be so bad as a team.

SOPHY: I'm glad to hear you say that. I was thinking the same thing.

No mention of their relationship outside the teamwork aspect is needed in this conversation as Sophy and William confirm several key points about their special relationship-generated productivity: (1) the new job would be a positive career move, (2) the prospect of doing it together makes it attractive, and (3) the company will benefit by their combined skills and motivation to take on the new challenge together.

Conscious management. In order to consciously sort out the potentially competing forces of sexual attraction from honest working motivation, both of you should arrive at certain agreements. Among them are the following:

- Agree to note instances in which you are willing to expend additional effort on projects when you wouldn't invest comparable energy without the relationship's incentive.
- Agree to observe situations where the sexual attraction surfaces, acknowledge it, and transfer it to the working energy of the project.
- Agree to verify, to your objective satisfaction, that the team effort is yielding more impressive results than previous initiatives by either of you performing alone.
- Agree to decide when professional opportunities are conducive to your combined talents, and to seek your partner's support in pursuing them with relationship-generated initiative.

Relating to Colleagues

At first, your coworkers might find it noteworthy that the two of you persist so willingly in your shared endeavors; they are impressed with the results of your labors. Because your own early feelings are ambivalent, you become conscious of the potential for misunderstandings and try not to provide any fuel for the office rumor mill. Though you are anything but an *item* at the office, you begin to realize that the potential exists for people to think you are, unless you are discreet.

As you consider how colleagues might see you, you realize the need to consciously manage your behavior in public settings, recognizing that much of what you do, while not wrong, might raise eyebrows among those not familiar with the broader understandings existing between you.

Even if your company's policy is to monitor so-called inappropriate attractions, you can avoid scrutiny by being sensitive to a few areas that give managers legitimate reasons for concern, regardless of the policy:

- bias in the treatment of the one who shares your attraction—favorable or unfavorable
- bending company travel policies to promote or discourage your attraction
- devoting company time to personal interests
- behaving in a way that discredits the public image of the company

When you present your relationship de facto in the workplace as precisely what it is—a natural outgrowth of good working chemistry between colleagues—its acceptance should be easy for your business associates. What everyone gains is the comfort of a well-functioning team that doesn't put a strain on the working environment.

Secrecy, of course, is neither necessary nor appropriate. You will find the change of relationship tenor in public and private settings to be a natural one. It is automatically invoked when your relationship reaches that comfortable point, where you indeed begin to function with your attraction safely compartmentalized.

Of course, during the discovery stage you will want to be sensitive to lapses in the personal/professional balance, where what you are wrestling with might momentarily be inappropriate for group consumption. For example, the urge to extend a particularly warm compliment uncharacteristic of your usual office banter might best be saved for a private time.

The fact that you have a thoroughly proper, if special, working relationship is nothing to deny if asked. However, the details of how it operates, its special character, and the details of your discussions of such things as work-related personal boundaries are private matters you will not find it necessary to share with others.

In time, your relationship becomes self-proving. Your associates know you well enough to notice the irregularities that come with a too-close man/woman association at work. When they don't materialize, you will find yourselves with little to explain about your relationship.

Contracts. Presenting a comfortable image in the workplace is something that comes naturally when you contract:

- to remain conscious of the possibility that colleagues and staff might find your relationship worthy of their curiosity
- to maintain a cordial but professional distance in the group workplace lest you give a mistaken impression
- to answer honestly, within mutually agreeable disclosure boundaries, should someone probe into the nature of your relationship
- that coworkers—unless there is relevance to your work—will not generally be the focus of your relationship discussions

Conversational gambits. For Bruce and Ardis, discussing how others at work might perceive their relationship was approached tactfully but directly:

BRUCE: I know we aren't doing anything wrong. This is not an affair in any sense of the word. Yet I feel worried about what the others might think.

ARDIS: Of course, people could misunderstand—we *are* pretty friendly. I guess we'd better be sensitive to what others see, or think they see.

By discussing the subject openly, an obvious potential source of misunderstanding becomes a matter of joint awareness and responsibility. Betraying your feelings about your partner can be as damaging as actually doing something wrong in the eyes of coworkers who don't understand the relationship.

BRUCE: I think Felicia is starting to suspect something between us. She gets that look in her eye whenever I mention you.

ARDIS: Well, maybe we should have a little talk with her after the others leave this afternoon.

BRUCE: No. I think we just need to watch what we say around her. Remember how enthusiastic we were getting about planning our Cleveland trip last week?

ARDIS: You know, you're right. I overreacted. Let's try it your way.

By discussing the possibility that their relationship might be misunderstood, Bruce and Ardis not only avoided exaggerating a minor situation but also brought to their mutual attention the need to monitor each other and keep a lower profile before their coworkers.

ARDIS: Christie has been my closest friend here at work for so many years. I'd feel better about not letting her find out about us from someone else. I'm going to have a talk with her.

BRUCE: What do you mean "find out about us"? What's to find out? Have I been missing something?

ARDIS: You know what I mean. We both know it's only a special friendship, but if she heard it the wrong way, without me there to explain, she might get the wrong idea.

BRUCE: I think you and I need to have another look at what kind of relationship we really have before you have a talk with Christie.

Ardis became a self-conscious partner and made the mistake of getting carried away with worrying about what others might think and was on the verge of giving them what they didn't then have—reason to suspect that *something* was going on. If you are true to your boundaries, you have no reason to be self-conscious or feel as if you have a guilty secret.

ARDIS: It was nice of you to have Robin bake me a birthday cake last week, but it's something we don't do for the rest of the staff, and I think a few of them resented it.

BRUCE: I was careful to have someone else do it.

ARDIS: But she was quick to let everyone in the office know that you were the one who virtually mandated it. Her message to me was pretty clear: I was to understand that you had a *special* interest in my birthday, if you can believe that.

BRUCE: I had no idea it would end up being portrayed that way. Live and learn.

Here, Bruce's subconscious affection for his partner came out before the group in a way that he never anticipated. It is important to be guarded, but not paranoid, about paying any special attention to each other that betrays a depth of caring that might send a wrong signal to coworkers.

Conscious management. Openly agreeing to remain conscious of the following issues can be helpful in maintaining a professional image in the workplace.

- Agree to communicate with each other when you sense that a wrong impression is taking root among members of the staff, and to alter your behavior to correct it.
- Agree to monitor each other for behavior that might lend itself to being seen as overly caring, too pleased with the prospect of engaging in a certain activity together, and so on—anything outside the pattern you've always shared as colleagues in this group.
- Agree to avoid dwelling on office politics as a team lest you engender an us-and-them atmosphere that can invite unwanted resentment, scrutiny, and suspicion.
- Agree to have an unemotionally honest answer ready for anyone who poses a question about your relationship. Don't be surprised or unprepared and overreact.
- Agree to use a cooling-off period during which you studiously keep your distance at work if you think that one or both of you is bringing the intimacy of the extended workplace into the day-to-day office environment.

Making the distinction between your intimate behavior when working alone and your behavior among your coworkers becomes much more natural and easy as you advance in your relationship and attain comfort with your places in each other's lives.

Dealing with Family

In the beginning of your more-than-friends-less-than-lovers relationship, neither you nor your spouse has any reason to expect anything other than an ordinary working relationship. However, as you and your coworker begin to sense attraction and become gradually more intimate, you must be sensitive to possible storm signals from your spouse. But don't make the mistake of anticipating what may never come; for most secure marriages, a properly conducted more-than-friends-less-than-lovers relationship will not cause a domestic crisis.

There will be instances where a two-couple relationship existed between the attracted coworkers and their respective spouses or lovers before the more-than-friends-less-than-lovers linkage materialized. Or others in which spouses meet, like each other, and set the stage for a friendly foursome. In such cases, you can enjoy social time together, and the intimate qualities of your work-based relationship need not be a problem. Spouses observe and are part of your interaction, and they know that you and your work partner are close friends. Your behavior is both honest and natural.

However, for most more-than-friends-less-than-lovers relationships, your coworker probably is not a close social friend of your spouse, and just as you feel no obligation to socialize with other colleagues, you should feel none to include your teammate in your social life. Neither should you avoid it if it happens naturally. For instance, you and your partner might meet your spouse for lunch in the course of doing business if your schedules coincide, or you may meet for a drink after work. But, on balance, your intimacy remains in the extended business environment. Unless there is a compelling reason to mix the two, you most likely won't. You aren't attempting to disguise your association, but it is primarily work-based and deserves no more mention than any other relationship you have outside the home. At the same time, when questions are asked they should and must be answered candidly.

Most modern spouses understand the necessity of working relationships between men and women. However, it would be wrong to assume that spouses instantly understand such unconventional working relationships. Chances are, they think men and women who have an intimate relationship are probably involved romantically.

Working intimacy may be viewed by a spouse to be as threatening as sexual intimacy. Many people find the prospect of their lover sharing understandings and discovering truths with someone besides them hard to accept; they fear they are being pushed aside or that they will be replaced. To succeed, the more-than-friends relationship can't be allowed to reduce the intimacy you enjoy in your marriage.

If you cannot manage your relationship in such a way as to keep it from becoming a point of contention in your marriage—as you would any other association or friendship—expect the usual problems of a disapproving spouse. If you conduct your work-centered arrangement honestly and unobtrusively, it will not interfere. It is not a secret; you undoubtedly will mention your work and your partner at home in the course of normal conversation. If your spouse asks questions, you should answer them honestly. Provide a statement of what your relationship is—a mutually advantageous, close professional working association with a colleague who has a life of his or her own, just like you do—and make it clear that both of you are firmly committed to keeping it that way.

However, if your spouse simply isn't receptive to your working closely with a member of the opposite sex, you have a fundamental problem to deal with that in all likelihood precludes a workable more-than-friends-less-than-lovers relationship—for which a secure and trusting spouse is a prerequisite.

Contracts. Keeping the right perspective on your domestic and intimate work relationships is crucial to the viability of both. To make it possible, both of you need to contract:
- to confine your overt enjoyment of the relationship to the shared work environment
- to be sensitive to the potential your work relationship has for detracting from your marriage, and to guard against it
- to stand ready with an honest and complete explanation of your special working relationship

- to remain realistic about the limitations of your special relationship, and to keep it in the proper perspective of your overall life
- that personal, family matters will be of limited relevance to this relationship and will not be the focus of discussion unless they are directly affected by it

Conversational gambits. Some of the most sensitive conversational exchanges of a beginning more-than-friends-less-than-lovers relationship can take place around family matters. Initiated intelligently and handled candidly, such open discussion can serve to clear the air in a positive way. Consider this exchange between spouses Ron and Paula.

RON: You've been spending a lot of time working lately. Should I be getting jealous of the job or someone in particular?

PAULA: Neither of the above. Let me tell you about it. [She tells Ron about the special project, and the colleague who goes with it, including the fact that he has an equally committed partner at home and that there is nothing to be concerned about.]

RON: Okay. Just thought I'd ask. Guess I've seen too many movies.

PAULA: No. It happens. Carl and I have talked about it, too. Believe me, it's nothing that either of us wants. I almost mentioned it to you earlier, but I thought you might get the wrong idea.

Paula and her spouse are having their first discussion of her special work association. She takes pains to explain the importance of the project and her and Carl's roles in it. She also emphasizes how committed she and Carl are to their domestic situations and their shared concern over creating no impressions of impropriety. Paula says nothing overtly about the attraction; it goes without saying that the team is well matched and motivated. Assurance has been given that romantic involvement is consciously off the table.

RON: Don't you realize that Carl is all you talk about anymore?

PAULA: No. I really didn't. Are you sure you're not exaggerating?

RON: Last week, it was the wonderful proposal. The week before, the presentation to the venture-capital group. Tonight I'm unloading my full briefcase, feeding kids, and hearing about how much you enjoyed your planning session over lunch at the club.

PAULA: You're absolutely right. I had no idea.

Depending on how solid the domestic relationship is to start with, the kind of discussion Ron began can be the occasion for making important changes in how you portray work at home.

PAULA: I'm going to have to cancel out on our plans to review the proposal tomorrow evening.

CARL: Oh, come on—you know we'll do a better job of it over dinner than at the office Friday morning.

PAULA: My kids are having a school play that I had completely forgotten about. Sorry, but you're out of your league trying to compete with that!

CARL: You're right. I understand. Let me see if I can't get a few ideas together for when we hit it Friday morning.

Paula knows that her personal priorities must be maintained. Her work relationship with Carl is secondary to her family and must be treated that way. Neither she nor he has any reservations about what comes first when such choices must be made in busy lives.

CARL: It's very thoughtful of you to invite us to your lawn party, but I think we'll take a rain check, if you don't mind.

PAULA: Why? A prior commitment?

CARL: Not really. This might sound a little crazy, but you're the kind of a business partner I'd be more comfortable not making a personal friend.

PAULA: Well, thanks a lot.

CARL: Think about it. We've never run in the same circles before. Why start now? It's not like we're going to be able to relax and do what we enjoy doing together—no professional problems to solve or after-the-fact intimate small talk one-on-one. That's what we do well. Let's skip the formal friendship thing and enjoy what we have when work brings it our way.

PAULA: Coming from anyone else, I'd be offended. On you, it fits. Agreed.

Carl and Paula have no interest in extending their limited relationship to their domestic lives. After talking, they realize that the separate social lives they've always led are probably best maintained in their particular case. This is not a requirement for being more than friends and less than lovers, but neither should it be an uncomfortable stance it it fits your temperament and situations well.

Conscious management. There are several understandings you should develop if you want to keep your relationship from becoming a problem at home. For instance:

- Agree to avoid making a major issue of the fact that your working relationship is especially fulfilling.
- Agree to monitor each other for signs of critically comparing spouses with work-team companions. They interact in a different arena and are not in a contest.
- Agree to answer honestly and unemotionally should questions be asked regarding your relationship.
- Agree to resist the temptation to include your work partner in your usual circle of friends unless he or she is already a part of it or it happens naturally.
- Agree to monitor any imbalance in the time and attention being devoted to the two relationships.

The story of Alexia and Paul, a pair of college recruiters who mixed very different backgrounds and current lifestyles to enjoy a rewarding relationship of their own, centered around the seasonal work assignments that brought them together, illustrates the different approaches that can be necessary to keep your office relationship from having any unsettling impact at home.

> *The autumn months are nomadic ones for those who man the information booths, touting the attractions of their institutions, at college nights around their regions. Alexia and Paul performed that task for two small private colleges that didn't directly compete for students. They served different campus environments, attracting opposite types of students. Paul's college was a church school with a nonsectarian student body, while Alexia's campus was a technical institute. Not unlike their schools, they were opposites. But they found a common fascination in the course of many nights spent talking during the off-peak hours in high-school gyms while their adjacent booths stood relatively empty.*
> *Alexia was in her late thirties, a woman who was more*

sexy than pretty. Divorced, she was in a stable relationship now that finally allowed her to be herself—a woman who enjoyed men. She was almost driven to befriend them, charm them, and then enjoy their complimentary responses without sexual involvement.

Paul was a good-looking man, the same age as Alexia. He lived a thoroughly straight-arrow lifestyle, with a pretty wife who had a home studio where she produced research books on a regular schedule for a major publisher. He spoke of much-enjoyed frequent trips with his wife during college breaks, but she had neither the time nor the inclination to accompany Paul on the fall recruiting circuit.

Talks at the booths led Paul and Alexia to dinners in small-town restaurants and eventually to even longer exchanges in the hotel lounge. Slowly the obvious attraction was acknowledged, but kept in place by mutual agreement.

In time, Paul came to know Alexia's lover casually. He was a former college athlete who was now in sales and doing well. His schedule put them in the same city a few times during recruiting time, and Alexia made it a point for the three of them to have dinner. None of them felt threatened or uncomfortable. Paul was secure in his marriage and got his satisfaction from sharing a nonpossessive work-based intimacy with Alexia. He viewed her as someone who would never have been a part of his life in another way. Her somewhat younger, athletic companion was secure in a relationship that was obviously very satisfying for both him and Alexia.

What worked for her—bringing her attractive coworker slightly into her domestic life—was not reciprocated by Paul. He was confident that his wife would not resent an intimate friendship with a woman who shared his working life a few months a year, but he felt no desire or need to interweave the two relationships. And Paul also knew that the two women he cared for in such different ways would not likely mesh well; they were different in too many ways. Besides, his wife was most comfortable doing things with him alone and was visibly relieved when a call from her publisher made it impossible to accompany him to their periodically mandated social activities at the college. She was a one-on-one person, and they both liked it that way.

So as they began their more-than-friends-less-than-lovers relationship, Alexia and Paul discovered and nurtured a common bond that was narrow, genuine, and promising for them in the limited world of their interaction. The exchange of ideas, personal and professional, and the safely stimulating company in the midst of the highly public but essentially lonely working lifestyle they shared did good things for them. The way it played in their homes was equally satisfactory, but in totally different ways—hers, selectively integrated; his, private, out of preference for time alone with a wife to whom he eagerly returned after each trip.

The secret to successfully keeping your working relationship in its appropriate place relative to the domestic one is found in the proper reading of your own unique circumstances. There is no formula other than good judgment and sensitivity to the loved ones involved.

MONITORING EACH OTHER

Developing and sticking to mutually accepted standards for avoiding temptation, maintaining the relationship safely, and keeping it focused on productivity can be achieved only through monitoring each other. You may recognize this as the *monitoring system,* in which two people agree to keep tabs on each other for signs of difficulty or danger and to notify the other if any are detected. In the more-than-friends-less-than-lovers relationship, you use it to monitor each other for signs of attitudes and actions that could compromise or harm the relationship or its two members: jealousy, possessiveness, favoritism, impaired job performance, and indications of difficulty in keeping the sexual element safely under control.

Warning Signals

Part of the process is the willingness to monitor, to be monitored, to listen to feedback, and to change your behavior as necessary. Monitoring each other for the following signs and discussing them as soon as they appear let problems be corrected before they grow larger. Events that can sound a warning signal at the discovery stage include:

Unbalanced attraction. One partner shows early signs of wanting more from the relationship than has been agreed.

Exploitation of the employer. Personal pleasure begins to dictate business arrangements instead of vice versa, and the partner who notices this must draw the relationshp back to the proper priorities if it is to survive. Meetings called for the purpose of sharing each other's company, with little business in mind, are an example.

Family and workplace neglect. As the attraction becomes a relationship during the discovery stage, it requires monitoring to see that it doesn't come to dominate either of your lives. Too much time and attention to business and too little at home are often as immediately apparent to one of the more-than-friends-less-than-lovers partners as to the affected spouses or coworkers. When such a growing imbalance comes to the attention of one partner, she or he bears an obligation to bring it to the other's attention.

Poor initial judgment. The first impression of a work partner is not always a complete and unbiased one. While knowing each other at work is a preliminary screening device, monitoring each other in more intimate settings can be revealing. If one partner sees something that is not what he or she hoped for and expected, it is time to cite the problem and exit the relationship if a satisfactory correction cannot be convincingly achieved.

Examples include unwanted sexual overtures, lack of respect for a spouse, and an inability to keep a low profile at the office. Before either partner can hope for intimacy, he or she needs to establish harmony in the parts of her or his life that the other will share.

Inappropriate control. Most people attracted to a more-than-friends-less-than-lovers relationship have the ability to accept the ambiguity of a caring liaison free of all-encompassing loyalties and mutual obligations. For those who do not, it will become apparent in the monitoring process, and this ability will need to be cultivated if the limited relationship is to be enjoyed and not turned into a source of unwanted jealousy and possessiveness.

While issues that might send up a warning flag are too numerous to mention, the concept of monitoring each other for their damaging effects is easily grasped and should become a part of your routine early in the discovery stage. These important sources of potential discord and many minor ones unique to individual relationships are bumps in the road that can be leveled as you grow increasingly involved with each other. The conscious monitoring of each other for potential problems is done for purposes of prevention and easy correction. While most problems can be solved, it is more easily done at the early stages, when they first come up.

Dr. Peter Rutter writes, "Critical information about what is happening at the boundary of intimacy is not easily visible through one's five senses but can be monitored instead through one's intuition and feeling. . . . It is extremely dangerous to dismiss the validity of boundary information received through feeling and intuition. While they are not infallible, such perceptions are likely to contain a wealth of important and accurate information about events that are not yet visible. They are likely an early warning system. Intuition and feeling reach directly into the deeper psychological dynamics that determine so much about what happens at the boundaries between a man and a woman."

Monitoring can be personal and focused internally as well as on your partner. Your own feelings and motivations are not always in concert with what you know to be the limitations of the relationship. The task of correcting the difference is largely a personal one, even if that means showing vulnerability by airing the concern and paring it down to realistic proportions with the help of your coworker. You come to appreciate that you can accomplish change for the better in each other. It comes from monitoring and feedback—both the vigilance and the structured expectation of confronting your differences and finding common ground.

In spite of these necessary cautions, the overall rewards make the discovery stage a satisfying one. Without looking for it, you may both have found an important source of renewal in your work. There is an excitement with another person that you haven't experienced before in quite this way. Work is blending with this excitement in a most productive way, and it is looking as though it just might be able to go on and on—and get better and better.

Progressing through the stages of the more-than-friends-less-than-lovers relationship can also be trying. The beginning stage is filled with wonder and promise, the advanced stage with satisfaction. The intermediate stage involves the processes of turning the former into the latter on a sustainable basis. You validate your resolve and mettle as the simplicity of the entry stage blurs into the testing times of the intermediate.

This challenge comes as you grow less dazzled by the uncomplicated attraction that started it all. You begin to sense that nothing is simple. Time and familiarity bring dilemmas to even the most ideal and limited relationships. There are still matters to resolve. Early rational discussions of boundaries have yet to translate well-intended words into what the hard experience of living with them eventually will teach—knowing when to break new ground, sensing when to stop, appreciating what you have together, understanding and accepting what you don't.

You have conceived a special relationship, but have only begun the process of implementing it. While you will find both pain and pleasure along the way, the more-than-friends-less-than-lovers relationship will lead to a genuine intimacy you will come to cherish as one of the most valued interpersonal experiences of your life. The intermediate, or establishment, stage we are about to introduce you to is well worth the aggravation you will sometimes encounter there.

4. *Sorting It Out: The Establishment Stage*

YOUR FEELINGS ABOUT your special working relationship get more ambivalent as you go from the simple attraction that sparked it to a deeper level of intimacy. All the momentum of your experience in past intimate relationships sweeps you emotionally beyond what being more than friends, less than lovers intends. Biology, anthropologically imprinted behavior, and social habit all tell you that this kind of closeness between a man and woman has to lead to physical intimacy.

On conscious levels of doing and saying, you don't seriously question the need to restrain your actions, but on unconscious levels of thought and feeling, you puzzle over your respective roles and obligations within a relationship that you have limited in terms of roles and commitment. You actively strive to achieve a convincing understanding with yourself and your partner that what you are doing and feeling on the personal dimension of this essentially business relationship is appropriate. You feel a strong need to define an acceptable position in the relationship because you sense the potential for personal embarrassment if either of you goes too far emotionally. In order to preserve the overarching business and personal character of the relationship, you feel it is imperative to know that you are in an acceptable balance emotionally—caring and being cared about enough, but not too much. In this phase, the magic of new beginnings yields to the realities of managing a complex relationship.

- Simple attraction is complicated by getting to know each other well, adding substance to what, in the beginning, was merely a more-than–interesting association spiced with casual sexual attraction. Now you must seriously consider where your growing intimacy might lead.
- Spontaneity yields to conscious behavior that you direct toward defining, understanding, and shaping your relationship.
- Work continues to provide the basis for your relationship, but it has blended sufficiently with personal attraction that the two are inseparable and thrive on each other.
- You operate on a dual track: you have clearly drawn and accepted rational limitations, but emotionally you continue to be puzzled by occasional urges to break your own rules and push the boundaries aside.
- Your repeated exposure to each other has dispelled earlier images of perfection. You sometimes wonder, "How could this warm and charming person be so cold and grumpy until at least 9:00 every single morning? I used to think this was amusing, but after two weeks on the road, it's wearing a little thin."
- You sometimes feel the need to restrain spontaneous intimacy and warmth in order to deliberately lower the relationship's temperature.
- Sexual desire doesn't disappear simply because you've decided to become more than friends, but less than lovers. You struggle to establish a convincing distinction between restraint and rejection as you deal with the frustration that accompanies your efforts to channel sexual energy into work instead of romance.

- The more you care about and identify with the relationship and your partner, the greater the urge to possess and control; jealousy becomes something with which you may need to deal.
- You find yourself sufficiently committed to the relationship that it is no longer easily expendable, like other, more casual friendships and business associations. The way out is no longer a painless step back; you would now incur a measurable loss, professionally and personally.

The character of your more-than-friends-less-than-lovers relationship changes significantly at its midlife as you seriously ponder potential risks that were latent in the discovery stage. Unconsciously, your commitment to each other has become institutionalized: you have a team identity that business associates see, and personal sensitivities that the two of you feel. Altering either would disrupt your work and necessitate lifestyle adjustments that would not have been required at an earlier stage. While the ups and downs are difficult and sometimes painful, you have invested too much to give up as you attempt to establish a mature, responsible relationship that respects the need to preserve the basic status quo, while enhancing it with carefully limited but significant pleasures. The light at the end of the relationship tunnel is the promise of the advanced stage of your relationship—relaxed personal and professional interaction within deep but consciously managed intimacy, where both of you are comfortable with the rules.

An extra dimension of professional satisfaction and achievement has materialized as a result of working together. You recognize new capabilities in yourself and link them with your partner. A caring opposite-sex companion is also personally rewarding, and gratifying to your ego. During this stage, you fight the natural urge toward total involvement that conflicts with your underlying differences and need for independence from each other. You are an attractive but imperfect match, with personal obligations and concerns about compromising your professional objectivity that rule out an unbounded relationship. This creates potential for conflict in several key areas:

Openness versus respect for privacy. Your relationship demands candor as you fashion deep yet limited roles in each other's lives. However, personal privacy is a boundary that can't be violated; you have deliberately drawn lines around the level of intimacy you will share.

Commitment versus the limited nature of the relationship. When you give significant measures of commitment in order to earn intimacy, you also risk the temptation of making it total—an outcome that is inconsistent with your agreements.

Exclusiveness versus freedom to separately pursue broad personal interests. You limit your interactions to the business venue, yet you occasionally chafe at not being able to enjoy the territorial prerogatives that normally accompany intimate man/woman relationships.

As with other intimate relationships, after long, sometimes difficult discussions, you find unanticipated middle ground on most conflicting points and agree to disagree on others. This disagreement can bring about personal growth. Dr. Lillian B. Rubin, in *Just Friends,* writes:

> *Where creative struggle is possible between two people—a struggle that might well have its origins in the envy of one of them—the discovery of the mismatch and the feelings it stirs can become a spur to personal growth. Then each partner can use the safety of the intimate environment, and the model of an alternative way of being that the friend or mate provides, to develop in self the part that was missing. As each moves in the direction of a firmer sense of a separate and autonomous self, the stage is set for a freer, more differentiated and more mature relationship.*

Which way it will go depends on the individuals involved, on their capacity to use an intimate relationship to learn about self and other, on their ability to tolerate ambiguity as they search for a new balance, test out new ways of being, discover unknown strengths. Not an easy task, to be sure, but within the reach of us so long as we can conceive of such shifts and changes in a relationship as challenges and opportunities rather than as setbacks and betrayals.

What you learn about yourself as you work through the establishment stage of becoming more than friends and less than lovers helps make you secure enough to better succeed in other relationships as well. You find a sort of *stimulating serenity.* On the one hand, you uncork a new flow of energy, both intellectual and sexual. On the other, you resist the urge to break out and behave in ways that, without careful management, might become dangerous.

Thinking about a secondary relationship also causes you to think about what your primary one means to you—the commitment and love you don't want to jeopardize for any reason. But regardless of the status of your primary relationship, you and your work partner will rarely be in perfect balance on the *feelings* aspect during the establishment phase. You are two individuals with different biological drives and inclinations, and maybe with different views of the attraction itself. One might be satisfied with his or her marriage, while the other is not. Your focus in this stage is on ironing out your differences and coming to understandings that will let you live with them as your relationship flows around the boundaries, finding satisfaction in the areas you *can* exploit fully—inspired work and nonloving intimacy.

Private lives might change in the course of a more-than-friends-less-than-lovers relationship, and quite independent from it. Divorce can affect it, for example, and its impact is apt to be greatest at the establishment stage, where critical boundaries are drawn and important emotional questions are resolved. With the loss of a primary relationship, one partner may feel less concern about avoiding deeper involvement, while the other's feelings on this issue haven't changed. Most often, divorce has no impact on a more-than-friends-less-than-lovers relationship, especially if it is long-standing and the routine of leading separate lives has been well established. In fact, the state of being separated from a lover and thus freely available gives you the opportunity to confirm that your relationship is genuinely limited to work.

ENTERING THE ESTABLISHMENT STAGE: THE CONTINUING CONVERSATION

By now you are faced with an established attraction that has a growing influence in your life, and you want to make sure the leash is strong enough that you can walk with it safely. For all of the agreed-upon reserve and practiced limitations, without conscious control your relationship could take on a romantic character that you can't afford and that you want to avoid. Fortunately, that danger is balanced with the proof of success so far: you are working well as a team, enjoying each other personally, and communicating with a candor that seems to indicate that conscious management is working.

Nonetheless, at this stage conversations grow more intense and less peripheral in probing the relationship's possibilities and potential outcomes. Sexual tension between you becomes overt at times, and you wonder whether there really is an alternative to the two options that course through your minds most often—walking away from the relationship and its temptations, or acting on its occasional passion. You resolve that quandary by establishing firm boundaries that address these tough issues. In the process you give up the spontaneity of your initial times together and develop direct understandings that let you go on without having an affair or ending the relationship entirely. With each other's help, you build a strong professional relationship from your awkward and conflicting establishment-stage feelings.

Still, sometimes you wonder, "With this deep mutual commitment and trust, why not give more? Haven't we earned the ultimate reward of physical intimacy, and aren't we in fact experiencing a form of compartmented love that would justify it?" In a carefully managed more-than-friends-less-than-lovers relationship, careful monitoring enables each of you to spot these signs and remind your partner, with compassion but with firmness, that your boundaries and limits are always to be respected. There will be no place in this relationship for romantic love.

As will be the case throughout, work stands firm as you struggle to turn sexual tension into productive energy. Your ambivalence at the discovery stage as to whether it was the work or the attraction holding you together is gone now: it is the work. The attraction is strong, but it is increasingly apparent that without the payoff of what you've put together as a working team, it would fade to mere friendship.

But the challenge to the relationship's underlying tenet continues: "Why not? We have a lot of class in dealing with each other. Sex wouldn't change what we've always been together, just make it better." One partner may try to rewrite the rules, and the other ultimately will have no recourse except to jerk the expectations firmly back into line—bruised ego and all: "But I'm not interested. We're not in love, and that's the only way I'd consider sleeping with you. You're not the right person and never will be. Besides, romance and work don't mix. Reputations are ruined, job integrity is compromised. How many more reasons do you need?"

It is at the establishment stage that for the first time in the relationship, you may actually reach the brink and turn away. Now that the prospect of a sexual relationship has been eliminated, you may look to see whether enough substance remains to build on. "When we discussed the personal side of our relationship the other night, it sounded like there really isn't anywhere else to go with it." To which the answer might come,

"You're forgetting what we agreed to all along. We use the energy in our work and we enjoy the pleasure of each other's company. We don't act like lovers and never will."

"You really think we can keep growing, feeling the temptation to get physical, and never act on it, don't you?"

"That's the only reason we're still here talking about it. There have been plenty of people who I could have had an affair with—some of them more desirable than you, if sex appeal were the only criterion. But we have a lot more going for us than that alone."

Then it sinks in more indelibly than it ever had in the theoretical discussions of the discovery stage that actual rejection at the establishment stage may in fact open more doors than it closes—that there are alternative ways to keep the relationship lively.

Pamela and Warren's story shows how the objective restraint of the discovery stage changes to the emotional testing of the establishment stage, resulting in the reaffirmation of the boundaries essential to remaining more than friends, less than lovers.

Pamela manages a health club, and Warren works there as a trainer. They are both in their late twenties, with finely conditioned bodies and fresh good looks. Pamela has been engaged for a year to the health-club chain's East Coast regional manager, who spends much of his life on the road. Warren is waiting for his live-in fiancée to finish law school, at which time they plan to return to Southern California and marry.

Pamela and Warren close the health club every evening at ten. At 9:30 the television soundtracks and rock stations zoned into the different equipment clusters are interrupted by an announcement that the facility will close in thirty minutes.

As the last member is let out the door, Warren secures it and goes back downstairs to help Pamela shut off the machines, lights, and audio equipment that bring the area to life. Neither would deny the attraction they find in their common work and interest in exercise, and they've enjoyed sexual sparring with no expectation of anything more.

Tonight the tone is different. Pamela has never been completely sure of how she feels about Warren. He joined the staff after her engagement and her fiancé's promotion to the road job that is now straining their relationship. She is committed to her fiancé, but at times Warren seems an ideal match for her. He's good-looking, fun, and intelligent, but most important, he's there when she needs him. Something moves Pamela to test the relationship's boundaries.

"Well, I . . . we have the run of the place until the cleaning crew arrives at midnight," she says. "Seems like a perfect time to use all this padded equipment to live out the fantasies we've kidded about for the last two years."

"I think we need to talk. Let's make a pot of coffee and go into the lounge," replies Warren.

An hour and a half later, when they greet the cleaners after a long discussion, they've acted out no fantasies, but they have reached a milestone in their relationship. What Pamela and Warren have resolved is that unless their lives change significantly, their working evenings won't end romantically. As inviting as the prospect sounded to Warren, he'd seen a similar digression wreck a friend's relationship and realized while talking to Pamela how much his fiancée and their kids-on-the-beach dreams really mean to him.

A long talk and heartfelt reaffirmation of their sexy but not sexual relationship kept Pamela and Warren focused on being colleagues who bring an extra measure of attraction to their work—but have firmly agreed to leave it at that. While they cared about each other a lot, they decided that adding sex to their relationship was not the right move for either of them. They would be more intimate than everyday friends, but not become lovers.

Understandings and resolutions to problems posed by situations like this one come only from talking out the conflicting feelings that lie beneath them.

ISSUES FOR DISCUSSION

The discovery stage demonstrated professional compatibility and mutual attraction that led you to evaluating whether or not you want a closer relationship. You enter this new stage by setting up and living through real-life encounters that will either drive you apart in frustration or meld you together with deeper professional understanding.

With personal attraction firmly established, you now test its limits. The objective is not romantic conquest of your partner, but confirming that you share something more valuable than friendship. Commitment between men and women is demonstrated in many ways, only one of which is sexual intimacy. You and your coworker have decided that a physical relationship is off-limits, but you openly discuss sex, love, and expectations for the future to verify your commitment to your special limited association.

Along with an established identity as a work team come practical obligations, expectations, and tests of your resolve to nurture the positive aspects of the shared image. Your family relationships and their obligations are taken as givens. Proprietary feelings should be limited to the working environment, but in spite of your agreement to a no-strings attachment, they may surface as twinges of jealousy when you see your partner enjoying the company of another coworker.

Working through inappropriate feelings will again require open discussion in this stage, where you provide reassurance that your identity as a team stands but reaffirm that your personal interactions with others are your own business. By the time this stage is over, you will probably have established that your relationship, like a friendship or marriage, has intrinsic value and that neither of you need fear that the other will be stolen away by social interaction with someone else. In fact, you probably will bring valuable insights to each other from noncompeting associations, just as your limited relationship enhances your marriage.

To get to that point, though, you have to pursue honest answers about your feelings and behavior, about avoiding romantic designs on each other, about not being physically intimate, about living separate personal lives, about functioning quite independently, and about strictly avoiding actions that might alienate or displace the affections of your spouses or lovers.

Attraction and Sexuality

During this stage, the attraction between you becomes more than casual interest in a good-looking, competent work partner. You have openly acknowledged that your attraction exists but will be restricted to genuine liking, mutual interests, and respect—not sexual desire. More time together promotes a deepening of your feelings about and knowledge of each other. You search for substance and find it in your common working interests, and you discover more common ground than you anticipated. You might begin to wonder if your feelings could turn to love.

Idealized visions of the perfect companion are still a factor in your partner's magnetism. Despite visible faults, which illustrate that your partner really isn't a prospective mate, you see a kind of productive synergy that makes tolerating minor irritations worthwhile, especially since tolerance is required only for limited amounts of time. Since you do not merge lives, your work and time together remain special, rather than ordinary and routine.

It is at this point that firming up your boundaries and respecting those of your partner become critical to successfully managing your attraction. What concerns you now is putting the relationship in its proper place in your life—letting it become more than friendship but keeping it from turning into love. You deal with this by overriding your natural inclinations through open discussion.

Contracts. The basic understandings necessary to keep your attraction safely managed are created when you contract:
- that you feel sexual desire and that the thought not acted upon is natural in your relationship
- that your sexual desire, aside from its obvious biological drive, carries with it a deeper quest for satisfaction and security that is fulfilled in other ways in this relationship
- that love remains the principal criterion for sexual involvement and that neither love nor sex is among your objectives
- that you will respect each other's personal boundaries, which do not allow for physical intimacy
- to discuss the issue of sexual desire and assist each other in its satisfactory resolution

Conversational gambits. Elevating sexual tensions from the level of privately felt frustrations to that of rational, two-party discussion is shown by the way Mike and Megan began these conversations.

MEGAN: As I've come to know you better, I find myself struggling to keep from caring for you more than I want to. Sometimes I feel like I could fall in love with you if I let myself. Even though I won't let it happen, having to consciously think about the whole idea scares me.

MIKE: What are you worried about? We have discussed this rationally, and we have our actions completely under control. You love someone else and so do I. Your feelings are natural ones that come up from time to time when you like someone as much as we do each other. You shouldn't feel guilty about feelings. You can't control how you feel, but you can control what you do.

Here, Megan and Mike demonstrate how one partner can usually assist a colleague with an uncomfortable or worrisome moment. With such an empathetic response, the boundary against loving is reaffirmed but not barbed with unnecessary rejection. Prospects for a loving relationship are extinguished, leaving the essential nonloving attraction unscathed.

> MEGAN: Even without sex, our relationship is still pretty special. How many people share the kind of understanding we do?

> MIKE: Probably not very many, and it didn't take an affair to get us there.

> MEGAN: You know, part of the secret is in what we *don't* do together. As much as I care for you, I'm glad I don't share everything with you. When work gets tough, and we've spent too many evenings and weekends at full throttle, I look forward to a different face across the dinner table.

> MIKE: Tell that to someone else and you'd insult them. But I know just what you mean.

Mike and Megan agree that sex is not necessary or desirable for two people involved in an intimate work-based relationship. Mutual confirmation of the relationship's worth is separated from sex, one of the traditional measures of man/woman intimacy.

> MIKE: Sometimes I'd like to grab you and . . .

> MEGAN: Yes? Choose your words carefully!

> MIKE: . . . choke you! You can irritate me more than anyone on earth!

> MEGAN: That's not what I thought you were going to say. But look at the great work we do—it makes all the frustration worthwhile.

MIKE: Most of the time. However, remember the final days of our last trip? You couldn't stand the thought of cold pizza for breakfast, and I'd had it with your constantly changing the station on the car radio. We couldn't wait to get away from each other!

Mike, at ease with the openness of establishment-stage communication, laces a conversation with lighthearted humor about real flaws in their personal attraction. They both admit that after getting to know each other intimately, their images of each other are no longer ideal. They've discovered some personal traits that would be intolerable in a lover. But they don't have to tolerate them for long since they don't live together. Because Megan and Mike share each other's lives only for short periods, such things amuse more than they irritate. The two of them don't let familiarity and the recognition of faults cause them to lose sight of the magic they share during their limited, special times.

MIKE: When we're in a situation like this, it can be so difficult. Making love seems to be the natural thing to do sometimes. I know better, but the thought just doesn't go away easily.

MEGAN: Well, you'd better get used to it.

MIKE: You're really sure about this, aren't you?

MEGAN: You bet I am. I learned to separate what I might *want* from what I *do* a long time ago, and it's time you did the same.

Mike ends a discussion with one more probe of the possibility of bringing sex into the relationship. Such an approach made one too many times draws a more direct response from Megan than it has before. At this point, her boundaries are secure, so she doesn't need to rudely reject overtures that are really little more than a way to express frustration. Megan views Mike's occasional advances as a compliment that she doesn't need to return.

Conscious management. You have decided that a sexual relationship between the two of you would be wrong for a number of reasons. Probably the most important is that sex would irrevocably alter your relationship by binding you together and blurring the differences between you in a way that neither of you wants. To ensure that you keep this focus consciously in mind:

- Agree that your objective in dealing with sexual attraction isn't renegotiating whether or not to change the rule and have sex, but accepting the irrevocable decision that you will not.
- Agree to assist each other in comprehending that your relationship has valued objectives, but that love and physical intimacy are not among them.

Commitment Level and Expectations

You are fully committed to your work together, but now there is also a limited personal commitment to the relationship, if not to each other. Your expectations wax and wane with your ambivalence about exactly what you want from each other and where you are headed. You choose a simple working arrangement that will let you enjoy sharing an uncomplicated attraction, but you can't help thinking about what you might be missing by keeping things so limited.

On the one hand, there is your firm belief in the wisdom of a cleanly limited relationship. On the other, you hypothesize about what it would be like if it were wider ranging. Your rational thoughts win out, but nettlesome feelings, such as jealousy and possessiveness, sometimes suggest behavior totally inconsistent with what you have both agreed to. These feelings are hard to dismiss because they are so normal.

"In our head, we remind ourselves that this is *just* a friend, that we have no right to these feelings," writes psychotherapist Lillian B. Rubin. "But the heart has other concerns. Suddenly, friend becomes someone else—the cruel depriver, the purveyor of the pain of unfilled longings. Suddenly, we are no longer with a friend, but with a representation of every person who ever left us with needs unmet."

At this stage, you confront your ambivalent feelings by discussing them with your partner. This is when expectations and commitment, as well as boundaries, are shaped and firmed. You are sure of what kind of relationship you *don't* have, but you're not so sure about what you *do* have as two people involved in a deliberately limited but intensely intimate working association.

Coming to terms with the precise nature of what remains is a task unique to the establishment phase. It is where you actually commit to expectations that are different from those you've been accustomed to in dealings with the opposite sex. They may require substantial new thinking. As thoughts of sex and caring surface, you learn to link them automatically to your work as inspiration and energy, not to developing a romantic relationship with your partner.

While you've talked about your expectations and commitment on many occasions, just rationally discussing them doesn't always suffice. Understanding guides only emotions; your behavior has to be literally trained into following a new course. As you act on your conflicting emotions, you get feedback from your partner that encourages or discourages doing the same thing again. The term *limited expectations and commitment* finally means something when you put it into practice. You begin to understand what agreeing to no social life together without a valid business purpose really means when you propose dinner for largely personal reasons, and your partner suggests that the business you're supposed to discuss can be settled with a phone call.

You might begin to view the relationship itself with exclusivity. It suddenly matters whether your ethical and moral standards are compatible with your partner's, just as they must be with other close friends or intimates. This is a reasonable expectation up to a point, but you know rationally that you have no *rights* when it comes to prescribing behavior or associates for your partner. The extent to which you will affect each other's behavior outside your relationship is a matter you establish at this stage. While your prerogatives are legitimately quite limited, this issue must be resolved. It is time to evaluate the concessions you are willing to make in order to maintain the relationship. After all, your livelihood is directly related to successful interaction with your partner.

You comfortably keep the same distance in your everyday lives as you always have. You aren't social buddies and don't share each other's nonworking lives unless such patterns predated your relationship, or occur naturally and spontaneously. The role you have assumed in each other's lives while working intimately has grown substantially. Your association is no longer casual and easily discounted. You have come to matter to each other personally, and to depend on each other professionally, in ways you didn't anticipate when you began. At some point during this phase, the door finally closes on thinking from previous man/woman relationships and you realize once and for all that this one is going to be different.

Contracts. To establish a basis for maintaining similar commitment levels and expectations, contract:
- that when you feel perplexed by the sometimes hot, sometimes cold feelings you experience, you will seek each other's help in working through them
- that if you drift over the line, your partner will help pull you back when necessary
- to refine your expectations and commitment levels as your relationship matures
- to demonstrate a believable commitment to your work and relationship by enduring the frustrations and making necessary adjustments

- to assume joint commitments professionally that bind you for their duration, regardless of personal feelings—making the role of work preeminent and demonstrating faith in the practical value of the relationship
- to test the range of the relationship and define the amount of social interaction that will be considered work related

Conversational gambits. As establishment-stage restraint begins to work in actual practice, you may find that, like Susan and James, you can enjoy the stimulation, make it a part of your working energy, and still not let it dominate the relationship.

SUSAN: I *can't* be jealous. I'm happily married, and we're not even romantically involved. Why do I feel like this?

JAMES: Think about how you sound. You have a husband you love, but if I find a lover, you're going to be jealous? Besides, even if I find the person of my dreams, I'll still want you to be what and where you are in my life. What we do together can't be replaced. So let's get back to work.

For Susan, territoriality came close to being jealousy. However, by bringing the subject up, she was able to enlist James's help in keeping her on the right track.

SUSAN: I didn't expect it, but you've carved out an important niche in my life. I can't imagine working without you now.

JAMES: When we began this project, my life was so busy and committed already, I didn't know I had room left for what I've found with you, either.

SUSAN: There's a touch of "I can't live with you, and I can't live without you" developing that we need to resolve. I don't need it and neither do you.

Susan and James face the quandary of coping with the fact that they need each other, at least professionally, while avoiding dependency.

> JAMES: Your letter suggesting that we free-lance as a technical-writing team is appealing. But I think it would make having an affair harder to avoid. Besides, we've got a great boss, wonderful working conditions, and we make a lot of money here. I understand you feel frustrated and alone since your lover moved out, but I can't encourage you when it comes to getting something going with me. I'm not ready for that, and you're not the right person to make me be.

> SUSAN: I guess I knew that. You know how much I care for you, and I didn't want to leave something behind that might have worked out if I asked one last time, one more way. I'm satisfied now—consider the issue closed.

The establishment stage often ends with a final test of the relationship's romantic potential. This can be particularly true if changing circumstances in your lives find you unobligated at the time. While this might remove one of the reasons you chose to be more than friends, but not lovers, you will probably discover that the other reasons are still valid.

Conscious management. To make the refinements needed to move from awkwardly emotional expectations and not-quite-understood commitments to conscious standards for the long-term management of your relationship, the two of you need to:

- Agree to protect the boundaries and freedoms that you require, but to clarify your reasons for your partner when necessary.
- Agree to expect some territoriality and attempts to control as commitment increases, but to provide feedback to keep them from assuming proportions that have no

place in your relationship. As you do with the sexual energy, sublimate feelings of territoriality into your working relationship, where limited exclusivity is acceptable. You can make your work yours alone, but this is not acceptable on the personal side.

- Agree to manage the attraction, to continue to monitor your expectations to keep the relationship within its prescribed niche.
- Agree to communicate with a warmth and honesty that neither undervalues nor misrepresents your intentions.
- Agree to distinguish between what you *feel* and what you *do* as you transition from early emotions to mature understandings. You may not be able to prevent feeling jealous, possessive, or sexually attracted, but you can control your actions.
- Agree to compartmentalize your expectations. Even though you've spent a great deal of time together, you still have no right to project your intimacy outside the context of your work. While you care for each other, it is the ability to channel the sexual attraction into satisfying work that justifies the relationship.

Boundaries, Intimacy, and Trust

Intimacy at the establishment stage is deep and meaningful, but still uncomfortable at times. If boundaries have been respected, trust will have developed to the point that, within the relationship, there are few things left undiscussed; most of what might be relevant has been revealed in the course of your time together. What you talk about now might be as casual as tastes in music, or as sensitive as health problems. You have come to know each other intimately.

After long days and nights of working together and sharing intimate thoughts, your trust in your partner deepens further and you know that the security of your boundaries is not seriously in question. What you still puzzle over is how much they should be probed—how firm and permanent they are in the eyes of your partner. Many boundaries are never verbalized—and are seldom enforced by words. Receptiveness to the relationship's constant flow of little initiatives is most apt to be shown with a smile or *voting with your feet*—readily joining in the activity, or walking away. No matter how intimate you become and how automatic the trust, your boundaries are no less real or inviolable. They are the license under which you allow your intimacy to operate—and without continuing respect for them your relationship loses its trust and ability to grow and provide stimulation.

Issues you broached and handled superficially earlier may resurface now with an urgency that demands in-depth discussions. As you become more intimate and vulnerable, you have to consciously decide where your boundaries are drawn and communicate them clearly before you risk deeper involvement.

As in sexually intimate relationships, you face the question of *how much* and *what* you need to know. As more than friends and less than lovers, you may have even more trouble than lovers in deciding what you should reveal about yourselves to each other. How much can you know and reveal, and still keep the desired distance? As intimacy and trust develop, consciously defined boundaries are critical if you are to funnel willing and purposeful intimacy into matters important to your joint productivity and not stray into inappropriate areas or behaviors.

Contracts. To clarify and maintain the boundaries that create trust and intimacy, begin by contracting:

- to deal with unsettling issues on which you hold differing opinions until you reach agreement, even if it is an agreement to disagree
- that against a backdrop of rising personal interest and sensitivity, the objective of your relationship remains to achieve a uniquely energized working arrangement

that accommodates your attraction without romantic
involvement
- that the conflict you experience in resolving differences
will be the basis for achieving even deeper intimacy and
commitment
- that trust and intimacy are essential to the relationship
and must be achieved by clarifying any remaining am-
biguities; they are not discretionary
- to respect at face value each other's judgment regarding
the safety and appropriateness of your interactions
- to deepen your tolerance for behavior that tests but
doesn't threaten boundaries and not to jump to conclusions regarding perceived threats not intended
- that as the level of intimacy rises, you will confront any
unacceptable personal objectives that are still on the
agenda—from sex to jealousy

Conversational gambits. When partners have built trust during
the discovery stage, dealing with boundary and intimacy issues is not so difficult, as Daryl and Betsy found.

> DARYL: I used to know when to stop pushing, but since
> we've gotten so much closer, I'm not really sure.

> BETSY: I've told you sex between us is always going to be
> out of the question for me. I think you're bright, sexy, at-
> tractive, and fun, but I'm just not interested in becoming
> lovers.

Here, Daryl and Betsy's expectations for the relationship
become unbalanced, and discussion is necessary to reassert its
limited nature. Knowing that absolute parity isn't necessary
and that differences will likely remain and occasionally come
to the surface, they have learned to deal with limitations rather
than be frustrated.

DARYL: It feels so great when we work sometimes. It would be wonderful to have that excitement all the time.

BETSY: But you wouldn't. When things aren't new anymore, they *not* so exciting. If feelings like that lasted, they wouldn't be special. If we were lovers with all the routine of daily living, work would just be part of the drill.

DARYL: But don't you ever have trouble finding the line between our working and personal feelings?

BETSY: Sometimes. When work gets intense, it would be very easy to get carried away. But we just can't do that.

DARYL: I know, but it's frustrating, especially after something's gone really well and we're excited and happy. That's when I ask the personal questions you refuse to dignify even with a grunt. Why can't we trust each other enough to at least talk about everything?

BETSY: Because we have boundaries, and they're not all physical. The last thing we need is a relationship so intimate it seems like a marriage without sex.

Frank discussion helps Daryl and Betsy focus on a payoff as unconventional as the relationship itself; they openly discuss the frustration that energizes them and the determined discipline that holds them back. Both have agreed to boundaries that keep a lid on their intimacy.

DARYL: I want to talk about how we feel about each other, but when I try, you give me the cold shoulder. Maybe I shouldn't bring it up, but I need to know where I stand.

BETSY: Okay, let's talk about it. But my silence should tell you something. Sometimes you just need to back off. I've made it clear that you're pushing for explanations that I'm not willing to give you.

DARYL: I could live with that if I thought I really knew why. It's not like my world revolves around you, but we've grown close enough that when you won't even talk to me it makes me a little crazy!

BETSY: All right, it's only fair to tell you. [A long-withheld explanation about a past relationship puts everything in perspective.]

DARYL: Sorry. I had no idea I was forcing you to think about something so painful.

At times, a nonverbal no is enough to give the intended answer when you are pressed on a boundary issue. When it is not, you should speak up with an unequivocal reading on where you stand. Sometimes a boundary has to fall in order to shore up a more important one. In Betsy and Daryl's conversation, her reluctant explanation about a personal hurt from the past helped Daryl understand the importance of a boundary. Such revelations are given only when intimate trust has developed. The willingness to expose such sensitivities reflects a commitment that, in its own way, compensates for some of the caring that making love would demonstrate.

DARYL: I keep wanting to ask you about personal things that you've made perfectly clear are none of my business. I don't mean to be obnoxious, but I feel a little jealous when you happily go out the door to lunch with someone and I feel like giving you the third degree when you get back.

BETSY: We're on totally different wavelengths on this topic. Ownership is *not* part of our relationship—we're not even dating! My feelings about other people don't change how I feel about you. How would you like it if I started asking personal questions about your social life?

DARYL: I'd hate it and tell you it's none of your business.

BETSY: Of course. That's why we agreed that some areas are simply off-limits—always. This is not a love affair, and we aren't each other's keepers!

Daryl got possessive in spite of his rational acceptance of boundaries that say it's inappropriate. Open discussion with Betsy helped him work through the problem, get feedback, and find out how he needed to change how he was acting.

Regardless of the point of contention, one way to resolve an issue is talking about what the two of you understand to be the basic agreements of your relationships. It isn't a matter of your both reaching total agreement on an issue as much as accepting that the boundary must stand in order to protect an area about which you may always disagree. In doing that, you each learn more about what the other intends and is apt to accept.

Conscious management. Conscious management of boundaries at this stage becomes easier when you:
- Agree to push a boundary only until you get an answer that is definitive enough for the situation, or until your coworker makes it clear that you should stop. Since nearly all boundaries are negotiated verbally, open discussion is how you probe the limits.
- Agree to communicate honestly as you repeat the pattern of testing and responding until you are satisfied that you know (or have communicated) what is expected, wanted, and will be tolerated.
- Agree to extend as much intimacy and trust as you can within the limits established, and to remain open to growth except in areas such as sex and love.

- Agree to avoid prying merely for the sake of curiosity, but to push for revelations you need to understand your partner's position and tolerate the ambiguity of the relationship.
- Agree to raise sensitive questions only when circumstances will let you see them through—not when you are tired and rushed.
- Agree to stay true to what is vital to you; if you need to know, ask; if you can't reveal, don't; if you can explain in a way that makes your relationship more viable, do it.
- Agree to respect the confidences that are shared as you are allowed deeper within each other's most private thoughts.
- Agree to accept levels of discomfort that you would not welcome in less purposeful exchanges, with the understanding that they will result in avoiding the same uncomfortable issue in the future.
- Agree to demonstrate total reliability by stopping a line of inquiry or a physical advance when it becomes apparent that your partner does not want to proceed.
- Agree to approach the boundary-testing process with the basic attitude that you will respond positively to further flexibility unless a real need for continued restraint is apparent. When in doubt, say yes to growth rather than retard it with a halting approach inconsistent with your trust in your partner.

The main difference between your feelings and actions with respect to boundaries, intimacy, and trust at the establishment versus the discovery level is the urgency of the need to establish *real* understandings. You have a substantial emotional and professional investment in the partnership at this point, and you want assurance that it is well founded—secure enough to base the comfort of your ego and the course of your working plans upon with confidence. These understandings must provide safety in the sexual/romantic area so that you needn't fear potentially disruptive imbalances in expectations; they should also provide assurances that you are each committed enough to warrant the personal and professional investment required by the relationship.

In the beginning, you discovered the need for limits and awkwardly began to delineate them, but since you assumed no long-term period of dealing with each other, they weren't very elaborate. At the establishment stage, you learn to care a lot about each other and develop trust based on the exchange of intimate knowledge and a willingness to be vulnerable within your boundaries: you won't have sex, but you will admit desire. You establish parameters within those limits: you won't fall in love, but there's more affection than in ordinary friendship.

Understanding which boundaries can be expanded, which ones must remain rigid, even which ones might fall, sometimes comes from direct discussions, and other times from your feelings and intuition. For example, in *Sex in the Forbidden Zone,* psychiatrist Peter Rutter tells us, "The sexual boundary is very easy to see once one has accepted its existence. At the moment of acceptance, it is as if a special light has gone on that illuminates previously invisible particles and projectiles crashing into a thin, flexible barrier." Spilled-over emotion from exciting work may put pressure on the physical-intimacy boundary, but at this stage, you know it will stand.

Your description of your establishment-stage relationship to a friend would include the same remarks you made about it in the discovery stage: you're a terrific work team and you like each other personally, too. But what you don't say is that you still feel confusion about your attraction as you draw realistic boundaries within the relationship. You know you want the relationship to go on, but it isn't stable enough that you are sure of the outcome. While you generally have faith in your ability to establish an enduring work relationship that is both stimulating and restrained, your conviction sometimes wavers. You have rationally dismissed the possibility of romantic developments, but have not yet removed them from your occasional wishful thinking.

There's no doubt that you will continue to work together; what you are thinking about now is a long-term professional partnership. But you are concerned about its effects on your personal and work lives. You realize you will have to continue to consciously manage your behavior if you don't want to end up with a broken marriage or ruined career.

Work remains the unchanging constant in the relationship. You love working together, do a great job, and everyone knows it. Most of the time you feel pleased about the way things are going between you personally, too. You're drawing closer, within your limits, and everything seems fine, but then something happens and there's more distance between you than when you were barely friends. For example, you press your partner too hard for intimacy in what you didn't realize was a forbidden area, and conversation either becomes superficial or shuts down entirely. To avoid making things worse and to cushion yourself from disappointment or rejection, you temporarily become defensive and retreat, realizing that you don't have carte blanche to ask about anything you might want to know.

You are optimistic that your future together will be professionally productive and personally satisfying but aren't so sure your unwritten contract with each other is the best way to get there. You wonder if you could do as well by merely consulting each other when specific aspects of your work call for it. Maybe you should pursue the project alone, you think. But you know it wouldn't work; the results of the team effort really are better. You don't just combine your working knowledge. The emotional part provides extra motivation, too, making the outcome special.

Communication is no longer the simple exchange of information it was in the discovery stage, where you learned about the major aspects of each other's lives. You now exchange personal details that let you understand and trust each other enough to move your relationship forward. You've laid open some sensitive areas of your inner selves and not had them turned against you. You know how important personal success is to each other and get a lot out of achieving it together.

Relationship-Generated Productivity

Work is fun and exciting, and the result is at least partly the product of your chemistry as a man and woman. What you have to do now is fit the personal attraction into a success formula that can be sustained at length in your professional lives. It is one thing to be new and exciting to each other, and quite another to preserve the special energy project after project without going too far into a personal involvement.

The attraction has several dimensions and offers a number of incentives for your work. You pause at this stage to sort your priorities and clarify what makes you work so well together. By now you know it is more than the physical attraction, because you've not become involved sexually. Still, that part of working together has remained central to what you do. Keeping it in bounds and refusing to indulge it has made your attraction even stronger in some regards (the unknown remains exciting), but you wrestle with the ultimate disposition of all that energy.

At the establishment stage you have begun to successfully sublimate it into your work, using it as a creative force and motivator, but you are still sometimes frustrated at not being able to enjoy it physically. Once you accept the sexual boundary, although desire remains, the prospects for making love fade, and you are more willing to put the energy into professional achievement. You will always feel a little ambivalent—who wouldn't want to consummate a tempting relationship? But you both come to accept the wisdom of limiting your relationship to work as you discover that your professional success provides immense personal satisfaction and gratification in its stead—enough to keep you going and looking for more.

Contracts. The understandings that lift your professional work together to unprecedented levels are given great effect when each of you contracts:

- that because the sexual energy is with you to stay, you will help each other find a constructive role for it
- to help each other keep your sexual energy directed away from making love and into the working process you share
- that you will look toward the long-term professional relationship rather than the short-term sexual one an affair would bring

Conversational gambits. At this stage of the relationship, you may have mixed feelings about your motivation for the hours you spend working so intensely. The value of the work is confirmed by outside sources, such as your boss and business clients, but you are sensitive to keeping balance in your motivation for such persistent effort. In time, like Bobbie and Warren, you accept the payoff comfortably as it becomes apparent that, while personal attraction drives the working relationship, your achievements are more than an excuse for indulging it. The work/pleasure combination is in reasonable balance.

BOBBIE: To be honest, I originally thought I was carrying you on this project—and now I can see that's anything but the case. You've come up with ideas that changed the whole approach for the better.

WARREN: Why in the world would you *carry* me?

BOBBIE: It was worth it to have you around, I guess—a way to ensure your continued company more than acknowledgment that I needed what you add to the project.

WARREN: That must have changed quickly. I'd never have stayed if I had caught any hint of that.

BOBBIE: I apologize for doubting your ability. Since we started working on this together, I've worked harder than I ever have in my life. And I really don't think I'd do this if it weren't so obviously important to you as well.

WARREN: That makes two of us. I've questioned the hours and what it's taking away from other things in my life a number of times, but you're right—there is a sense of owing it to the other to hang in there.

BOBBIE: I've never experienced the same driving motivation before. I wouldn't do it for work alone, or for someone I was just trying to impress. It's sort of a combination of the two, and that's new to me.

Here Bobbie reveals early motivations that were not entirely professional. In revealing her early doubt, she acknowledges Warren's unquestioned value and confirms the balance essential to their continuing as genuine peers.

Bobbie and Warren uncovered the secret to their lasting attraction. It isn't what they feared in weaker moments—just an excuse to be with the other. And it isn't the mere love of work; such extended effort wasn't the norm for either of them before the team was formed. It is a synergetic combination of attraction and the rewards of combining their capabilities that drives them in such a powerful way.

Conscious management. A central task at the establishment stage is retaining the energy of your attraction while consciously working together to build a conduit to carry it to a safe and productive place in your professional relationship. You establish this conduit when you:

- Agree that you are performing exceptionally together and look for a way to do so again and again with ever greater effectiveness.

- Agree to maintain an emotional *safe zone* that can absorb the missteps and shocks that come with exploring new sources of energy for the way you work.
- Agree to stay honest about the combination of incentives that drive your work—the sexual attraction, the restrained redirection of its energy into professional excellence. You won't continue to expend extraordinary effort without them.
- Agree to restrain your behavior, not letting enthusiasm and exuberance at success turn to unmanaged emotion that can threaten your professional objectivity and productivity.

You both know there is more to your relationship-generated productivity than work. Instead of suppressing sexual energy so that it either fades or blows up in your faces, you incorporate it in the highly personal formula for success that you have found. You manage and cultivate it as you would any other valued component of your life and career.

You have consciously chosen to be more than friends and less than lovers, and the rules stand: no sex, no love. At the same time, there is no reason to pretend that the sexual feelings aren't there, or even to put them aside. Instead, you can safely enjoy your sexual feelings and the spark they bring to the working relationship. In doing so, you find extra satisfaction in your work, getting immense productivity benefits from a wellspring of human energy seldom approached as a manageable resource.

Relating to Colleagues

At the establishment stage, you may be more interested in what your colleagues think than they are in what you are doing. Your coworkers have known for some time that you are close friends and work together as a team most of the time. Unless you behave in a way that generates gossip, they take your relationship at face value.

As with any other personal relationship in the office, you can't let it interfere with work, or be perceived as a duo that functions only together, independent from the rest of the staff. You need to be discreet about your personal relationship and not flaunt it if you want to remain outside the rumor mill.

Working through your feelings of ambivalence, setting boundaries, and monitoring your actions are all done when you are alone, causing no ripples in the workplace unless your own bouts of self-consciousness and frustration are poorly managed and are allowed to become apparent. You reserve intimate interaction and discussions for your private extended workplace, making no secret of your close friendship, but behaving as professionals who are at work to get a job done.

During this stage, while you think what you have is special—sexy, but innocent—you might sometimes have to resist the temptation to share it. You've discovered a new kind of relationship, and like anything new, it's something you'd like to talk about. You already are linked professionally, you're proud of this relationship you've developed, and you think that maybe you could teach some of your office mates a thing or two. Therefore, you sometimes feel a little disappointed that you can't just announce it as something positive and enjoyable in your life, a source of satisfaction, the sort of things others might find useful. (Of course, if your coworkers are familiar with the more-than-friends model, or have seen a copy of this book lying on your desk, and seem supportive of the idea, you may want to be more open.)

Contracts. Ensuring smooth, positive interactions with colleagues at this stage is done from a base of understandings in which you contract:

- to focus your obvious enthusiasm for each other on your professional achievements and not on personal aspects that may lend themselves to misinterpretation
- not to be coy; everyone knows that you spend a lot of time together and know each other well
- that the sometimes tumultuous nature of your relationship at this phase is largely internal, personal, and apparent only to you; it doesn't show unless you don't manage your behavior, and it shouldn't be the basis for self-conscious overreaction to what others might think
- to remain receptive to explaining your relationship objectively, but to recognize that the intimate aspects are personal and not subject to in-depth description to others
- that your working relationship will be confined to the two of you and that each of you is entitled to interact separately with others at work unless it interferes with your productivity as a team

Conversational gambits. This is how Louise and David dealt with workplace issues at the establishment stage:

LOUISE: Sometimes *I* don't even know if we're friends or more than friends or what. Do you think other people in the office think we have something going?

DAVID: Of course not. They know we're close, but it's not as if we sit and talk in the office like we do when we work evenings. I think you're seeing suspicious minds that don't exist.

Louise found out she was too quick in assuming that others suspected something improper between them. As David pointed out, unless you've dramatically changed your behavior in some way, chances are that this concern is unfounded. By discussing the issue with her partner, Louise got a balanced view.

> DAVID: I know I don't even have to ask this question, but I will anyway. Would it bother you if I took on a second project like ours with someone else on the staff?

> LOUISE: The objective answer is "That's up to you"—but my gut reaction is that our work would suffer.

> DAVID: I guess you're right. But we need to help on some of the other projects when we can.

> LOUISE: Of course. I didn't mean we shouldn't, just that we can handle only one big project at a time. And I still think we do our best work together.

> DAVID: So does the regional manager.

You feel some measure of exclusivity at the establishment stage because you've worked together closely and been successful as a team. Remember that work is the only legitimate excuse for your relationship and that you can't let your feelings turn into jealousy and spill over into personal areas, such as relationships with others at the office or anywhere else.

Conscious management. You focus on keeping your behavior within normal bounds so that others will not make wrong assumptions about the relationship.
- Agree to manage office behavior and keep it professional and friendly without showing intimacy that may be perfectly appropriate in a private setting but is inappropriate in the business environment.
- Agree to be discreet about discussing team working arrangements where they might raise others' curiosity.

Trip planning with personal overtones, weekend work at the other's apartment, and so on are best handled privately.
- Agree to be honest with each other about your feelings regarding third-party relationships in the workplace, but make it clear that jealousy is not appropriate.

As you draw closer at this stage, your task is to continue your intimate development privately without generating rumors by spending too much time on your personal agenda. Concentrate instead on bringing forward the benefits of your strengthened teamwork, comfortably showing the natural effects of any two people sharing the intense communication and interest associated with common objectives. You find that most of what you do to adapt to each other has little to do with your coworkers; the changes taking place are in you and in how you function during your private working time.

Dealing with Family

The more-than-friends-less-than-lovers model offers a way to expand your horizons both professionally and personally with those of the opposite sex without undue risk to your relationship with a spouse or lover. With its disciplined, limited objectives, the relationship can make you a better companion at home. The business relationship you build is both fulfilling and productive, and you bring your happiness home. Your feelings for your husband, wife, or lover are unchanged.

Many marriages are composed of two busy and secure partners, and for them this kind of relationship probably will not cause a ripple. It will be seen as precisely what it is—a no-threat situation—or simply not noticed in the course of positive, fast-moving lives. In fact, husband and wife might each have such associations at work, which makes understanding come easy.

Although there is no need to dwell unduly on the sexual element, as one involved in a more-than-friends-less-than-lovers relationship you have no reason not to discuss the relationship openly with your spouse or lover. If he or she asks, answer honestly that you have a special working relationship, that it involves an intense sharing of your talents, that it is essentially professional in nature, and that you also are good friends. Describe the workplace project in a way that would have meaning for your spouse, talk about the contribution each of you is making, and explain that you are achieving impressive results that are recognized at work. Explain that it all began with an assignment neither of you sought, but that now it is both enjoyable and in your mutual professional interests to continue.

If asked about looks, sex appeal, intellect, and so on, be honest, and stress that you have a carved-in-stone agreement that personal involvement outside work is out of the question. If asked about how you feel about your coworker, again be honest, but stress the irreplaceable and different role your husband or wife plays in your life.

Contracts. To resolve what, on the surface, could seem to be competing loyalties between the attraction you feel for your spouse and that which you feel for your work partner, it helps to contract:

- to regularly affirm that your relationship is to remain secondary to and will not compete with your home life
- that you will address questions from your spouses or lovers honestly
- that any unsettled emotions regarding such things as loyalties and priorities are transient, to be resolved as you firm up boundaries, and not to be discussed at home unless questions are asked
- that you will not allow yourselves to displace spouses or lovers—the main intimate focus of your lives

Conversational gambits. The following conversations show how those involved in three different more-than-friends-less-than-lovers relationships handled the subject when asked about it at home.

> VIC: It sounds like you and Jake are really doing some impressive work together.

> JAN: We are. It's grown a lot since I first described the project to you a few months ago. Let me bring you up to date. [She goes on to describe a more mature and productive working arrangement and talks about its growing promise and some of what might be anticipated in the future.]

> VIC: So he won't have any problems keeping it all going while we're off to the sun for a few weeks?

> JAN: No. That's one of the nice things about the team approach.

Here, Vic's curiosity about the growing relationship is handled by Jan with the emphasis where it should be—on the work. In the process, it is reaffirmed that vacation plans remained central and dominant, with no more than the usual keep-in-touch-with-the-office expectations made on behalf of the work-based secondary relationship.

> ALLISON: I don't want to sound like a jealous wife, but you are treating this thing with Jill a lot differently than any business relationship you've ever had before.

> MACK: What do you mean?

> ALLISON: It's not like you're putting me on the back burner or anything, but I clearly feel the presence of another important person in your life—and I know it's Jill.

MACK: You're right, and you deserve more of an explanation. [He explains that this relationship is different, more personal because of genuine liking and common interests, but that the emphasis really is on work, and is in no way a competing relationship or a budding romance.]

ALLISON: So you're asking me to trust you and make room for this?

MACK: It would mean everything to me if you could. I didn't go looking for anything special, but Jill and I just clicked somehow, and it shows in our work, as you can see. And talking with Jill has made me think about how important you are as the center of my life. I'd never do anything that might make me lose you.

Allison, a concerned wife, asked for and got some honest answers about an outside relationship that she sensed was special. Mack reassured her that the secondary relationship posed no threat to the marriage. Their conversation also leaves the door open to future questions, because answers were given willingly and without hesitation.

BILL: I want you to stop seeing Sam.

GAIL: Where did that come from?

BILL: He's obviously becoming more important to you than I am, and you are going to have to make a choice.

GAIL: You're wrong! Sam is important to me, but only as a friend and someone that I work with.

BILL: And happen to find very good company, from what I can see.

GAIL: Yes, but not like you're implying. Let me explain. [She goes on to describe her association with her work partner.]

The kind of reaction you get at home depends on several things, including: (1) the stability of your marriage; (2) how you have portrayed the working relationship at home; and (3) your own comfort and lack of guilt feelings about the relationship. No amount of explanation will compensate for a seriously flawed marriage, but being honest can put a potentially serious misunderstanding by a caring spouse on the road to resolution.

Conscious management. To keep your special working relationship from becoming a problem at home, consciously:

- Agree to keep your relationships separated and remain honest and open in each. You shouldn't feel guilty because you share something special with someone outside your marriage—as long as it doesn't interfere.
- Agree to clearly delineate the priorities of your life and keep your working relationship focused and limited to where you have agreed it should be.
- Agree not to make light of your spouse's curiosity or concern about your relationship.
- Agree to keep your spouse informed, as you always have, about life at work, including the people you work with—in this case, your opposite-sex partner. In the process, you will deflate possible concern that might come with a sudden revelation that there is an all-at-once new and wonderful focus in your life. Be honest about the fact that *work* is especially exciting, with the emphasis correctly on its quality, and appropriate credit given to the partner who is an integral part of it.
- Agree to perform regular reality checks on each other and provide feedback to verify that your priorities are in order, that your relationship is within its boundaries, and that it is not taking on the aura of a romance.

The establishment stage is when you may acknowledge that you have broader needs than a single relationship can supply. As you sort through the feelings and establish boundaries, cast a realistic eye on your marriage. Properly managed, the satisfactions found in your more-than-friends-less-than-lovers relationship can relieve pressures that might otherwise build with your spouse. Your work partnership should supplement but not threaten or compete with your marriage.

OVERCOMING UNCERTAINTY

Uncertainty characterizes the establishment stage. While sure of their ultimate intentions about each other, men and women in the midst of dealing with this special, limited attraction wrestle with a confusing residue of traditional feelings. Before they finally work through them, intermediate-stage partners have perfectly natural human bouts of near-love feelings, sexual desire, jealousy, and possessiveness—all areas they have to resolve to achieve disciplined intimacy outside its usual romantic habitat. "In order to express differentness, judgment must be removed from the feeling area," writes Shirley Luthman in *Intimacy: The Essence of Male and Female.* "Feelings are not right or wrong, good or bad, they are just feelings; and they must be understood as such so that they can be shared and understood in terms of what the feelings mean in relation to the individual and the relationship."

Here are some of the warning signs that you or your partner may be having real difficulty in resolving those feelings.

Communication can be imperfect and lead to serious misunderstandings. While this is true in any relationship, for a work team the problem is compounded because deep communication is limited to irregular periods of working together and requires a private setting. A quick, superficial exchange in the business-conversation tone of a crowded office hardly satisfies the needs of a partner who is grappling at that moment with his or her feelings about the attraction, or experiencing a twinge of jealousy or any of the other feelings that continue to surface and may require intensive discussion to resolve.

The lapses in quality time together sometimes result in confusion. A concerned partner might interpret a perfectly innocuous noncommittal response in a public setting as confirmation of a fear of unmatched enthusiasm and commitment to the relationship, just when warmth and reassurance are needed most.

Behavior you know is inappropriate may surface periodically even after you thought an issue was resolved. For example, you know it isn't right to try to build a protective fence around your partner, but you find yourself doing it anyway. You must continue to provide each other with feedback when unpleasant incidents like this occur, and the offending party needs to adjust his or her behavior accordingly.

Commitment to problem solving provides relationships with strength and vitality. Because of the rewards and satisfaction resulting from your achievements and intimate caring, your relationship enjoys a staying power not found in ordinary colleague or friendship-based teams. Therefore, if you have a serious disagreement and ignore it, your work will suffer. You make this partnership work by turning personal attraction into caring, and work that you love into a prosperous and successfully shared professional life.

In the case of Jocelyn and Troy, work tempered the response of the offended partner, who found a reason to make the effort to solve the problem due to the promise of an exceptional professional relationship.

Jocelyn and Troy had worked together for a trade association as a team of lobbyists for six years. She was single, but had enjoyed a prolonged relationship that ended months before she came to know Troy well. He and a longtime companion had parted within the past year when she returned to her native Australia.

A written memorandum from Troy and a response from Jocelyn follows. The partners tell us that, to this day, they will sometimes put important thoughts in writing. Their reasoning is that some of their best reflections on their relationship occur while they are apart, and they want to capture and share them when they come to mind rather than wait. Another point they made was that some things might never be said in a face-to-face conversation. They might be too busy with work or, even though they know each other very well, feel reluctant to hammer home the bottom line. The exchange that follows thus represents bare feelings deliberately expressed for maximum impact.

Jocelyn was flabbergasted at Troy's reaction when he returned from an autumn trip and unexpectedly confronted her with his dramatic rendering of her behavior with an associate. His tirade-by-memorandum had been pecked out on a laptop computer at an altitude of 35,000 feet, when he was tired to the bone and on the way home from a frustrating ten days of rushing around the country alone. She became the focus for all that wasn't right in his world that day.

October 19th

Jocelyn—

As you have probably sensed, something has been troubling me. It's been there for a while, but this trip brought it to the surface and I have to get it out of my system. I don't mean to hurt you in doing so, but it's time to clear the air. A conversation would be hurried and incomplete—an inquisition is not what I have in mind, so let me just tell you what's been troubling me.

I know we have no claims on each other, but when you started another relationship it so changed your status in my life that ours ceased to exist. When the new interest apparently took hold, I felt the loss, but kissed it off to no time together recently. As implausible as it seems to this moment, you began the very

*office relationship you were so dead set against and, over the
months that followed, thoroughly trashed my perception of you.*

*I found out that my trust had been misplaced. My connec-
tion to you crumbled and I couldn't put it back together again.
Not intellectually, not even the attraction. It just wasn't the
same. I reached for a feeling that used to leave me anxiously
awaiting our next exchange of ideas, and it wasn't there
anymore.*

*You of all people deserve to know where my limits are—
since you were so instrumental in defining them. I hope the new
relationships of your life will lead to happiness. You are quite a
woman, Jocelyn—do your thing and thanks for sharing what
you could with me along the way. I guess it was even more limited than I thought.*

*If I am wrong, enlighten me. If I'm right, stay my friend
and colleague through the contract and let's give the world something it wouldn't have had without us. How many people are
privileged to get that far? In our case I am at a loss to tell you
whether one moved on or the other stepped back, but the gap between us has grown too wide. It was a wonderful path of discovery we walked, now we've reached a gate we won't go through
together. It was nice and more Jocelyn—much more . . .
"I wouldn't have missed it for the world, wouldn't have
missed . . . " . . . you know the song. But I did . . . and
I'm sad.*

—Troy

*Troy's memorandum speaks for itself in terms of underlying
feelings and expectations that grow in spite of best efforts to limit
a relationship. Jocelyn's spontaneous and effective rebuttal shows
the depth and breadth of their bond. She stresses that personal
feelings are not what they count on for being more than casual
friends—that they are incidental. If a loving commitment was
being demanded, she would have run the other way. She knew
from their long intimate hours together that Troy was after some-*

thing else, and she found the relationship worth defending for the same nonromantic reasons. They were personally and professionally valuable to each other quite apart from the alleged incident that now threatened them. Jocelyn's resilience in the face of such a hit, her unyielding and yet soothing candor, speak eloquently of the value she attaches to what she and Troy share.

October 20th

Troy—

You need a vacation or you've lost your mind or you've been working too hard or something!

First, you're wrong about my personal life. I think you've been seeing things with me and other people that aren't there, not that they're any of your business. As you should know, it's not the time for even Robert Redford or Tom Cruise. I've got some very close friends (including you, I thought), but I'm actually happier than I thought I could be being on my own right now. Frankly, I have too many other things on my mind, including our project, my father's health, the puzzle of what is to happen in several important aspects of my life. Some of that is painful for me and will just take time to resolve. With all of it, I'm hardly in a position to deal with the love affair you implied I'm having.

But why am I telling you all of this? How many times and ways have we taken a difficult knot of feelings, discussed them, understood them, even felt regret, but decided to keep on going? The relationship constantly evolves due to situation and context, but it's also influenced by external factors that have to be dealt with constructively.

Though you say you don't, you want to draw a box around us, and we'll become like everyone else. The reason we've done so well is that we're not like everyone else and we have something to offer as a team that's different. That's what our clients *see! These people see the chemistry without the usual routine familiarity and they love it.*

Sure, I'll be a bit sad when you find the Asian beauty you dream about, but I'll also be inspired to be better, more interesting and more desirable, and she'll be inspired to do the same. And you and she will be bound closer, while you and I will go on as we have. I would hope the same would happen if I find someone who makes me happy. This is one of the things that make us special and prove the real affection we've shared all these years.

So, my cherished friend, think carefully before you send us down the tubes. I think you're dead wrong!

—Jocelyn

These notes to each other—and the resolution they brought about—demonstrate the integrity of Jocelyn and Troy's relationship. In the turmoil of disrupted personal lives, they remained limited but uniquely vital focal points in each other's value systems and relationship networks.

After a few days of rest for Troy and several long private discussions over working dinners, the biggest test to date of this very special bond was passed. Jealousy was acknowledged as unfounded and appropriate. Possessiveness and control were renounced as inappropriate. And their need for continuing the unique roles played in each other's lives was reaffirmed. Through uncommon forbearance, understanding, and communication, two more than friends were again secure in being less than lovers.

As we've moved through the first two stages of the more-than-friends-less-than-lovers relationship, we've seen the emergence of an unexpected attraction; watched it grow into something worthy of keeping; seen the partners decide that since they would not become lovers, they would divert the attraction's energy into their work; and observed the sometimes wrenching process of converting an intellectual accommodation into a living one through the testing and boundary adjusting of the establishment stage. Next comes the payoff, where the man and woman involved are playing basically the same tune.

- They aren't lovers—and they're glad of it.
- They occupy a valued niche in each other's lives—and feel secure about it.
- They do great work together—and they enjoy it.
- They live comfortably with each other's personal lives—and aren't threatened by them.

They are poised to enjoy the advanced, or consolidation, stage of their more-than-friends-less-than-lovers relationship.

5. Reaping the Benefits: The Consolidation Stage

I N THE ADVANCED stage of your more-than-friends-less-than-lovers relationship, as you focus on consolidating an association that is both professionally productive and personally satisfying, you achieve a degree of symmetry that was lacking in earlier stages. The tug-of-war that characterized the establishment stage, where you were vulnerable players gradually yielding more trust as you negotiated boundary and expectation issues, finally ends. Standing securely as more than friends, and less than lovers, you no longer feel the need to protect yourselves from potential threats to your ego, your professional integrity, and your marriages. The embarrassment of an unreciprocated attraction no longer threatens. Neither does the question of where it will lead. You've come to rest safely short of sexual involvement, falling in love, and inflicting or feeling pain by misunderstanding the other's expectations.

Now you are reaping the benefits, pursuing a common goal—maintaining your relationship at its current comfort and satisfaction levels—and not individual agendas. The two of you are more in harmony than you have ever been. Prior concerns about each other's loyalty and intentions are resolved. You've become a balanced team, with interdependent skills— an operating entity with a character of your own that commands respect in the marketplace. You don't anguish over how to deal with the personal attraction you inadvertently discovered in the beginning, or with the intimacy you developed and nurtured along the way.

Even though your boundaries are firm, some of them will always remain matters of reasoned contention—things about which you will never totally agree. One partner may forever seek to define the relationship with more certainty, while the other derives satisfaction from its ambiguity. One has blind faith that the association will accommodate whatever the future holds; the other never shakes a foreboding that more orthodox closure still lurks somewhere down the line. One may hope that the sexual boundary, though firmly in place and unquestioned, might at some unspecified time be pushed aside; the other feels that the issue is forever closed. These kinds of differences are not focal points at the consolidation stage, only evidence that you will always need to tend the fences of your relationship; conscious management doesn't end with success.

Your relationship continues to grow, but the pace is more even, less erratic. Unlike in earlier stages, you have established enough common ground that your relationship is in little danger of foundering. Regardless of how it is challenged, you view it as a highly valued and positive force in your lives—one you would abandon with great reluctance.

You have established a pattern of doing professionally significant work successfully and realize that it is all underwritten by tremendously strong personal ties. Along with consciously disciplined limitations, you have established a faith in each other that opens the way for maximum achievement as a team.

Until now a substantial amount of your energy was spent actively probing the dimensions of your attraction and how you might comfortably live with it. By consciously managing your behavior, you have been able to care for each other deeply, know each other intimately, and share professional success fueled by sexual attraction, while keeping your personal lives separate in order to preserve the status that makes it all possible. What you've ended up with is a positive force for stimulating each other to new levels of achievement and satisfaction. By this time, you specifically have:

- learned to work together with intimate personal sharing that few colleagues achieve
- deliberately remained free of the entanglements of broader personal involvement, either romantically or as close traditional friends
- learned to focus a combination of sexual energy and complementary skills on achieving extraordinary productivity
- realized that your relationship is no longer a struggle for understanding at fundamental levels and accepted that some of your expectations will never perfectly match
- moved distracting behavior to the background
- resolved any traces of the competition and defensiveness that arise uniquely between the sexes—the potential for hurt that stings all the more when inflicted by an object of your affection; balance and mutual worth are apparent, and concern for ego injury has subsided
- comfortably placed your relationship in your total lives, remaining sensitive to its impact on spouses and coworkers
- agreed to continue pursuing an intimate mix of growth and achievement, both personal and professional, as mature attraction continues to inspire the relationship

You appreciate what you have together and don't bemoan what you may have forgone by avoiding a sexual involvement. Your relationship has become a primary part of your lives and provides you with enough productive purpose and satisfaction that it successfully rises above moments of professional or personal discontent.

By consciously managing your behavior at each step

along the way, you have progressed beyond pitfalls—such as failed communication, unbalanced expectations, jealousy, and possessiveness—that threaten most friendships and marriages. You have avoided these problems by agreeing to expand your relationship at a limited pace as you monitor each other for signs of too much or too little commitment, of falling in love, of breaching boundaries, and so on, remaining largely insulated from the complications of total involvement.

In the beginning you communicated at a superficial level, getting to know each other's basic home situations, backgrounds, and professional and personal interests. Later your communication increased in both depth and sensitivity, while you drew and tested boundaries to get important issues like romantic and sexual prospects, values, expectations, hopes for the relationship, and career objectives out on the discussion table. At the consolidation stage, you are comfortably open and forthcoming about what you mean to each other, the value attached to the relationship's limited nature, and the reasons you want to see it continue. You respect each other's right to privacy on personal issues, but you freely discuss feelings or events you consider relevant to your relationship. As is true of marriages, friendships, and other important personal relationships, you know that you should not take your association for granted and that you need to work at it if it is to grow and last. Therefore, you rely on good communication to bridge the gap when your intermittent time together denies you the opportunity to monitor your boundaries and reestablish the intimacy so vital to your special status.

REACHING THE CONSOLIDATION STAGE: THE ULTIMATE DIALOGUE

In the discovery stage, you talked to each other as an attracted getting-to-know-you man and woman—superficially, lightheartedly, much as any two people who are casually interested in each other do. Next came the establishment stage, where you began to invest in the relationship and see prospects for its becoming important to you. You began to talk in depth about hopes and dreams, values, and career and professional goals, ending up a deeply committed business couple with a great deal of knowledge about each other. In the process, you laid the groundwork for a long association by agreeing on boundaries, rules, and goals for the future. And you did it primarily through open, direct communication that was sometimes painful, sometimes embarrassing, and sometimes fun. At the consolidation stage, communication continues to be the tool that keeps your behavior and your relationship on track, moving in the direction you have laid out.

On topics you've agreed to share, you speak openly, but there are plenty of things you don't know about each other and never will—a multitude of differences outside the limitations you've placed on your association. You talk about some issues and events, and not about others; you can tell which ones are over the boundary now. The dividing line falls somewhere between your mutual working interests and your private lives. There is overlap, of course, but experience in testing boundaries has made you excellent judges of what you will share and what you won't. You've defined a wide swath of common turf, and you know every inch of it. With all the limitations, you continue to explore broad areas of inquiry—the working world of your relationship, and personal aspects of your lives that touch it as well.

The difference between consolidation-stage communication and earlier discussions is an ability to focus your energies and get productive results without rehashing old frustrations. Awkward inquiry and learning were part of building your relationship, but replowing old ground is a mistake you don't make at this stage. You know the difference between refining sophisticated understandings and bludgeoning dead issues. Serious disagreement and awkward moments are now rare.

The secret is your common insistence on growth. Another angle, a reason to reconsider a point, a change of circumstances—all are legitimate grounds for rethinking something from the past, but always with respect for arguments previously made. Reexamining your attraction never gets tiring because you find new facets each time you look. Sexual attraction remains the untiring engine of your relationship because its inspiration is crucial to your motivation and productivity. The keystone of consolidation-stage communication is that you have moved beyond simply exchanging information to attaching real meaning to what is being said. You know your partner so well that you no longer just speak and listen; you comprehend his or her deepest meaning.

Your sexual attraction, for all its compelling qualities, gets bumped a notch down motivational psychologist Dr. Abraham Maslow's hierarchy of needs, in which "needs are arranged along a hierarchy of priority or potency. When the needs that have the greatest potency and priority are satisfied, the next needs in the hierarchy emerge and press for satisfaction." Satisfying sexual needs is basic, but other things actually do come first with more than friends. Economic, self-worth, and personal-identity satisfactions transcend this relationship's sexual drive, accompanied by your determination to be faithful to spouses or lovers. The discipline isn't as difficult now that you've settled on what your priorities are. While sexual energy underwrites your association, it is secondary to the goals that you've set for yourselves and the satisfaction you get from resolving problems and issues that might get in their way. Open discussion provides the feedback you need to keep yourselves true to the contracts you've drawn.

The story of Heather and Greg illustrates the power of communication at the consolidation stage.

Heather is a research physician at a prominent teaching hospital. Greg is an established free-lancer and successful ghost writer for people in the scientific community. A catchy journal article by Heather attracted the interest of a major publisher. When she responded that she'd love to do a book in her specialty but had neither the time nor the skills to write a popular version, the editor suggested an agent known to represent the kind of writer who might assist her. A few calls and weeks later, she found herself having dinner with Greg—her prospective writing partner.

The first book succeeded dramatically, and Heather and Greg's relationship as coauthors has gone on for more than six years, through as many shared projects. All the while she has pursued her medical career and remained happily married to a university professor. Greg has continued to publish in his own right. While he's never married, he remains deeply committed to the woman who was in his life when he met Heather.

Over the years, long hours of working on manuscripts triggered an attraction between Heather and Greg that, retrospectively, should have come as no surprise. What could be more intimate and fascinating than the systematic struggle to communicate your deepest understandings to another person? After years of finding time to talk and think privately, whether over working dinners at local restaurants or during rare weekends closeted at his lakeside cottage hammering out a final version, they came to know each other very well.

While Greg and Heather worked separately most of the time, even their exchanges of draft chapters became intimate experiences. Many times nothing was said of it, but each saw in the writing of the other the bits and pieces of answers to questions they'd wondered about, curiosities not previously satisfied about the other's values, thinking, and attitudes. Communication was their ultimate intimacy—a subtle and powerful bond that made them special to each other and gave them power as a writing team that was prized by their publisher.

Heather and Greg discussed their fascination with each other and their work, and it eventually evolved into a more-than-friends-less-than-lovers kind of association bounded by their personal circumstances and inclinations. They loved their work together, not each other. There was a sexy undercurrent that made the time spent groping for the right thoughts or words especially satisfying and fun, but never uneasy or threatening. Personal feelings remained a part of their overall energy mix, but didn't smother their central purpose—writing good books, enjoying the experience, challenging each other professionally, and never having to overlook or apologize for the man/woman attraction they shared as well.

Gregory and Heather found that they thrived on not becoming day-in, day-out fixtures in each other's lives. Those roles were reserved for others. Their time together was limited and almost always a stimulating high that was easier to achieve because both knew it wouldn't have to be sustained. Theirs wasn't everyday reality, and they knew it shouldn't be. They unabashedly enjoyed a sex-tinged intellectual turn-on that never got out of hand or had to deliver too much for too long.

As the years passed, Heather and Greg marveled at their growth as a writing team. For two people matched entirely by the machinations of a distant publishing house, and with fully functioning lives already in place, they found room for a complete and and intimately private realm all their own. After getting over the early bouts of discomfort as they discussed everything from how they felt about extramarital relationships and what kinds of locations were acceptable for working alone together, to their fears that the relationship would end if one of them came right out and said no to a romantic liaison, Heather and Greg settled into the business of putting their attraction to work for them instead. They communicated with total honesty, sometimes by mail as they exchanged manuscripts, and the result was a relationship with an indefinite future. Her scientific knowledge and his ability to coax it out of her gave their writing a quality that appealed to the mass market and produced an exciting series of popular books on medical subjects.

It was more than a technician/ghost writer collaboration mechanically getting the facts down on paper. Heather and Greg lived their books, got inside each other's heads, and genuinely made the whole of their thinking greater than the sum of their individual contributions to it. They could never have generated, much less produced, a book a year without the benefit of the very sophisticated personal communication that enabled them to identify what they did best together, use the special fire of their controlled attraction to keep them motivated, and maintain the stability of their existing personal lives.

ISSUES FOR DISCUSSION

Like marriage or friendship, your relationship is subject to decline for all the usual reasons—intruding interests, loss of shared interest, employment changes that separate you physically and professionally, simple indifference, or taking it all for granted. Consolidation-stage discussions deal with these pitfalls. The momentum of a dramatic project can give you a false sense of security, making you feel as if the relationship is so natural that it can take care of itself. Like any significant relationship, it can't. Continued growth and vitality demand consideration of a number of questions:

- How do you plan to keep personal attraction alive when the prospect of sex and love have been removed from consideration?
- What else can you add to the commitment level and expectations that have been set?
- Where do you go with boundaries that have been tested, intimacy that seems to have retreated from its most tantalizing point, and trust that appears to be fully established?
- How will you add to the workplace magic that you've already demonstrated?
- Can you now offer coworkers an explanation of this relationship model for them to try out?
- How can you keep your family's trust and understanding through the course of what is looking like an indefinite secondary relationship?

Attraction and Sexuality

You sense your attraction at the discovery stage, define its boundaries and wrestle with it at the management stage, and give it an affirmed, comfortable place in your life at the consolidation stage. You have come to appreciate the existence of a substantive attraction that includes more than physical attributes and superficial personality traits. It is solid and no longer needs constant reaffirmation or restraint. During the emotional upheavals of the management stage, you learned to sublimate your attraction into your work. When sexual tension was in the air, you directed conversation and energy immediately to the work at hand, achieving excellent results.

At the consolidation stage you consciously use the energy of your sexual interest as a positive motivator and creative spark. You are no longer uncomfortable about discussing it, so instead of deliberately sublimating your feelings and changing the subject, you freely discuss why the air is suddenly charged, bringing the energy to the surface and then focusing it on the project at hand. You feel tremendous excitement as you admit that work is downright sexy. You learn to deliberately harness a force not available to mere friends, and feel even more excited in the process. This is a battle you've won by hard work as you've talked at length and kept each other in line through direct monitoring and consciously managed behavior.

The discovery-stage halo you drew above your partner's head, nearly lost during the reality testing of the establishment stage, returns now—but the fit is much improved. While you haven't found the love of a lifetime or gained the working company of a matinee idol, on balance you rate your partner a wonderful human being, and the association as a warm and productive one you'd definitely like to keep. You focus idealization primarily on yourselves as a team, a man and woman who are essentially satisfied with working together. You no longer look at your partner as someone whom you have to make a place for in your life; his or her place is assured. The relationship is specifically bounded and purposeful.

The power of your sexual attraction is undiminished at this stage, but you are more experienced in handling it. *If only we could . . .* has become *I know we won't, but . . .* , and the energy continues to swirl about you, challenging you not only to keep it in its proper place but also to use it productively. You have neither spent the sexual energy nor removed it from your dealings with each other. You realize that you are not going to have sex, but you continue to wonder what it might be like. The emotional and biological stimulation continues, and you retain your own minute trace of wondering that keeps the feeling alive. Neither of you fears that the relationship will end for lack of sexual fulfillment, but sexual feelings have much to do with the spark you bring to your work, and you make no attempt to extinguish them. Caged but not vanquished, your sexual attraction is something you put out of tangible reach and use to your advantage as a work team. You have a relationship with an open-ended future that remains vibrant as the *what if* provides an eternal excitement not found when you know how the game ends. And in the process, you continue to light the fires of sexual attraction and channel their heat constructively into your work.

Contracts. At this stage, you keep sexual interest alive and still controlled when you contract:
- to respect the limited place of your attraction in your total lives and avoid letting it compete with your marriages or love relationships
- to freely share your attraction, and to use it to fire creative energies that don't receive the same kind of stimulation elsewhere
- to make use of sexual energy, not in each other's beds, but where the creative spirit needs a boost
- that it is desirable never to remove totally the power of sexual attraction and the fantasy of possible fulfillment

- that sexual attraction and its attendant energy are meta-phors for the deep mutual commitment that fuels your uniquely productive effort
- that your mutually accepted values still link romantic love and sex, and that neither is an objective of this rela-tionship
- that the prospect of having sex can be effectively re-moved without eradicating its energy or legitimacy as an aspect of your relationship

At the consolidation stage, your attraction has been enor-mously simplified by honest communication about how you feel and by agreement on where it will and will not lead. While sexual attraction continues to give your relationship its special vitality and professional applications provide the outlet and tangible rewards, it is the combination of all these aspects of a complex attraction that finally lets your professional relation-ship come into its own. You have moved from an individually guarded sexual attraction to a mutually disciplined one—two people agreeably seeking the same result, free to enjoy the never-ending stimulation of the process together, and never complacent enough to take it for granted.

Conversational gambits. Here is the way Dirk and Sandy dealt with the issue of sexual attraction at this stage.

DIRK: You're still a turn-on for me, but I don't feel guilty about it anymore. It's finally clear what's *not* going to happen.

SANDY: And you still think about it?

DIRK: Sure. You'd think by now we'd have this thing back in the bottle, but it never seems to go away.

SANDY: You still find me exciting sometimes?

DIRK: Just enough to keep the pot boiling.

SANDY: That's okay. Now that I feel safe, I consider it a compliment.

By now both Dirk and Sandy are clear that sex is off the table, but the look, feel, and mutual understanding of the attraction are not. While only periodic and never protracted, such exchanges can provide an outlet for honest feelings—and confirmation that they're very much under control.

SANDY: There are things about you I don't like at all, and you know that. But for some reason, I find you even more attractive than I did when I was looking for perfection. Only someone who knows you the way I do could say that.

DIRK: Yeah, I'm more than just another handsome face now.

SANDY: You laugh, but it's true. Somewhere between the sex we haven't had and all the work we have to do, life might not be long enough to finish it all together. I guess I can take you for a long, long time—in small doses.

Sandy and Dirk's attraction is acknowledged as a total mix of imperfect looks, unfulfilled sexual desire, and endless plans to finish important work together, made safe for the long haul in a relationship that won't deliver on the sexual side but is obviously important and special to both of them. As consolidation-stage partners they can enjoy their sexuality and attraction without every thought leaping to the threshold of love, or each word of criticism delivering a mortal blow to the ego.

SANDY: We made everything seem much more complicated than it needed to be for a long time.

DIRK: Once we decided to stop feeling guilty about a sexy thought every now and then, everything got simpler.

SANDY: Yeah, and when we realized we weren't falling in love, we were able to relax and enjoy the good feelings.

DIRK: No matter how you cut it, we do share a chemistry.

SANDY: There's certainly been *something* over the years that's more than mere biology.

DIRK: Yeah, I think a lot of it is our backgrounds—both coming from the country, growing up the same way, and feeling the same way about so many things, including working ridiculously long hours to get something done.

Sandy and Dirk have come to understand that their attraction has a magic about it that is more than any of its components. Sex alone doesn't account for it, nor does a certain kind of appearance. There's a bond that grows out of looks, intellect, cultural background, values, interests. The sum of what they are produces an identity and gives both partners an ability to understand each other in a special way. This consolidation-stage realization displaces the insecurity of more superficial attraction.

DIRK: Do you remember how awkward we used to get maneuvering around polite little discussions about sex, trying to figure out just what the other was thinking?

SANDY: And now we know.

DIRK: And now we speak right up.

SANDY: That's because we know most of the answers.

DIRK: Oh, I don't think we'll ever know most of the answers. But we've asked the right questions and know how to behave if we don't want to wreck everything.

The lasting value of the relationship is acknowledged at this stage. Dirk and Sandy have revealed a lot about themselves on their way to this point, but their knowledge is anything but complete. There are aspects of their feelings that range beyond what each of them is willing and able to share, and these preserve the mystery of the unknown. They realize that they can never be sure what the ultimate future of their relationship will be, and that total revelation is not among the obligations of a more-than-friends-less-than-lovers couple.

Conscious management. To exercise conscious control over the consolidation stage, you both need to:
- Agree to enjoy the moments when you idealize your relationship. Use them to add color and vitality, but never think that they represent reality.
- Agree to keep your rationality, because it gives you control over your behavior. Your magic together is a controlled mix of the rational and the ideal. Total rationality would strip your relationship of much of its energy, and too much idealism would reduce its ability to last in the real world.
- Agree to reinforce your establishment-stage agreement to be open about sexual desire, keep it alive, control your actions, and consciously direct sexual energy into work, thus lessening the prospects for unwelcome forms of sexual expression.
- Agree to maintain the kind of intimacy you need in your marriage, and don't try to compensate for problems there by turning up the intensity level of your limited working relationship.

Commitment Level and Expectations

At this stage you recapture the simplicity of your relationship's beginning in the form of understood and mostly balanced expectations. Establishment-stage apprehensions about who was giving, who was taking, and whether or not you were coming up short have vanished. Trust has become a pragmatic faith that the relationship is equally important to you both, yet you accept the fact that you can't will, arrange, or otherwise guarantee its continuing value.

Much as it does in a marriage or friendship, commitment to the relationship will last as long as both of you want it, need it, and are willing to work at making it grow. The commitment is a simple one: you will stay as long as caring, interest, and mutual satisfaction remain. You are totally free to go—no marriage license, no romance, no written contract. But you're strongly predisposed to stay because you've worked hard at building an enduring, valuable association—one that is based on natural personal attraction and caring, in which consciously sublimated sexual energy turns your work together into something far better than either of you ever had alone.

At the beginning, there was no jealousy and possessiveness because you expected no exclusive treatment. You weren't yet committed to the relationship, and you felt no inclination to exercise your rights because you didn't think you had any. As you increased your stake in each other's lives, you experienced some of these feelings, worked through them, and came to understand that, just as you placed limits on your total relationship, you also needed to place them on the natural inclination to keep your partner only unto you. If your involvement were a courtship, you would focus on each other and give up competing relationships. But this relationship is not a courtship, and proprietary feelings and twinges of jealousy have mostly disappeared after many frank discussions that made you realize you were trying to match apple and orange

relationships—the more-than-friends-less-than-lovers relationship, based on work, with personal aspects clearly secondary; and the marriage or romantic liaison, based on love and
emotions, with external aspects clearly secondary.

At the consolidation stage, you successfully limit proprietary feelings to your specialty; they do not intrude into
your lives or work in general. Now it honestly doesn't matter
to you how your partner spends his or her nonrelationship
time. You know your legitimate territoriality begins and ends
with issues that touch your work as a team. Occasionally one
of you might step over the jealousy boundary. This calls
for the ability to say, and to accept being told, "It's none of
your business." One of the greatest ongoing relationship-
management challenges is in keeping perspective on where
your prerogatives stop with your partner. It becomes easier at
the consolidation stage, where you are reaffirming what is already established instead of thrashing out original boundaries.

You used to be self-conscious about your working relationship having a personal side that mattered a lot. Without
flaunting it, you have integrated the caring into your lives
without awkwardness or apology. Everyone knows you spend
much of your time working together and are good friends. At
the same time, you have been able to detach yourselves from
each other's everyday lives at the office and at home. The dating mentality of having to do things together whenever the
two of you are present is gone. It simply doesn't fit at work,
where each of you needs to be socially and politically independent. The need to cultivate those who can help get you the next
raise, or help those who need your expertise, doesn't go away
because you are an identified work team.

You have an uncanny ability to sense when you need to
talk about the future and reaffirm your commitment to the relationship. It won't do to stretch an aging infatuation across
lives that are changing and diverging, as you knew they
would. With so many things off the table as you accept your

boundaries at this stage, you need something very real and valuable around which to rally your relationship commitment and expectations. As before, you find that needing each other for inspiration and substance in your work, along with personal caring short of romantic love, gives you the basis for continuing together.

Contracts. To help bring both your expectations and commitment into line, you need to contract:
- that the measure of your commitment will be what you give to your relationship, not what you withhold from lovers or spouses
- that less is more at this stage of your relationship and that you will emphasize quality time and effort together instead of expanding its scope
- to accept the validity of your commitment at face value; if it is working and the results are productive, you have no need to define an explicit proof of it
- that your relationship has minimum standards of commitment to which you will be sensitive, not taking it for granted in the face of more immediately demanding requirements in your life
- to remain realistic about what you define as reasonable to give and expect in terms of relationship exclusiveness—nothing in your personal lives, and limited business exclusivity when it involves your shared tasks
- to reaffirm as needed that there is a special place for each of you in the limited life you've defined together
- that you will remain focused on the original motivations for limiting your relationship if it becomes tempting to alter or escalate your commitment and expectations as you grow comfortable with each other

Conversational gambits. This is how Nick and Nora's discussion of commitment and expectations sounds at this stage.

NORA: You finally seem to understand that I'm committed to what we do together.

NICK: Yeah, it took a while. I guess you really *can* give enough without giving it all. I think we'll be working together a long, long time.

NORA: Why did we ever make this relationship so complicated? What we want from each other is pretty simple after all.

Achieving focus is your greatest challenge at this stage. If you insist on full commitment, your relationship will fail. If you can settle for the work and limited personal involvement Nora and Nick have agreed to share, you find security once unproven fears about rejection, loss, and disappointment are finally allowed to fall aside.

NICK: There was a time when if either of us had accepted a road assignment with someone else, it would have been curtains for our relationship.

NORA: Yeah. It really wouldn't make much difference now. We both realize that what we have is based on what we do together, not on what we do with someone else.

NICK: I still wish we could have spent more time together at the annual meeting, but the chairman insisted on having me with him every minute.

NORA: That's no problem. I hear you're being groomed for a promotion, and it's because you've made yourself a key person.

NICK: But I don't want you to think that it means I'm giving up on our project—it means so much to me.

NORA: Hey. We decided a long time ago that outside the project hours we'd live our own lives and build our personal careers. Our relationship will work for us only as long as it's special and no longer. That's how it has to be.

Here, at the consolidation stage, Nick and Nora show that they don't try to limit each other's association with others. They realize that everything they do contributes to a running value judgment each makes on whether to remain in a relationship neither can take for granted. As coworkers they take care of the dual tasks of being sensitive to competing interests and letting each other know that it's okay. While neither is a requirement, both are essential bits of relationship management at the consolidation stage, where individualism is assured but caring is always appreciated and strengthens tolerance for necessary independence.

NORA: A Saturday afternoon at the office was never my idea of a vacation, but I have to admit I'm enjoying this.

NICK: Yeah, it's been a while since we've been able to work on something by ourselves without the rest of the world intruding.

NORA: I can remember when we weren't so easily satisfied.

NICK: Like when this wouldn't have been any good unless we puzzled over the indefinite future of our relationship, and would have gone to dinner to hash it out?

NORA: Yeah. We can still have dinner, you know.

NICK: Sure. And not because there's some profound question hanging over our heads—but because we're hungry, like each other's company, and the conclusions for this report need some brainstorming on the way home anyway.

Now that they have settled the major issues surrounding their relationship, Nick and Nora are at ease with each other. They place the emphasis where it belongs—on work and on enjoying each other in the way they've decided will serve their mutual interests.

Conscious management. In order to consciously manage your behavior to reflect mutual levels of understanding on commitment and expectation issues, you need to:

- Agree to leave third parties out of your problem solving; the only behavior that is fair to judge is that which affects your special work.
- Agree to find growth and new challenges in deepening your existing work interests instead of trying to engage each other more broadly.
- Agree to assume the best in your relationship and not to look for reasons to doubt it or insist that its course has been run.
- Agree to assume a stance that lets you derive satisfaction from seeing your partner get pleasure from other things in his or her life, not just from what you do together.
- Agree to remain alert to doing your part to preserve your value in your partner's eyes for as long as you want your work to continue as it has.

Enjoy the less-strained commitment and expectations of the consolidation stage, but don't become indifferent to a relationship you value because it takes effort to keep it fresh. At the same time, don't take it for granted, assuming it will always be there, exactly the way it is, whenever you want it. Remember, for the most part your expectations and commitment levels are in sync, but don't assume that periodic reinforcement isn't necessary.

Boundaries, Intimacy, and Trust

The interactive qualities of intimacy, trust, and boundaries have progressed from general formulation through firm definition, probing, and adjustment and on to the intuitive understanding of the consolidation stage. As with marriage or friendship, you now know where boundaries stand with your partner and when they need to shift naturally or be adjusted to accommodate either of you. Tacit understandings bound even the most intimate areas of your interaction. You deal with each other based on unquestioned trust, and you are confident that it won't be betrayed; the track record together is long now, and there's no reason to expect betrayal from a person you know so well. If asked, you would say you share a terrific working relationship with an attractive colleague and that you have crafted an ideal team for your limited purposes.

As trust deepens in your advancing relationship, fears of being exploited have disappeared. If concerns remain about sex, they are the general ones posed by the intimate relationship itself and not fear of your partner. Dealing with sexual temptation will always require conscious management, but sex will remain a matter for discussion, never action. At this stage, you acknowledge the temptation and then deliberately put it in its designated place as an issue you have firmly resolved. If the unwanted proposition resurfaces, either let it die or retrace the reasoning behind your refusal, reaffirming the sexual boundary. You know what you don't want and by now are confident of your ability to avoid it.

It is in this stage that you finally appreciate the real limits of your relationship and comfortably accept its boundaries. You feel at ease extending intimacy and are not afraid that, by doing so, you will spread the relationship ever wider and thinner into private areas of your life. Disappointment comes only when you ask for something that your partner did not agree to give or for more than you can hope to sustain together.

At this stage, you stop wasting energy on the negative

practice of reining each other in and concentrate instead on looking for an unending chain of irresistible challenges to meet together. Just when the intimacy seems as complete as it is going to get and you expect no more, a new professional task unearths a facet of your partner you'd never dreamed would be revealed. In turn, you may learn something about your own feelings or abilities that surprises you just as much. Rather than looking back nostalgically to your first moments of intimate disclosure, you leap ahead to what you could never have anticipated had you managed each other instead of your relationship.

Willingly leaving each other free to enjoy others keeps fresh breezes blowing through your relationship as you draw on the inspiration of an unending cast of characters from both your lives, whose ideas and behavior give you food for thought or discussion. Some of these are people whom you'll never meet and with whom you'll never exchange a word because they are part of your separate lives, but they add color to what you know about each other. This is a gift that you share by not clamping down the possessiveness lid that tends to close over many conventional relationships. Remember the fresh thinking and different perspectives that attracted you to each other in the first place? The magic of consolidated more-than-friends-less-than-lovers status is sharing highly advanced intimacy within boundaries that give each of you the privilege of remaining your own person, free to range through life with enough abandon to bring back ideas, thoughts, and questions worth sharing.

Contracts. To ensure that both of you respect each other's boundaries, keeping your trust and intimacy intact, you will want to contract:

- to keep the reasons for enjoying your relationship clearly before you: the first is business; the second is personal intimacy tempered by limitations that direct your sexual energies toward your work

- that while intimacy and trust are givens at this stage, you will reaffirm them frequently to keep your maturing relationship charged
- to trust your partner to function fully in his or her professional and personal life, being receptive to sharing the stimulation found there in your own relationship
- to pursue growth together by deepening intimacy and trust in your professional specialty rather than extending your relationship beyond your shared interests
- to adapt to accommodate possible changes in work and lifestyles that may separate you physically but allow your work to go on under different circumstances
- to collapse old boundaries that are no longer relevant, but to honor the essential ones that continue to define your relationship

Conversational gambits. Lee and Helen helped each other cope with boundaries and trust by remaining open and honest with each other.

LEE: It's funny. I used to be concerned about whether I could trust you when we worked alone and got so wound up solving something. Now I have to fight off a trace of unwillingness to trust you with other people on the staff.

HELEN: Hey, we're way too far down the line together for that kind of talk. I think we're talking about jealousy, not trust.

LEE: I know, but this project we're working on matters so much to me that I still have to work at disconnecting it from the other things we do on our own.

HELEN: Well, don't worry. What I'm doing on Adam's project in no way interferes with what we're doing.

While jealousy of other people who you feel indirectly threaten your relationship is essentially a solved issue at this stage, both of you have to remain sensitive to it and not hesitate to work it through again when it makes you uneasy.

HELEN: The report we did together last year took a lot out of each of us personally, and what we're planning next is going to make that look like child's play. Are you ready for that?

LEE: I don't see where there's any question about it—this is what we do together. If we're going to grow professionally, we need the intensity.

HELEN: We could try something lighter.

LEE: And what's going to liven up our time together? Hard work is our substitute for sex . . . and we can handle it that way. I don't want lighter work—or heavier personal involvement. Let's do the report!

As long as Helen and Lee agree to share intimacy via work and stick to their agreement not to make it personal, they need to accept greater challenges together professionally. Lee and Helen recognize this as they acknowledge that by involving themselves in intensive work, they remain exciting companions while they offset any temptation to end up in a sexual relationship.

LEE: Well, we got the news today. Marsha and I are heading for the Midwest in two months. I hate it, but I guess that's it for our plans to develop a consulting practice on the side.

HELEN: I don't see why. Nothing is changing but the geography. You'll still be back here monthly, and I'll be out your way now and then. Let's give it a try.

Boundaries serve their usual function at the consolidation stage, but they can also be used to place limits on the operating environment of the relationship. Here Helen and Lee decide to work together from different parts of the country by coming together as time and circumstances permit, each still making his or her special contributions to the work they share.

> LEE: There's something I've never told you about me . . . always considered it none of anyone's business, including yours, but now you're about to get an earful.

> HELEN: Why now?

> LEE: This project is going to take us into an area of research that is a very sensitive one for me. You're going to need to understand how I react to some of this stuff.

As Helen and Lee advance more deeply into their relationship, they find it appropriate to share personal confidences that would have been out of the question at earlier times. Their boundaries have fallen back as intimacy and trust have extended to a much greater depth than before. This is a necessary part of growing together and an endorsement of their maturing relationship. The enduring boundary even in this situation is relevant to shared work; the revelation, though very personal, is made to satisfy a working requirement and not personal curiosity or objectives.

Conscious management. Because you have both earned each other's trust, boundaries are not as difficult to manage, but you will need to:

- Agree to keep your priorities in order, and not be lulled into thinking your relationship with your work partner is on a par with your primary obligations. Respect the boundaries between your relationships as well as between the two of you.

- Agree to reaffirm in subtle ways—discouraging a new level of intimacy, initiating a cooling-off period on your own—the reasons for maintaining your boundaries when long-term comfort with your relationship makes them seem less essential.
- Agree to deal with the landmark issues of your relationship with the security that comes from knowing and understanding your partner and managing your behavior. For example, you may express sexual frustration with a knowing look or even in easy conversation, rather than with an awkward apology or by avoiding time alone; likewise you can deal with possessiveness by a temporary distancing instead of making plans to withdraw from the relationship.
- Agree to talk about anything in your relationship, but feel free to protect matters you still consider off-limits. At this stage, you know each other well enough that you probably will not probe forbidden areas or be offended if your partner lets you know you've stepped over the privacy boundary.
- Agree to take the initiative when you sense your partner needs an answer to a question or clarification about an issue that hasn't been discussed or resolved.
- Agree to cherish the faith and trust you have and not to take for granted or use them to exploit each other.
- Agree to keep your relationship fresh and lively, looking for new ways of doing your work as you avoid the tendency toward the predictability of knowing what you can and cannot do, what will and will not happen as you grow and change, and so on.

In the consolidation stage, intimacy is as complete as it gets among nonloving adults. Your boundaries are there now for the purpose of defining the relationship, not for protecting you from each other. You have answered the essential questions about what you want from each other, what you are willing to give, and what you expect from the relationship itself, and your major boundaries reflect those agreements.

You are left with the challenge of overcoming complacency and not taking success for granted. As in marriage, to keep it fresh you need to figure out ways of preventing familiarity and predictability from making your relationship mundane. The irony is that the comfortable intimacy you've worked so hard to achieve can become complacency if you let it.

Your happiness with the relationship will always be contingent on your ability to provide each other with the stimulation that attracted you in the first place. So it's important not to sacrifice that quality by making boundaries so rigid there is no room for growth. Even more destructive is the individual version of the same phenomenon—thinking what used to be a sexy, promising thought that really gets your energy flowing, and immediately calling on your emotional sprinkler system to put out the fire because you *think* you know the answer. If you find that you do indeed know the answer every time, your more-than-friends-less-than-lovers relationship has stopped growing, and you have stepped backward to become ordinary friends or colleagues; all the mystery and excitement are gone.

Most boundaries, even as they are being respected, have some aspect that can be safely surrendered or shifted, allowing you to continue the process of desirable growth. In earlier stages, you defined your own boundaries, and probed and tested those drawn by your partner. Now you share enough trust that, working as a team, you can define and widen the boundaries of the relationship itself. Little about your partner surprises you. At this stage, you naturally draw closer and share areas of your lives that you couldn't share without absolute trust and security. For example, talking about something as unromantic as financial goals or problems, or a phobia or fear you think is silly, might be the source of renewed sharing that meets an important need. You want to talk about it with someone you trust, someone who cares about you but who won't be directly affected or worried by the confidence you're sharing. And your partner is there to listen, understand, and share the same kinds of things with you. These are the kinds of exchanges that deepen intimacy, shift and redefine boundaries, and keep your relationship moving forward. At the same time, remember that the more you share without inhibition, the more your relationship requires conscious management and intelligent monitoring.

Relationship-Generated Productivity

Work has become a mature pleasure for the two of you performing as a consolidated more-than-friends-less-than-lovers team. You are beyond the excitement of plunging into work and sorting personal from professional feelings. The new excitement comes from using your personal stimulation in the lasting role you've finally agreed to give it. The mystery of *Will or won't it turn romantic?* has been replaced in a most satisfying way by a solid residual attraction that still says, in no uncertain terms, "You do something special for my work."

You have redefined *work* together. What used to be tasks to endure and finish quickly, to bang out with minimal effort and put behind you, are now labors of love—love of accomplishment that you know wouldn't happen without combining your talents with your partner's. The time dimension of work has changed. Where you once prided yourself in knocking out projects expeditiously and wondering how others could dwell on things that seemed so straightforward, you now have so many ideas that you look for enough hours to finish projects together.

But don't take your good work together for granted simply because you're successful at what you do. The quality of your work is directly related to the energy your relationship brings to it. Look for new ways to use your intimacy in upcoming projects. For example, you thought you'd never describe a certain personal tragedy to anyone, but it bears such a striking resemblance to the case the two of you are trying that you decide to do it—and your defense-team effort takes on a brilliant new dimension.

You are clear as to the source of your unique strength as a team: a personal attraction carefully managed to create just the right balance of energy and control. You use it to drive a genuinely inspired working relationship that yields tangible benefits in both professional and personal satisfaction. You are an accomplished team that thrives on a delicate blend of temptation and restraint and a solid set of complementary skills.

Contracts. The challenge of keeping your relationship-generated productivity at a peak can be met when you contract:

- to renew your working inspiration constantly as the unknowns that drove you to explore each other's minds so vigorously, and in turn propelled your work, get solved and leave your team verging on ordinary energy levels—to keep uncovering new unknowns together
- to shift more emphasis to the productivity aspect of your relationship as the sexual attraction achieves a vibrant but supporting quality that promises a level of inspiration more on a par with the work itself; you have been building toward that mix of motivations and need it now to carry your maturing relationship successfully into the future
- to reinvest a significant portion of the economic gains that your relationship earns through its productivity into your future work; as you prosper, buy the time and circumstances needed to support your work and become even more productive as a team
- to work without reservations, leaving the topics for your future exploration contingent only on your combined interests and abilities, never hesitating to alter negotiable boundaries to unveil new capabilities together

- to abandon some of the reserve you previously used to maintain the limited character of your relationship, so that you can acknowledge your work together as the best you've ever done
- that a cooling-off period of indefinite length might occur now and then as a result of changes in your lives, but it will not destroy your firmly established working relationship

Conversational gambits. Here is how Joe and Edie discussed relationship-generated productivity at the consolidation stage of their relationship.

> JOE: You know, there's something we've never talked about that has always held a real fascination for me. If we get the results I expect, our professional image would become a lot more high-profile. Frankly, that's why I've never broached the topic before. Nothing crazy, really, but different. We'd be opening up some new windows on ourselves for all the world to see. Are you game for a whole new line of thinking?

> EDIE: Sure—it's hard to think of a project I'd say no to with you. I hadn't brought it up either, but I've been getting the feeling that we've done about all we can with the track we've been on for the last year. So let's hear it.

Joe and Edie consider expanding the scope of their work, realizing that it will have ramifications for their overall relationship. Boundaries that might have blocked certain categories of inquiry in earlier stages are now made flexible in the interest of keeping fresh challenges and growth before them. Changes that open such doors include expanding areas of common interest and cultivating still further their trust in each other and their ability to deal with sensitive topics together.

JOE: It's no news that I find you attractive in a physical sort of way. We've woven that topic into and out of everything we've ever done together.

EDIE: And now you've decided I'm losing it? I think I know that look.

JOE: No, you're not "losing it," but I'm ready to admit that all these years of pounding on me not to over-emphasize that part of you has taken its toll.

EDIE: Positively, I assume?

JOE: Yeah, I think so in our particular case. I find myself thinking about your *thinking* as much as or more than your other attributes . . . and that wasn't always the case!

EDIE: Will wonders never cease? The next problem I'll have is figuring out how to keep you interested!

JOE: Anytime you'd like to test my remaining interest . . .

And with some lighthearted discussion of the state of their attraction relative to why they still find each other inspiring, Edie and Joe acknowledge that their relationship-generated productivity is still very much dependent on physical attraction, but that their equally beautiful minds are major contributors. They understand the need to remain sexually interesting and acknowledge that they still are. They've balanced the sex and working attraction and told each other so.

JOE: Now that we've won the poor man's Nobel Prize—a healthy retainer on our next contract—what do you say we take a few days and do some creative thinking together?

EDIE: That sounds wonderful—the way we used to when we had the fishing-industry account and used to end up with a few days at the shore between appointments!

JOE: Gene won't mind?

EDIE: Gene will understand, and I assume Vera will too. We should be thankful they've been so wonderful about the time we've spent together over the years.

JOE: They really do seem to understand that we need to go off and brainstorm once in a while to keep the engine on the old productivity machine up and running.

EDIE: It helps that they're creative people themselves. They know you have to reinvest if you're going to keep coming up with new ideas.

Whether it's a weekend away to brainstorm together in a totally different environment, finishing off a working space in your respective homes, or tacking some time onto a business trip to explore a new business prospect on the way home, you need to provide for the future of your working relationship with the proceeds you earn today. At the consolidation stage, Edie and Joe need to make providing for future opportunities together a regular part of doing business.

EDIE: It's great to see you again—it's been much too long!

JOE: I've thought about you and the stuff we used to do together so often.

EDIE: Even though there were no guarantees when we went our separate ways, I always had the feeling we'd be working together again. You look wonderful.

JOE: I know you've read the proposal, but let's get something to eat, and I'll tell you where you fit into this thing—I couldn't begin to do it without you. I was so glad to hear that you've got the time to take it on with me.

EDIE: All work . . . you haven't changed a bit. So what's the story with this thing? Let's get going. We'll fill in the personal gaps along the way.

JOE: Just like always.

There is nothing that says a more-than-friends-less-than-lovers relationship has to be lockstep and continuous. Like Edie and Joe, you can take a breather from the sameness of working with each other and come back later. Or you may bow to the realities of changing lives that take you separate directions for periods of time. The bottom line is that the two of you once enjoyed a unique gift for productive work and are able to reignite it. As long as you maintain that ability, you can lapse in and out of working commitments with whatever frequency the two of you find satisfactory.

Conscious management. If relationship-generated productivity begins to drag, you can consciously put it back on track when you:

- Agree to frequently reaffirm that your sexual attraction continues to supply welcome stimulation to your work—not too much, not too little . . . just the right touch that revives the relationship's creative juices, and your interest in each other.

- Agree to take the trouble to pause and look often enough to recognize how professional effort that uses the energy of your attraction is what your relationship is all about—sexy gaming that gets transmuted into working productivity.
- Agree to take the initiative to inject new life into your relationship; avoid both complacency and the conservative approach of relying on your partner's coming to you to prove continuing interest before you risk an investment of yourself.
- Agree to show that you see the potential for keeping attraction alive by finding ways to verify for your partner that the sexual thoughts live on and continue to contribute desirable energy to your working interaction; in this way, you avoid neutering the relationship.
- Agree to reinvest the proceeds of your present relationship in your future together; take the time and resources made available by your current success to ensure continuing opportunities for the team.
- Agree that, when circumstances call for a hiatus and do not reflect a basic loss of interest in working together, you will trust your relationship enough to give it a substantial cooling-off period rather than declaring it ended.

The intimacy you've developed, fueled by your carefully managed attraction, truly stimulates creativity and ideas. These are the outlet for the emotions you alternately generate and field with each other as sexual messages are exchanged—verbal and otherwise. The torrent of communication surges between you until it finds a direction you can follow together. The instant that occurs, you're off on a creative binge that lasts until you've again cooled to less impassioned thinking. The ultimate benefactor is your work. Often you find an angle that is fresh and new, something neither of you would have come up with unless the other had triggered the thinking that got you going in productive new directions with some kind of man/ woman mental tease. The relationship-generated productivity at this stage is no less charged with sex and its energy; you're just far better at comfortably keeping it within the boundaries.

Relating to Colleagues

The peace you've made with each other at the consolidation stage is apparent in the ease with which you operate among your colleagues. Since you've been a stable, long-term team, you may get some questions about what makes things work so well between you. Your overexuberance of the beginning has faded, and your enthusiasm no longer requires containing. Your self-consciousness at the establishment stage no longer threatens to invite misunderstandings. It is at the consolidation stage that you may feel enough comfort in the relationship you've so carefully built and managed that you can answer your colleagues' questions by telling them about the more-than-friends-less-than-lovers relationship model. Remember, you aren't the only ones ever to have had a relationship like this, and some of your coworkers will likely reply, "Oh, I have one of those!" Others who are struggling with the feelings and confusion you fought through during the earlier stages will be intrigued by the possibility of building a successful professional relationship with sexual attraction as the catalyst.

How much you volunteer about your relationship and what you've accomplished as a work team depends on your circumstances. Imagine that you began your association within a company environment, then found that your attraction, common interests, and complementary skills stimulated a kind of creativity that led to a joint project outside the office—a magazine article, a novel, a documentary film—that is about to receive publicity. You may decide to do your manager and coworkers the courtesy of telling them about the event before they hear about it elsewhere and feel excluded. After all, you are still part of the company family.

Others of you will continue to do the same work you've been doing since you became a team. Even without elaboration on your part, your coworkers have long since realized you have a special relationship. But because you are discreet—friendly but not overtly affectionate—they correctly perceive you as colleagues who also share a personal, but nonromantic, relationship.

This stage is also the point at which you have the poise as a professional team to consider homogenizing your relationship more into your total network of colleagues. Now that you've worked through the most difficult parts, you feel secure enough to include others to a limited extent in an association that in earlier stages was a more private arrangement.

The key to dealing with colleagues at this stage is, in a word, *comfort*. You have solved the riddle of the two of you and are far more at ease in dealing with the rest of the working world around you. You have a relationship you never imagined could exist without an affair or utterly changed lives and careers. You've negotiated your way to uncompromising personal intimacy and a particularly strong position professionally. You have your work and each other, and the lives and careers with which you entered the whole unintended adventure are intact. Professionally, the two of you have clearly become better together than you were individually. It shows in the feedback you've gotten from management, and in professional options for the future. You are enriched personally, which has made you a better companion for your spouse or lover. All in all, you feel wonderful about how this relationship has changed your life, and about the fact that after the whole journey of discovery together, you have remained more than friends and less than lovers.

Contracts. The understandings necessary for interfacing comfortably with colleagues begins when you two contract:
- to share your experience with coworkers in limited and specific ways that are relevant to your overall working situation at this stage, revealing the nature of your rela-

tionship and of work you've done together that might
be important or useful to colleagues
- to use the skills you've learned with each other in dealing with other colleagues of the opposite sex
- to retain the privacy of your intimacies in the midst of
what might become a higher-profile relationship at
this stage
- to deal with significant team success in the same way
you built the relationship that produced it—with respect for each other's contributions, boundaries, and
expectations

Conversational gambits. The ease with which you can deal with
colleagues at this stage is illustrated by Jacob and Annette.

JACOB: I know how you feel about keeping the results of
the experiment quiet until the final results are verified,
but we're in for a lot of outside attention if this thing
works out the way it looks.

ANNETTE: But we've kept our boss up to date every step of
the way. And we're not really sure yet.

JACOB: Yeah, but he may want to warn the department
head so it doesn't come as a surprise. This could be a big
one, and they might want to think about marketing.

ANNETTE: You're right. The company will love the attention. And this *is* a spin-off of the main hypothesis that's
bigger than what they were looking for in the first place.

Because of their longevity as a successful work team,
Jacob and Annette realize that they need to be sensitive to the
needs of others who have a significant investment in the work
they do, sharing information as they go along and taking care
not to get lost in the privacy of their teamwork.

JACOB: How long are we going to stand by and watch management pussyfoot about putting men and women together in teams when it needs to be done?

ANNETTE: Yeah. A lot of them could handle it as well as we have.

JACOB: But it took a crisis to bring about our first assignment.

ANNETTE: Why don't we mention it? I'd be willing to talk with some people if it would help.

As comfort with their own situation increased, Annette and Jacob began to see the potential for extending some of what they had learned about working together to their colleagues. They had learned a lot with each other—and they were now willing to share that knowledge.

Conscious management. At this stage, your coworkers are aware of your special relationship. While you reserve your special intimacy for your private work time, you:

- Agree to the increased understanding of your status with each other to be less guarded in your relationship; retain your private intimacy, but otherwise relax and let your team effort blend into the workplace at large.
- If relevant in your situation, agree to prepare for the possibility that your previously low-key relationship will have a higher profile as your work draws broader attention at this stage; agree to a common approach to what you will reveal and what you will keep private.
- Agree to share with others, when it might be helpful, the knowledge you have gained by working together; depending on the situation, this could range from offering an office friend an informal bit of advice to making a recommendation to management.

Dealing with Family

With the passage of time, your relationship with your work partner has become securely drawn and bounded, making it easier to keep it distinct from your marriage. It is an integral part of your life by this point, and if you have successfully monitored your behavior and kept your priorities straight, you probably are not in danger of inadvertently hurting your spouse.

At the consolidation stage, you are excellent priority managers when it comes to the two relationships. Your relationship with your work partner is so thoroughly defined and integrated into your overall behavior that you no longer find yourself thinking of or treating her or him like a surrogate spouse, as you occasionally did at the establishment stage. Questions of infidelity have long since passed, and the only remaining concern for most spouses is that the adjunct relationship not detract from the family. You solve this problem by demonstrating where your priorities lie and continually making the distinction, in your thinking and actions, between the purposes and character of the two relationships. This has become a successful habit as you enter the consolidation stage.

If your spouse had concerns and raised questions earlier, they should now be resolved by the nondisruptive nature of your more-than-friends-less-than-lovers relationship—no infidelity, no displaced love, no interference with your home life. Even so, your professional relationship should continue to remain where the interaction happens—in the workplace—and not be forced on your spouses unless they ask, or unless the two relationships have become interwoven naturally. You should be sensitive to your spouse's needs and worries (explain unique work or travel arrangements, maintain interest in family matters, and so forth) and respect your obligations, allowing sufficient separation of the two relationships for them both to flourish in their separate environments.

You have made peace between the two relationships in

much the way you do with other overlapping obligations that contain both an inherent good and a built-in conflict—such as raising a young family and having the time to keep a romantic relationship with your spouse, putting in the long hours needed to become a partner at the firm and spending time with your family. You come to view your more-than-friends-less-than-lovers relationship in the same light at the consolidation stage—a sometimes demanding but generally limited intrusion on your family life that pays enough dividends to be worth it for all concerned. The professional growth and personal satisfaction gained there increase your prospects for remaining a successful and committed spouse.

Contracts. You both need to contract:
- to extend the contracts of the establishment stage indefinitely to include (1) reaffirming that the work relationship is secondary to the family one, (2) dealing honestly with questions, and (3) not displacing husbands and wives as the main focus of intimacy in your lives
- that it it not necessary to integrate your association and your family relationship; it is appropriate for them to remain separate
- to handle balancing your relationships as a long-term life-management obligation and not as a temporary accommodation

Conversational gambits. With an understanding spouse and tactful honesty on your part, simple dialogue can be enough to handle any problems that arise at this stage.

> PAULA: I see you and Theresa are still bringing in the contracts together. Don's wife mentioned the new one while we were waiting for the bus this morning.

> RON: Yeah, we just found out yesterday afternoon. Since I got home so late, I didn't get a chance to tell you last night.

This one's a three-year contract, so we won't have to worry about funding for a while.

PAULA: That's great. You know, I used to think you and Theresa would run out of new ideas at some point, but it really doesn't look like that anymore.

RON: And is that a problem?

PAULA: Now that you mention it—it really isn't. I guess I'm getting used to whatever it is that keeps you two in business. It also helps that I've become convinced over time that even though you're really good friends, business is the glue that holds you together.

For some husbands and wives, the continuing presence of an opposite-sex working relationship that is obviously close and long lasting is unsettling. But by the consolidation stage, even those who earlier had their doubts are convinced of the relationship's innocence, although they may never be enthusiastic about how much time the job requires. Ron's relationships with Paula and Theresa can coexist nicely without being fully integrated. In other cases, friendships outside the office may develop as spouses meet, enjoy each other's company, and begin socializing.

JERRY: I'm not sure I'd know Jim if we passed on the street, but he's sort of become a member of the family.

DIANA: Sure he is—a member of our *extended* family.

JERRY: The guy sure brought you to life career-wise. You used to have more résumés out than I could keep track of. Now I never hear a peep about moving on. I might actually get to retire here!

DIANA: Well, it hasn't been a one-way street. Jim and I stumbled onto the right chemistry together and the company has been great about letting us run with it . . . and so have you. I appreciate that.

Most families quickly get used to the presence of the workplace colleague in their lives. These people can become invisible members of the family, as Jerry observed. Had Jerry and Jim been social friends before, they might know each other well. But they weren't, and none of the players felt the need to make the job partnership more than a working relationship. That didn't prevent Jim from becoming a comfortable part of the extended family. Diana added a nice touch by acknowledging Jerry's acceptance of the working relationship and saying thanks.

ART: There's a special project team forming at the plant that's going to be causing me some long hours and travel.

LAURIE: There's not much either of us can do about that. Why did you bring it up?

ART: It involves nitrate residues in municipal water-treatment facilities again, and the logical person for me to be working with is *that woman!*

LAURIE: You mean Jenny Wilson? [She laughs, recalling when earlier business trips with Jenny caused a lot of tension in their relationship.]

ART: No problem this time?

LAURIE: Are you kidding—she can have you!

A working relationship that caused a domestic problem when dealt with the first time is reintroduced to a confident wife far different from the person who had felt threatened by

the mystery that surrounded her husband's attractive professional partner a few years earlier. After a period of time in
which Jenny's status relative to the marriage was accurately
portrayed, what previously evoked feelings of jealousy or irri-
tation became a private joke between Art and Laurie.

Conscious management. It takes less conscious effort to keep
your relationship on track at this stage, but you will still want
to:

- Agree to continue practicing the basic disciplines you
  applied to your dual relationships earlier, providing
  honest explanations when asked, maintaining priorities correctly, and viewing the marriage as your
  main source of overall intimacy.
- Agree to continue keeping your work relationship
  from becoming a mystery; talk about its work aspects
  when they would interest your husband or wife, and
  humanize your partner by mentioning him or her in
  ways that won't be resented.
- Agree to cultivate your conviction that the two relationships are of independent value, each of them
  providing something the other doesn't, and use that
  mind-set to keep them separate in your thinking.
- Agree to reaffirm that what you share with your spouse
  is irreplaceable, and to give him or her the opportunity
  to comfortably raise concerns about the work relationship even after it has become an established part of your
  life.
- Agree not to be tentative about your relationships,
  thinking that with both existing, neither can be lived to
  the fullest. The justification for the supplementary relationship is to be found in the benefits that accrue to
  your life in general, including your marriage; limiting
  its potential would be a false economy.

At this point, you are beyond questions of whether or
not to continue the relationship with your work partner, and

how it is to be understood in your family. On reaching the consolidation stage, you and your spouse have thoroughly discussed the idea that one relationship seldom, if ever, satisfies all of one's needs. You have explained and demonstrated that your relationship with your partner, like those with friends and other intimate associates, is supplemental to, not competitive with, your marriage. You also have said you understand that your spouse may well have relationships that satisfy certain needs that your relationship with her or him does not. Both of you have agreed that these associations actually make your marriage better and more complete, since what you share with each other is *mutually* interesting and satisfying.

You have reached satisfactory understandings with both your spouse and your intimate coworker. Both relationships are firmly established and coexist comfortably. With your coworker, you share a special type of intimacy that is centered around creating great things together professionally. On the other hand, you don't attempt to apportion your love or even your physical intimacy to more than one person; your spouse has it all. It is at home that you still find the intimate personal rewards of your life. Because you are a happier, more well-rounded person, you bring more to your spouse and your partner than you could if they weren't both significant parts of your life.

ROUTINE MAINTENANCE

You have attained your goal of safely forming a nonromantic intimate relationship focused on your work life. You didn't go looking for it, and there was a shaky period when the relationship almost dominated your life, but now it's a comfortable part of your way of doing business.

- The pyrotechnics of the earlier stages have passed. You are more settled into your jobs, you easily live within the boundaries you have drawn for intimacy, and you are committed to your relationship for the indefinite future.

- You have sorted your motivations for staying together, such as compatible career goals, and have decided that what you have is valuable both professionally and personally. You reserve your love and physical intimacy for husbands, wives, and lovers, yet experience unconsummated but nevertheless extremely deep intimacy with your coworker during your shared times of intensive professional effort.
- Your work partner is a best friend and more—someone you deeply trust and care for, and with whom you'll share anything but your love.

The consolidation stage is a time of backing off from the intensity of your relationship and enjoying the comfort you've worked so hard to achieve. Your lives take their turns and you stay connected through your work and the intimate personal exchanges that are now an integral part of it, but you are very much your own people, living two separate lives. To each other you are like no one else among your acquaintances— someone who came to visit and never left. You continue to consciously manage your behavior, to provide feedback to each other as you monitor both your own and your partner's actions for signs of trouble. But by this stage you have resolved the most prickly problems, and your major concern is maintaining what you have and continuing to grow. Your monitoring and feedback, no longer focusing on mismatched expectations or boundary violations, now center more around preventing stagnation and finding new challenges. In addition, although you are not integral parts of each other's personal lives, you know each other extremely well and care about each other's happiness and well-being very much. As you grow close over the years, your monitoring and feedback process includes those aspects of your personal lives that you choose to share.

Illustrating this kind of mature relationship is the story of Megan and Alex, who saw their marriages end in the course of their years together. They never seriously considered each other as life-partner replacements, but found themselves more than idle observers in the process of restructuring their respective lives. Megan had found a new love following her divorce of several years earlier, and Alex was about to embark on a search for one of his own.

While their relationship patterns are fairly typical of our society, there is nothing about the dynamics of their interaction as consolidated more than friends and less than lovers that would be inconsistent with two long-term lovers who choose to share an important confidence, turn a crucial corner in their lives, and go on productively working as an inspired team that has always been based on qualities that are essentially unaffected by changes in their personal lives.

Alex was in his early thirties, a financial analyst with a bank trust department who yearned to be a free-lance investment-newletter writer working from some hideaway a thousand miles from the nearest financial district; his wife loved the city and its social calendar. Megan sold analytical services to institutional investors like Alex. She liked his idea of the newsletter and collaborated with him while they both still worked for separate employers. Her husband was a corporate attorney so married to his firm that they eventually agreed they had no relationship to continue and parted.

As the years passed, the newsletter grew in circulation and sophistication. During their intense evenings of putting it together over restaurant and kitchen tables, Megan and Alex's attraction to each other grew and found its limited place, while the tale of two dying marriages droned on in the background—never a focal point of their discussions, but not a secret. One evening as Alex pulled out his draft of the next newsletter at a pub booth they'd sat in many times as they performed this same task, Megan announced a change of address; she had left her husband.

It crossed Alex's mind that their relationship might change now, but he wasn't sure how. More interest in each other? Probably not. That would be a total reversal of their pattern of several years. A new lover instead of a workaholic husband? Yes. That was more like it.

Alex decided it was none of his business since their relationship really didn't include day-to-day involvement in each other's personal lives.

The next year he and his wife parted for reasons of their own: he was seeing the light of day on his plans to leave the city; she had no desire to join him.

Through the unraveling of their marriages, Megan and Alex managed their relationship very much as they always had—supporting and caring for each other without any attempts to substitute for the missing spouse. Two individuals found two sets of solutions—the same way they would have had each still had a spouse waiting at home and the problem been something other than divorce.

Megan and Alex illustrate one of the underlying truths of the more-than-friends-less-than-lovers relationship: it is *not* a romance in waiting! You are *not* two lovers held at bay by the existence of family obligations alone. Megan's and Alex's marriages were not threatened by their special relationship, but by the same sorts of irreconcilable differences that end others.

Through all the unsettled emotions of leaving long-standing relationships, they kept their pattern of working together unchanged. This included a ringside seat at the emergence of their new personal lives.

Megan agreed to meet Alex for an unhurried dinner in a quiet place they occasionally patronized when their newsletter needed to be discussed. No agenda had been set. His invitation was a simple "Let's have dinner—it's been a while and I want to talk over something that might affect the next few issues of the newsletter."

When she joined him, he reached for his briefcase and pulled out a copy of the local city magazine, opening it to the "in search of" section of the classified personals, where the upscale singles take a shot at advertising for the person of their dreams. With his finger marking the spot, she read:

DWM 32 ISO attractive, slender, private, independent, natural woman, late 20s, to share—no immediate prospects of live-in or marriage—quiet, intimate, unpretentious, quality, 2-person life with successful (estabished, independent—not rich) consultant—6′ 1″ 185 lbs fit, attractive. Extended seasonal travel. Photo essential. Confidential but provide contact. Mutual health/character screening expected. Box ISO 3X-356-12.

They talked about it and kidded each other a lot. Why did he do it? Because he knew he wouldn't have any in-house applicants for the job—an acknowledgment that their long tease was just that and that when it came time to seriously look for company, she was not a player.

Megan and Alex confirmed what men and women at the consolidation stage of a more-than-friends-less-than lovers relationship need to know once and for all if they are to settle into a perpetual working arrangement that can flow successfully around their attraction, its limitations, and the fact that significant others will continue to play dominant roles in their individual lives. Two things of significance were related in their short exchange: (1) Alex was so comfortable with, and trusting of, Megan that he could share an innermost secret and deep personal need without embarrassment or fear of being judged unfavorably; and (2) he knew that, despite their intimate caring for each other and moments of temptation, with the moment at hand neither would she apply nor would he consider her qualified for this vacancy in his life. They genuinely had another role to play as coworkers who fanned, but never touched, the flame of their attraction. Even under the pressure of what must have been enormous temptation when they both lost their lovers, they resisted filling the voids in their lives with a loving relationship of their own. They knew better than to mistake their warm, genuine affection for love.

Although divorce was the event that set the stage for this proof of a more-than-friends-less-than-lovers relationship, it could have been life-changing events for couples who stayed together. Alex and his wife might have come to share the same dream and completely change their lifestyle, moving together to the mountains of New England or Arizona, where he could work on the newsletter from an idyllic setting. Had that been the case, the dinner meeting might have centered around a real-estate magazine describing a fixer-upper farmhouse instead of an ad detailing the woman of his next dream. Megan would have been as much on the outside of his deeply personal quest as she was before—not to be the lover, not to share the restoration of the farmhouse—but still central to the sharing of a turning point in her colleague's life. Where there was an implicit challenge to remain relevant in a life that was about to include a new love interest, there would have been a similar one presented by her partner's potential for getting lost in a new rural lifestyle without her. With modern personal business communications, mere distance wouldn't keep them from collaborating on the newsletter, and the chances are excellent that their established relationship would go on.

Divorce or marriage is no more the issue than the kind of life you individually live or with whom. What you share as consolidated more than friends and less than lovers is the challenge to remain a vital stimulus to each other in your work. The story of Megan and Alex, with the outcome centered on either a new love or a new lifestyle, merely illustrates that lives go on and the players manage to keep their connection. With each unfolding change of circumstances, you find a way to validate how uniquely important you are to each other in your special, limited way. As long as you have your work and make your contribution, you will continue to move ahead.

The Question of Endings

Many more than friends, less than lovers who begin with success lose their way in the complications of the establishment stage, where boundaries have to be drawn with just the right precision and flexibility to keep the attraction within limits and still allow growth. Those who don't have a substantive attraction to hold them to the task, an exceptional mix of chemistries to make it worth the effort, and a general stability in their lives to keep them from getting lost in the sexual energies they fire in each other will never achieve the status of more than friends and less than lovers.

For those of you who make it to the consolidation stage, the relationship still could end for a variety of reasons. As you monitor it, look for signs that any of the following events are taking place. The special balance you have worked so carefully to achieve may be lost, and with it, your relationship.

- The character of your relationship has changed to the point where it no longer exists as it was; it becomes all work, for example, and the magic of the attraction no longer surfaces with enough strength to make it special.
- You fail in the task of conscious relationship management and become lovers, taking on entirely different obligations together.
- You decide it's just become too much work to manage the relationship and that the personal attraction has lost enough of its zing that the relationship has become disposable, that there are more interesting people and undertakings in your life now.
- The working arrangement that provides the basis for your relationship ends due to a reduction in work force, loss of funding, shifting company focus, or any other reason, and with it goes the stage on which you play—unless your work has the kind of value that endures beyond a given job setting.

- Something changes in your marriage that requires all your energy, or a husband or wife forces a choice that ends your secondary relationship.

Threats to your relationship are often more convoluted and difficult to analyze into specific underlying causes than the problems just listed. A combination of dangers can manifest themselves in a relationship-changing event motivated by several things—diminished attraction that leads to less productive work, a competing interest that calls into question commitment to the relationship. For example, other very close friendships can exist, but there is an intensity about the more-than-friends-less-than-lovers commitment that makes it unlikely that most people could handle two at the same time. The story of Ken and Barbara illustrates what can happen when they try.

Ken was a graphic artist employed by an advertising firm where Barbara worked as a copywriter. They had collaborated on a number of accounts and become a close-knit professional team. Their combined talents with the words and images that made things sell put them in the forefront of their company's marketing effort. The hours were long, and there were weeks when they saw more of each other than they did their respective spouses. But the attraction they came to share was overwhelmingly professional in character. A relationship developed. It had its moments of upheaval when personal issues needed to be put into perspective, but they did all of that successfully.

Ken and Barbara's relationship matured into a stable and productive one that they assumed would go on indefinitely. They had worked together for five years. The projects they shared were clearly enhanced by their special relationship. They were an excellent creative team and knew it. Their spouses had grown comfortable with their closeness, saw the product of it in their work and in their profits, and showed no concern about what they saw as a nonthreatening relationship.

Then Barbara and Ken encountered problems from an unanticipated quarter. Ken became involved in an outside project with a woman from one of his company's subcontractors. An attraction arose that was quite different from the one he shared with Barbara, and he found himself devoting considerable energy to what eventually amounted to a second intimate relationship outside his marriage. He felt complimented to have another attractive woman interested in relating to him in depth, and the nature of the work was entirely different—one artistic, the other technical.

In time, Barbara felt the positive energy drain from her relationship with Ken. It wasn't traditional jealousy she felt, but she believed he had become considerably less involved and therefore less valuable to the work they had long shared. At some level, she even felt a sense of abandonment, but realized that Ken was not deliberately deserting her. He had merely found another area of professional interest on the new project, and a new someone with whom to share it. Barbara soon concluded that she really didn't need Ken to do a good job. He was still attractive, but was no longer a positive source of productive energy.

The story of Ken and Barbara shows how difficult it is to have simultaneous intimate relationships in the workplace. Experience indicates that a marriage and one outside interest are probably about all most people can handle if they are going to do both relationships justice. But other issues are raised by situations like this one. It is possible that Barbara will shift her interest to another coworker capable of supplying the mix of personal and professional inspiration that was formerly supplied by Ken and develop a new more-than-friends-less-than-lovers relationship of her own.

Once you have experienced the satisfaction and value of such an association, you might be more receptive to forming another if the opportunity presents itself. In the case of Barbara and Ken, for example, this would not be a jealous reaction ("If you can do it, so can I"). Rather, she would be making positive use of a relationship model to replace something she wants and needs and no longer has from the original source. Another possibility would be for Ken and Barbara to return to their former status. There was nothing abrupt or bitter about their parting, just a change in the value each attached to their work as a team. This could change in a favorable direction in the future. The controlled emotional level of the relationship makes it more likely that such accommodations can be made successfully, leaving the door always open to what is in their mutual working interests.

Growing Versus Ending

Becoming consolidated more than friends and less than lovers poses interesting choices. Embedded in each decision you reach together is the potential for your relationship either to grow or to end. You have lived an intense life together, limited in some regards, but amazingly complete, from unintended beginning—to the bitter end? Hardly. The ending won't come for most of you, because you have a good thing going. You've already taken your lumps and passed the tests. The real payoffs have just begun. Why quit now?

You know each other so well. The person who sits across the table from you is hardly the simple combination of flesh, feelings, and capabilities you saw there when you were first drawn to him or her. Piece by intimate piece you've dismantled each other, insofar as you've agreed, and she or he is no longer the puzzle that alternately charmed and tormented you as you worked through your relationship.

You realize now that a man is a man, a woman a woman, and that your reasons for confounding each other are seated in more than a desire to be difficult; they come from the valid sexual differences that give you the special characteristics you combine so effectively as a team. Women and men are more than just good fits when they choose to fall in love. Somewhere short of that, as more than friends and less than lovers, you find a union you'll also value in an enduring way. It is your own special means of combining the pieces of the gender puzzle so that each of you still taps the excitement of the other enough to propel you into a productive future together—without the obligation of merging your lives beyond the work you share.

Somehow in your advanced stage of working together you choose the positive side of these monitoring dilemmas:

Using each other without exploitation is a positive and caring act that drives your existing projects to exciting conclusions and finds you together looking for new worlds to conquer. You pool your talents, mutually sense the needed time-outs, and draw on the other's strength when yours is exhausted.

Drawing a narrow focus is an act of preservation and not denial as you steer your relationship clear of the broad sea it was never meant to navigate. Together you constantly recalibrate the scope of what you will and will not do as a team, how far across the line of colleague to confidant you will go, how deep into the intimate understandings that give your work its vitality you will venture—extending the stiff arm of restraint when either walks too boldly toward doors deliberately left ajar but never to be misconstrued as wide open.

Preserving your unknowns is an obligation to yourself and each other to grow together and yet remain separate. You become masters of the art of omission, sharing only that which you believe is relevant to the two of you. All of this is part of consciously managing the most complete of incomplete relationships, knowing when thoughts or feelings are best left in the individual worlds of your own unknowns—the things you needn't share and don't as more than friends who have other lovers.

Encouraging stability in your respective homes is accomplished by stressing in an unending stream of subtle ways that the ease of your relationship rests in the soundness of your family lives. To provide the inspiration you need for creative work, your relationship of necessity allows enough intimacy to occasionally cloud the gaze of a partner who looks too hard for a kind of love that will never materialize; you bear an obligation to discourage that view. Overcoming the urge to draw each other nearer in ways that most threaten the limited nature of your delicately balanced working relationship depends on not looking to each other for romantic love.

As you pause and look to the future together, try to take a fresh perspective. Retain all of the lessons you've learned, but none of the hurts you may have intermittently felt. They're history now, and the two of you are your own unique future—with all the promise of one of the deepest, freest, and most potentially enriching relationships you will ever have. If you are like most people who have had an intense experience together, you head for tomorrow with much of what you came for, and a few things you never imagined would be yours. True, one or two things were denied, but it's a balance you can live with, and you prosper tremendously from the resulting mix of what you do have. When it comes to sustaining a limited relationship, as the popular song attests, "some of God's greatest gifts are unanswered prayers!"

III

Impact of the More-Than-Friends-Less-Than-Lovers Relationship

6. *Enhancing Your Organization: Advice for the Manager*

THE MORE-THAN-FRIENDS-LESS-THAN-LOVERS model provides a proven framework in which employees who experience sexual attraction for each other can confront, accept, and consciously manage it. In an environment where people deal with their sexuality directly and rationally, illicit sex rarely becomes a problem. If their attitude is positive and their productivity high, the likelihood of a disruptive affair is virtually nonexistent.

Traditionally, managers have viewed a more than strictly business association between working partners already married to others as *bad business*. The typical solution was to separate the pair, often resulting in career-stunting reassignments and tainted reputations that were difficult to live down. But with an awareness of the principles of the more-than-friends-less-than-lovers relationship, you as a manager can help guide attracted employees through intense intimacy that focuses their passion on their work, not on each other's bodies.

The workplace is constantly evolving. Men and women working together are bound to be attracted to one another and wrestle with handling their attraction on a daily basis as they struggle to keep their eyes on maintaining successful careers and strong relationships with spouses or lovers. You can help them manage and refocus these natural attractions by being aware of these realities and by having faith in your employees' ability to deal with them successfully. To it all, you can add the offer of a workable solution—the more-than-friends-less-than-lovers approach to a work-based man/woman relationship.

Tomorrow has arrived for the American manager on the issue of intimate, nonsexual relationships in the workplace. According to a study recently completed at the University of Michigan School of Business Administration, "Not only are nonsexual love relationships common, with 22 percent of managers reporting involvement in such a relationship at work, but they were actually found to benefit both the 'couple' and the organization where they work."

Amy Levin Cooper, editor-in-chief of *Mademoiselle*, introduced the concept to her readers this way in early 1991:

> *Office affairs used to mean behind the doors, on the desk, after hours. And no doubt some skeptics will think we're crazy or naive to suggest a different scenario . . . two cute and smart people, both gainfully employed, who spend 8, 10, 19 hours a day together, eat together, perhaps travel together, share the same goals and passions—but no sex.*
>
> *Here is the new mating game. This platonic form of office romance doesn't present any emotional danger to the participants but offers all the charm, chemistry and special charge of the man/woman thing. It's a real collaboration, one with intimacy, intensity, respect and inspiration. You're in each other's offices hour upon hour, looking good, looking not so good. . . .*
>
> *You know how he takes his coffee, and you speak in a private shorthand. You can ask, "So what are we going to do tomorrow?" with the impunity and security that does not come in sexual relationships until you're paying for the children's orthodontia together. And whatever the job requires you to do tomorrow, you know he'll want to do it too. Failure looms large, and success tastes sweet, and you support one another through both.*

This is a different attitude toward women and men working together; these two people are willing, highly motivated coworkers of the best kind. They aren't having an affair, and it's obvious to you and their coworkers that they know how to handle their attraction without disrupting their lives, careers, or families. They aren't cheating you out of work time or hurting their spouses, and they love you for encouraging them to work so productively together. Give them the task and let them go. You, as a manager, can take positive advantage of this solid working partnership, and your business can only be improved with their high level of motivation and self-discipline.

Maureen Dowd, a reporter for the *New York Times'* Washington bureau, wrote in a *Mademoiselle* feature article entitled "Everything but Sex: The New Office Affair" that "letting the attraction work as an underlying charge rather than acting on it provides a high-voltage current to the day and an exciting edge to the relationship. . . . Hollywood has already figured this out—it's why TV producers are loath to let the flirtatious stars and colleagues of hit television shows such as *Cheers, Moonlighting* and *Who's the Boss?* consummate their desires: Things tend to get boring fast once the sexual tension is gone."

Dowd goes on to say that "people may be making more mature decisions about not acting on sexual attraction in the workplace—if only because they know that such relationships can damage the way your boss and coworkers perceive you, and haunt you if the affair ends and you still have to see the person every day." A twenty-six-year-old New York lawyer quoted in the same article told Dowd, "The tension is not a bad thing—sometimes it makes you a little more motivated. . . . If you're attracted to somebody, your mind is probably working pretty sharply and that can have a good effect on whatever you're working on. Also, if you're both trying to impress each other, you'll throw more ideas out and try to do your best."

Morale, motivation, willingness to travel and make extra effort—important quality-of-life and career issues—are enhanced in organizations that recognize the positive side of allowing colleagues to use the power of natural attraction to give their work an extra edge. Dowd noted that having an attractive coworker "not only makes you want to work longer; it also stirs the creative juices because you want to show off for the other person and let them see what you can *really* do." She quoted a male Washington, D.C. attorney who has had intense friendships with women over the years as saying, "The main thing about these relationships is that they psych you up to come to work. . . . The more you enjoy spending time with this woman that you're working on a project with, the more time you'll spend on the project." More time spent on work means higher productivity, and that translates to more profits and increased company morale.

Of course, knowing how to appropriately respond to and manage workers under these new conditions can be a challenge. As *Time* magazine reports:

> *The more subtle changes necessary to successfully manage a culturally diverse work force often scare the daylights out of even the best intentioned executives. Many find themselves for the first time adrift in uncharted territory. Workers don't follow familiar codes of behavior. Bosses must rethink the way they evaluate people and unlearn habits that can alienate or confuse employees from different backgrounds. . . . Difficult and slippery as some of these issues may be, companies must address them. . . . Learning to lead a diverse work force may be maddeningly complicated. But the alternative, management experts predict, may be alienated employees working at cross purposes. At Du Pont, an exhaustive series of new training courses helps employees explore sensitive issues dividing the sexes. . . .*
>
> *Another seminar explores a topic that only recently has gained boardroom respectability: how management attitudes affect employee performance. . . . At a time when corporations increasingly expect employees to work with minimal supervision and to show more initiative, cooperation and fresh ap-*

proaches are essential. . . . Encouraging diversity . . . can be another way of ensuring that workers can contribute their best ideas and efforts in an intensely competitive international arena.

You, as a manager of an increasingly male/female work force, find yourself at the forefront of this revolution in attitudes and approaches to team productivity.

MYTHS AND MISCONCEPTIONS

In the course of researching this book, we asked employers and employees what they thought about men and women who are sexually attracted to each other and work closely together. Their answers indicate a number of popular misconceptions that can lead to misunderstandings and counterproductive actions that could seriously impair the productivity of otherwise highly motivated man/woman teams:

- It is dangerous for men and women to work alone together after hours; they are tempting fate, asking for an affair.
- A man is incapable of spending long periods of time, after hours and on the road, with an attractive female colleague without making sexual advances to her.
- If a couple travels frequently or work long evenings and weekends, they are bound to have an affair.
- If someone is sexually attracted to a work partner, he or she can't possibly do the job effectively; the attraction will get in the way because his or her mind will be on sex rather than on work.
- If a man and a woman who work closely together seem to enjoy each other's company as well, they are having an affair.
- If you are a manager or CEO, you should discourage close relationships between male and female coworkers; affairs and all their embarrassing and disruptive consequences are inevitable.

- If two employees under your supervision become too close, you should counsel them immediately, making it clear that they must cool it, or one of them will have to go.

While a few of these beliefs are based on the way things used to be when individuals were forced to deal with sexual attraction blindly, they need not be true when issues are openly discussed and consciously managed with firm rules and guidelines. Current research indicates that the truth is quite a bit different:

- Sexual attraction is biologically natural; a marriage certificate or commitment to a partner doesn't make it go away.
- Coworkers can enjoy sexual attraction without sleeping together.
- Men and women can sustain deeply meaningful secondary relationships without ruining or diminishing primary ones—most of us need more than one kind of relationship to fulfill our needs for intimate interaction.
- If colleagues appear sexually attracted, they are not necessarily headed for or having an affair.
- Employees can share attraction and affection without losing their job effectiveness. Managers who handle the situation carefully will probably discover that their subordinates are even more creative and productive than before they became a steady team.

In spite of appearances, intimate nonsexual relationships between sexually attracted coworkers are possible, as one manager, Lena, learned when she made traditional assumptions about two of her employees.

Lena considered herself a thoroughly modern manager and a solid advocate of a progressive role for women. She had joined a federal-government agency as a trainee after completing her MBA about ten years before, and steadily moved through the ranks. Within the last year, she had realized her dream and was appointed the head of a major region. It was the beginning of her education in a few important areas.

Lena, who is attractive, had her share of bad experiences as a woman in the workplace—nothing she would describe as harassment, but comments and attempts at familiarity that left her a little jaded. Whenever she saw opposite-sex coworkers obviously enjoying a close relationship, she had a tendency to suspect the worst—either affairs in progress or a very real potential for their development, which could disrupt the lives of her employees and cause serious problems in terms of workplace productivity.

After touring the field offices in her region, Lena was convinced that she had a real management problem. Everywhere she went, she saw the very kind of relationships that gave her pause. She could pinpoint nothing as inappropriate; in fact, everyone looked happy, and productivity was at an all-time high. "Then why am I so concerned?" she asked herself.

It all came to a head after a staff meeting one afternoon. Lena had brought in Ted and Angela from out of state to cochair a committee on an important issue that affected their district. After an all-day session with the committee, the three of them went to dinner to prepare for the next day, laboring through a cognac and several cups of coffee before calling it an evening. When she got home, Lena thought of a key point and called Angela's hotel room, but got no answer. She then asked the desk clerk to ring Ted's room, but was advised that calling him would be pointless since his number and Angela's were the same. Lena thought her worst fears had been confirmed—that Ted and Angela were having an affair, courting disaster! She decided to discuss it with them over their scheduled breakfast meeting.

Breakfast quickly became an awkward confrontation. Angela and Ted were surprised and chagrined, and Lena was uncomfortable. Work took a back seat for close to an hour, but all three of them walked away satisfied. Angela and Ted explained that they had taken an idea from Angela's husband's company, whose long-standing practice was for business travelers to share corporate residential facilities. She was used to him and any com-bination of colleagues sharing a townhouse or city apartment while on a business trip. Spouses were forewarned and had grown comfortable with an extremely practical arrangement that saved the company money. Angela and Ted were pooling their limited government per diem and taking advantage of the suites-only facilities around the region. They saved money, had a comfortable area to relax and work in—a kitchen table for a shared coffee and Danish when they didn't have time for break-fast in the morning—and generally enjoyed the more domestic atmosphere. They had separate bedrooms, of course, and their spouses trusted them thoroughly. Now so did Lena.

Whether you are worried about the appearance of em-ployees shacking up on company per diem or are concerned that the men and women in your employ are courting danger because they enjoy each other's company too much, as a man-ager you are wise to take a second look.

Discuss your concerns in a nonthreatening, nonaccusa-tory manner, hear the suspected parties' side of the story, and be willing to consider intimacy as a positive stimulus to work-ing productivity.

MANAGING THE MORE-THAN-FRIENDS-LESS-THAN-LOVERS RELATIONSHIP

Managers can quietly foster a workplace environment in which intimate nonsexual relationships can function safely and productively by observing the following guidelines:

- Accept the premise that a man and woman working to-gether can develop an intimate relationship based on sexual attraction and common interests and keep it from becoming a love affair.
- Try to understand that such relationships can exist in-definitely in your work force and not disrupt it.

- Let employees involved in more-than-friends-less-than-lovers relationships know that you expect discreet, responsible behavior and self-discipline.
- Realize that the man and woman will likely be more productive if allowed to enjoy their relationship comfortably and to direct its energy into their work without undue scrutiny.
- Approach each management decision on the basis of competency and not gender, thus freeing up the most potent mixes of talent at your disposal.
- Avoid the temptation to be a mother hen to your employees and protect them from themselves.
- Apply a little bit of Zen to your management; you are part of a movement that is revolutionizing the way men and women relate in the workplace, so focus on the possibilities rather than the problems, and seek to guide rather than control workplace relationships.
- Make yourself an optimistic part of the new solution with an attitude that sees the possibilities and helps perfect new approaches, instead of shoehorning your organization into dated thinking in terms of stereotypes that carry negative expectations.

These few rules put you in a position to make the most of the changed mix of men and women employees who are bound to feel the pull of biology from time to time. Follow them and you'll find yourself directing a vital stream of productivity flowing from your work force, rather than struggling to plug a hole in the dike as you attempt to hold back a totally natural, potent creative energy source.

HOW YOU'LL BENEFIT

Your tolerance and understanding are not without their rewards:

- You can more easily make decisions on team building based on competence rather than gender. You don't have to eliminate the obvious choice of the best people for a project because they are a man and a woman. The subliminal concern that it is dangerous to pair men and women for extended periods in intimate, even private, working conditions for fear of romantic complications and workplace disruption is gone.
- Because they enjoy each other's company as well as what they do, the coworkers are willing to work harder and longer, and with more inspiration than they or you ever imagined.
- By allowing colleagues who fire each other's enthusiasm to work together, you can harness levels of enthusiasm and productivity that would have never been possible otherwise. Genuine teamwork develops because men and women who find natural pleasure in each other's company are allowed to work together to get the job done.

In addition, consider the burdens that helping coworkers through a consciously managed more-than-friends-less-than-lovers relationship can lift from your shoulders: (1) less grousing over long hours, intense work schedules, and business travel by workers who look forward to spending time together and know their working productivity will be the better for it; (2) less need to enforce cooperation in minding their professional image when workers have a vested interest in perpetuating a relationship that is both enjoyable and advantageous to their careers; (3) less likelihood that you'll have to be involved in resolving an attraction that has no suitable outlet, becomes destructive, and threatens to destroy a very productive team; and (4) less need to motivate and encourage greater effort from the team.

Even the most enlightened manager is entitled to some practical concerns about the impact of an intimate relationship between his or her workers. In *Office Warfare*, Marilyn Moats Kennedy points out a few of the main ones:

- Will business judgment be affected by the relationship?
- What about productivity?
- Are they concentrating on business or on their relationship?
- How will a nonamiable breakup affect the business?
- Will the relationship create adverse or embarrassing publicity for the business?

There is no magic way to implement inspired management of the sexes. You need to face sexual attraction among your employees directly as a matter of routine business and not let it get in the way. Of course, some workplace relationships do become problems. But at the same time, don't anticipate problems that will hang you up on a creative solution or team-building effort.

Here is a good example of how open discussion helped one savvy manager, Michelle, create a man/woman team that headed off the problems that might have been created by sexual attraction before they developed.

Michelle is a senior vice president for a multibillion-dollar regional bank holding company. She is responsible for the cash-management segment of their commercial business—lining up everything from utilities to small mail-order houses with sweep accounts that put their receipts immediately to work in interest-bearing investments when their clients pay their bills. It is very competitive, and her expertise is in building and motivating real go-getter sales teams to bring in new business.

The previous week, Michelle got the word that the bank had received regulator approval to serve a new section of the country. Six states with booming economies were ready to be tapped. She needed her best staff, and they had to be willing to burn the midnight oil for about a year until it all came under control.

Michelle called Alice and Dwight into her office to discuss what the job would require. She covered everything objectively and was gratified to see them excited at the prospect of taking on the challenge. As she got more into the demands that it would place on them, Michelle didn't shy away from admitting to them that sending a couple of bright, good-looking young professional people with families of their own off into a situation that would tax the energies of any marketing team might present them with special problems.

"Let's talk frankly about something . . ." is how Michelle began her approach to a touchy issue that was still very much a business concern of hers. Then she went on to establish that while she wasn't about to explain the facts of life to them, or how to handle their personal priorities, she did want them to know that—as one who'd been in the same situation—the assignment they were about to accept could present them with potentially destructive temptations. Dwight and Alice were taken aback, but only very briefly. Michelle was relating her personal perspective on what they might face, not giving a moralistic lecture on not sleeping together on the road. Without putting it this directly, she conveyed the message clearly: "You two are my brightest and my best. I expect a lot out of you and I know you can deliver. I also see two people who fit and will almost certainly have nights when you'll think more about each other than the people who are waiting at home. If you can't handle that, your lives will change in a way you probably wouldn't want them to—and I'll lose the best team I ever sent to look for business together. Do you know what I mean? And can you handle it?"

Just as those exact words were never spoken, no direct answer to them was ever given. But the team that took the assignment did so with an important part of their interpersonal challenge well previewed for them. It gave them a leg up on the competition. Lots of men and women are assigned together these days, but most are simply thrown into the sea with management's unspoken hope that they'll not sink together in an affair that will blunt their business effectiveness, if not ruin their personal lives.

Alice and Dwight had a better-than-average chance of avoiding that outcome because Michelle was gutsy enough to put the issue of sexual attraction and the need to deal with it directly on the table for them to consider and discuss before they took the assignment. While she didn't offer a solution, Michelle placed the issue before two people bright enough to work through the options. With sexual attraction brought up by someone they both respected and knew valued their work, Alice and Dwight didn't feel awkward about discussing how they would deal with the feelings that would likely flow from the intimate year they were about to spend together as a working team. It was up to them to decide whether that meant a close but deliberately restrained relationship that might inspire their work, an affair that would have a negative impact on everyone affected, or the improbable likelihood that neither would notice the sexual attributes of the other in their year of intensive effort and proximity.

As you can see, managing sexually attracted colleagues is nothing particularly mysterious or threatening. You don't need a soapbox or a particular position on the issue to bring some objective awareness to those who work for you. Instead, discuss the situation openly when the time is right.

Thus, you can accentuate the positive benefits of personal attraction in the motivation, quality of life, and professional productivity of your work force. And, as an enlightened manager, you can do your share to put to rest once and for all the belief that every workplace attraction ends in an affair.

7. *Enhancing Your Marriage: Advice for the Spouse (or Lover)*

YOUR HUSBAND OR wife has explained to you that he or she has formed something like a more-than-friends-less-than-lovers relationship and that it is a work-only relationship. Your spouse has given you either verbal or nonverbal reassurance that he or she is far too much in love with and committed to you for an affair to even be a possibility. But because the work partner is attractive and interesting, you sometimes fear that your spouse might not be able to resist such obvious temptation when you aren't around. While this kind of reaction is not unusual, unless your marriage is already in serious trouble, a relationship such as this will not harm your marriage and might even enhance it.

While at the beginning of a domestic relationship we may look to a mate for satisfaction over a broad spectrum of needs, in time we find that one person can't satisfy or complement every aspect of our personality and interests. "When we look to a spouse or a lover to meet all of our needs, to fulfill us, to bring us a lasting heaven on earth, it never works, does it? It's very natural for us to want to do that, because it's natural to want to have . . . one we can touch and hold and embrace and sleep with and maybe even possess. But it doesn't work," says psychiatrist M. Scott Peck.

Instead, we find satisfaction in different areas from a variety of acquaintances outside our domestic relationships— colleagues, friends, sports teammates, family members, and others. Our marriages are not a failure when our husbands or wives reach beyond us, or we reach beyond them, for certain kinds of fulfillment in nonsexual dimensions of our lives. Most of us gain insight and self-knowledge from our interactions with people outside our immediate domestic circle, and if we are interested in the growth and renewal of family relationships, we apply what we have learned to revitalizing and renewing these relationships.

M. Scott Peck says that "one of our myths is that we should be completely happy with and fulfilled by one woman or one man. . . . That's nonsense." He goes on to say that while he can't tell us conclusively what the right way to deal with sex is, he can illustrate the wrong way: "the couple who say, 'What's the problem? My wife and I have been married for thirty-five years and I've never even looked at another woman and she has never even looked at another man.' . . . The price people have to pay for that kind of repression simply isn't worth it." Dr. Peck says that we all go through a lifetime of "celestial boot camp" filled with obstacles designed to keep us learning and growing and that "the one most fiendishly designed is sex." We have the impression that we can figure it out (*max* it, in his words). He says there are several ways to approach that problem and they include finding "someone for a day or two or even a year or two, but then she changes or he changes or we change and we realize that we haven't maxed it [figured out our sexual riddle] at all. We either try again with someone else or go forward and learn about love and intimacy and how to whittle away at our narcissism, and some of us graduate from boot camp."

You don't need an expert to tell you that sex is a powerful

motivator. But you may never have dreamed that you'd need to accept it as a part of a relationship between your own spouse and an attractive coworker. Yet anytime a woman and man interact on a meaningful level, sexuality is an element in their relationship. In an article for *Health* magazine, Dr. Morton H. Shaevitz, associate clinical professor of psychiatry at the University of California at San Diego Medical School and codirector of the Institute for Family and Work Relationships in La Jolla, California, discussed the importance of the sexual connection in relationships between men and women:

> *She responds to him . . . early on. She . . . moves close . . . and in all those little body-language ways lets him know that soon . . . they will become lovers, or something akin to lovers. Then and only then can he begin to open up emotionally.*
>
> *A man doesn't literally need to score . . . but he needs some degree of sexual acceptance before even thinking about relationship concerns. He can't begin connecting until this is taken care of. A woman doesn't literally need a commitment right away, but she needs some degree of closeness, even a fantasy of closeness.*

The point is that sexuality is an essential ingredient in any meaningful relationship between the sexes.

Understanding the part that sexuality plays in relationships between men and women will help you to understand, live with, and manage a life that respects the realities of human attraction. With the more-than-friends-less-than-lovers model, it is possible for you to grow and allow growth in your spouse or lover, honestly deal with your mutual frustrations, and conclude that you have more reasons to stay together than to part. When the dust settles, you find that the special working relationship, whether it's your spouse's or your own, has stimulated you, as a married or committed couple, to grow and develop.

THE NEED TO TRUST

In order to grow together and make our lives more fulfilling in the long run, we all need enough trust from our spouses to be ourselves. While this may involve some risk taking, it should be considered an investment. We derive benefits from allowing each other to vary the routine of a long and committed relationship.

Julian Rotter, a professor of psychology at the University of Connecticut, has a theory of reciprocity that accurately describes this book's perspective on trust. It boils down to: "the more trusting we are, the more likely we are to be trusted by others. . . . Take the risk of trusting, and you may be trusted in return."

Caryl S. Avery, writing in *Psychology Today*, describes trust in this way:

> *Although trust in a partner means different things to different people—dependability, loyalty, honesty, fidelity—its essence is emotional safety. Trust enables you to put your deepest feelings and fears in the palm of your partner's hand, knowing they will be handled with care. While feelings of love or sexual excitement may wax and wane over time, ideally, trust is a constant. When you have it, you have it all. The challenge for most of us is not to let the specter of deception in love interfere with finding the intimate connection we want and need.*

Both the participants and the spouses of those who are involved intimately, but not romantically, with attractive co-workers must share a large measure of trust. Both husband and wife need to commit to their marriage and make it clear that it is their highest priority, something worthy of indefinite investment. Avery suggests that "how a couple demonstrates their dedication is . . . a personal matter, and often nonverbal: It can be a willingness to do things for each other, spending time together, making personal sacrifices on the other's behalf, being consistent. Self-disclosure is part of it too, because sharing what's inside—even if what's inside isn't pretty—is the supreme act of faith in another."

Scott M. Stanley, a psychologist and codirector of the Center for Marital and Family Studies at the University of Denver, suggests how you might best deal with feelings of hurt or anger that you might encounter as you discuss a perceived threat to your marriage.

> By identifying the immediate underlying hurt and expressing it instead of rage, you can use anger to increase trust and intimacy. For example: A woman is angry because she feels her husband doesn't spend enough time with her. She can either attack (You don't care about anyone but yourself) or express the frustration and disappointment underneath (I know your job is important, but spending so little time with you makes me sad).
>
> Most people attack because it's safer . . . Sharing your real feelings is riskier: On the one hand, it's your only hope of getting the caring acknowledgment you want; on the other, you leave yourself open to rejection.

But even if what you learn is painful, you know where you stand with each other.

Caryl Avery writes, "Your inclination may be to trust less—but you'll pay the price of being trusted less. Or you might be inclined to put less into the relationship, while researchers find that the more you invest, the more commitment increases."

Boston College sociologist Diane Vaughan, also writing in Psychology Today, states:

> Instead of complaining, initiators [those troubled by their marriage and considering leaving] may use sullenness, anger and a decrease of intimacy to suggest unhappiness. Having always remembered to buy a birthday present, they may bring an inap-

propriate or a thoughtless gift. The reporting of daily events, usually exchanged at dinner, may get briefer and briefer. When such subtle signals fail, initiators may then turn to interests outside the relationship. . . . In a healthy relationship, outside interests can add to the excitement and well-being of the situation because they are shared in ways that strengthen ties. In a deteriorating relationship, these activities exclude the partner and widen the already-open gap. . . . By sharing their unhappiness with others, they create bonds and begin (still unintentionally) to prepare for life without the partner. . . .

The signals become increasingly bold, however, as initiators gradually come to see the relationship as unsavable. As outside interests grow more important, they devote less and less time to restoring the relationship. They express discontent to convince the partner that the relationship is not working, rather than to change or improve things. . . . What begins as a break in the pattern becomes the pattern. Arguments, working late . . . even threats to leave lose their impact with repetition. . . . Repeated signals of unhappiness may be so inconsistent with the partner's conception of the relationship that they are denied or reinterpreted rather than confronted. . . . Nobody wants to discover that a valued way of life is ending. So the partner, too, avoids direct confrontation and gets to hang on a while longer. But, by helping . . . keep the [true] status of the relationship a secret, the partner is missing a chance to do something to solve the problem.

Indifference to the relationship grows, and it deteriorates further instead of getting the attention that might correct the misunderstandings that caused the initial concern. By withdrawing, you can encourage your husband or wife to turn the innocent and limited work relationship into something more—tempting him or her to find outside your marriage the caring and warmth once found with you. This is why one of the basic tenets of the more-than-friends-less-than-lovers relationship is the monitoring of each other for just such signs of

displaced domestic intimacy. Rarely would both members of
the team permit their relationship to go far down this road. By
monitoring your own behavior, you stand a better chance of
not inadvertently doing harm where open communication
might solve the problem.

Perhaps you have a nonromantic but intimate relationship of your own with someone besides your lover. If so, you
might consider that association—with a coworker, or maybe
with someone who shares your interest in sports, crafts, wild-
life preservation, the theater, or another area not enthusi-
astically enjoyed by your husband or wife—as a positive model
for a similar work-based relationship of your spouse. That relationship can bring the same kind of renewal you've seen
in your own life to your spouse, adding to the vitality of
your marriage with the self-knowledge and insight gained
from a secondary relationship, and validating for yourself
the strength and power of your own relationship with your
spouse.

"True trust is felt, not willed," according to John and Kris
Amodeo, authors of *Being Intimate*, in a *Psychology Today* article. "It must be developed over time, by sharing your innermost thoughts and feelings gradually and seeing how they're
received. . . . To be able to be oneself and not have to disown
one's values to please another—that's what intimate love is all
about." They maintain, in effect, that we have to give our
lovers enough freedom to realize how much they love us.
Overcoming doubt and learning to trust is something you
may be called on to do as the spouse of someone in a more-
than-friends-less-than-lovers relationship, as the story of Allison and Jerry illustrates.

> *Allison and Jerry were a married couple who each had careers of
> their own. They were in their early thirties and were much too
> busy to be watching for the other to show telltale signs of in-
> fidelity. The thought hadn't occurred to either of them. Then Al-
> lison had lunch with an old college classmate who worked at the
> same corporate headquarters as Jerry. While the classmate didn't*

*want to plant any suspicions, she felt an intense interest in hear-
ing Allison's version of her husband's stellar working relationship with a woman in the firm.*

*Before heading back to their respective offices after coffee,
Allison was treated to a very understanding explanation of
how in sync this woman and Jerry seemed to be—rushing down
the hall between presentations, cheerfully sharing a sandwich in
the archives while doing some hurried research, catching a taxi
for a rush-hour flight to the regional office. It all painted a picture
of a working relationship worthy of a budding affair; they just
looked and acted too happy together. Wasn't she concerned?*

*No, she wasn't. She honestly was not. Allison could re-
member doing some of the same things herself two years before
with a male coworker at her last job, which didn't bother Jerry at
all. The job ended and so did their relationship—he moved to the
West Coast. But they both had enjoyed their relationship im-
mensely while it lasted. And that was how she basically felt
about Jerry and his partner, now that it had been brought to her
attention.*

*But the seed had been planted; her classmate's account wor-
ried Allison just a little. Then Jerry came home, walked in just
like always, full of the usual "Great to see you, Hon. How was
your day?" genuineness that he just couldn't fake. She relaxed,
relayed her classmate's account to him one Saturday morning
when there was lots of coffee and bathrobes were the uniform of
the day, and came to the conclusion that Jerry had indeed found
someone special other than her—but the relationship really
wasn't any different than the one she had had two years before.*

*Intellectually, all was well. Emotionally, Allison watched
things closely for a while. In time, her optimism and faith in
Jerry carried the day. His career took off, and the woman was
clearly a factor in his success—but Allison was, too, and she
knew it. She was the lover; the other woman was an enduring
and especially valued professional associate who turned him
on—but not in a romantically competitive or harmful way. Allison could live with that; she had his love and full attention as a
domestic life partner, and she trusted him, just as he had trusted*

*her in the past. Career partner wasn't a role to which Allison
aspired, and she didn't mind that someone else did, as long as everyone involved knew their boundaries—and it became apparent as the months and years went by that they did.*

Like Allison, many of you will have enough trust and
security in your marriages to take your spouse's or lover's
more-than-friends-less-than-lovers relationship in stride,
with hardly an emotional ripple. Others of you will have perfectly natural and honest concerns to work through on the way
to accepting a new, different, and constructive force in your
lives. For a few of you, it may even be the occasion to face
long-standing problems in your marriage that were there before this nonsexual work relationship came into being.

Spouses or lovers might not notice, or pay little attention
to, their mates' close association with a coworker, or they may
acknowledge it as an important and positive addition to their
husbands', wives', or lovers' repertoire of friends and acquaintances, or they might view it as a threat to their domestic
peace. If you see that your spouse is involved in such a relationship, consider the benefits we've described so far, and try to
avoid or at least minimize creating any unnecessary emotional
pitfalls that might have a negative impact on your relationship.
Don't think the following:

- It is *wrong* to be attracted to anyone except your spouse
  or significant other.
- If you are even intellectually or emotionally attracted
  to someone else, you should feel extremely guilty.
- If you are intimate with someone of the opposite sex,
  you are likely to become sexual partners.
- You can't have more than one intimate relationship.
  Your spouse or lover should fulfill all your needs; if
  not, something is terribly wrong.
- If your spouse or lover spends a lot of time with an attractive, interesting colleague of the opposite sex, you

should be extremely worried about an affair, especially if they travel together.

Furthermore, don't assume the worst, act like a jealous spouse, and demand a choice of either your marriage or the more-than-friends-less-than-lovers relationship. In all probability this will leave you with either a mate forced back into line but with resentment always below the surface, or a broken relationship. Forcing the issue in this way is admitting that you feel you cannot command the love of your spouse on the merits of your relationship. Coercive bonds like the one resulting from such action may enforce superficial fidelity but deny you the underlying confidence that your spouse is the willing and trustworthy lover you seek.

Don't refuse to acknowledge or discuss the work relationship, letting your unhappiness build a wall of misunderstanding between you and your husband or wife. This approach eventually provides the basis for problems that the actual situation never warranted. By refusing to express your concern and face the possibility that it is unfounded, you compound it with an escalating series of intimacy-destroying actions that leave you with a relationship devoid of the very qualities you both need. By comparison, the outside relationship grows more attractive and, while the more than friend is probably no threat even under these conditions, you encourage the development of a less benign relationship somewhere else in your lover's life.

Don't accept the relationship grudgingly and make your spouse or lover feel uncomfortable about bringing up work topics at home, leading to your feeling further excluded from an important part of his or her life, and possibly forcing your spouse or lover into keeping secret thoughts and feelings that normally would be shared routinely with you. Partial denial is nearly as destructive as complete rejection. The essential step for you is to confront the cause of any unease that you might feel. If you are concerned about having your own intimate

relationship violated, say so! Get the matter resolved, understood, and put in its proper perspective. Don't settle for less
than the kind of understanding of the workplace relationship
that you need to regain any comfort or assurance that its existence has cost you. Be positive and receptive to the likelihood
of its innocence, but resolve the matter to your satisfaction.

Do believe that your spouse—or you, for that matter—
can honestly maintain a second intimate relationship based on
shared work, not romantic interest, and remain a loyal, loving
partner. This is the display of trust and understanding that
makes you the standard by which all other intimate experiences, no matter how fleeting, superficial, or outside the realm
of loving, are measured. It is the quality of committed romantic love that draws your spouse back and invokes perspective
when other interests have their appealing moments. If ever
there were qualities whose absence can be quite literally felt in
a relationship, they are trust and the will to love. Removing or
lessening them is the last thing either partner wants to do in a
relationship worth preserving.

In those instances where a more-than-friends-less-than-
lovers relationship becomes a source of jealousy, the solution
is direct communication rather than withdrawing your commitment. Adopting the following positive measures should
relieve your concerns.

Be optimistic about your relationship until you have actually
confirmed reasons not to be. Appearances can be deceiving,
especially if you begin by expecting the worst. The chances
that spouses will experience more than a prolonged dose of occupational adrenalin in the attraction shared in their more-
than-friends partnership are small indeed. It is a relationship
deliberately limited and stacked in favor of respecting the
marriages and loving commitments of the individual partners. The participants want their respective lovers to accept
their desire to pursue a valid course of professional growth together without assuming they have an interest in romance.
They can and will consciously avoid acting on the romantic

potential, remote or nonexistent as it may actually be for them. Giving up the opportunity to fulfill their professional promise together is their other option—the classic distancing solution that has long been the unsatisfactory alternative to the workplace love affair. As a husband or wife, you can make that solution unnecessary by extending trust and playing your own vital role as the stability-giving love of your spouse's life.

Avoid thinking and behavior that stem from your worst fears and become self-fulfilling. As research cited earlier attests, trust begets trust. The converse of that statement is, unfortunately, also true. In the unlikely event that you feel neglected or hurt as a result of a spouse's work partnership, take a positive approach to resolving it by means of objective inquiry and reasoning together. This particular workplace attraction will bear your scrutiny, and you'll spare yourself the added pain of contributing to the demise of your marriage.

Keep the channels of communication open; get beyond the comfort of simply saying the right things, and confront the real concerns that need attention. Heed Dr. Diane Vaughan's counsel on the tendency in many relationships to let familiarity erode those qualities of mutual inquiry that initially made you sparkle as you and your lover deciphered each other's meanings, hopes, and aspirations. Keep the fascination with your partner; stay a part of his or her reaching and dreaming. Take the trouble to ask the hard questions and dig for the truth until you can again stand comfortably together on the newly firm ground your inquiry has solidified. Fresh ideas keep our relationships alive and growing, while regurgitated niceties uttered in practiced tones leave us hungry for the newness of others.

Take the trouble to investigate and learn the real dynamics of the problem you think you see, and enlist the help of the person most central to your concerns, your husband or wife. Hear him or her rather than withdraw. Consider the plausibility of an attraction that indeed constitutes something far short of love and poses no threat to what you have together. You may even have similar relationships of your own that you've never considered in this particular light. Neuter the relationship in your own mind and see how much of the perfidious thinking remains when you face the objective situation rather than worry about what might be. Think of your spouse's more than friend as what she or he objectively is—a professionally fascinating adjunct to your lover's career pursuits who, were it not for the fact that he or she is of the opposite sex, would cause you no concern.

Change your perspective and picture yourself in your husband or wife's situation. If you don't already have a similar relationship, open yourself to the possibility that you might in the future. Even the mental exercise of putting yourself into such a situation will be enlightening. Think of a person of the opposite sex with whom you either now share or previously have shared a special connection—an immediate grasp of the other's wit or meaning, for example. Recall someone in that category whom you find attractive—someone you would not have spurned during your dating years. Now ask yourself if all of that adds up to anything even close to the intimate relationship you came to call love with your husband or wife. What you have synthesized is something akin to your lover's more-than-friends-less-than-lovers partner—an attractive object of affection, one who evokes pleasant thoughts and possesses a challenging intellect that complements your own, but not a lover.

Free yourself from the burden of being all things to your husband or wife, and concentrate on what brought you together romantically in the first place. Set a goal of systematically broadening the boundaries of your marriage to accommodate the growth that will be inevitable in the course of the long lives you are now privileged to live. Surely there is further distance to travel together down the road you love to share. Renew those journeys and reestablish the dialogue you began as excited strangers getting to know each other. Forget about trying to cover every base of each other's interests; accept the reality that no two people are totally compatible. Welcome rather than resent the trait in your spouse that keeps him or her reaching for ways to be more complete and productive in his or her own life, secure in the knowledge that you'll share it in your own special way. As it is true that the best part of a long journey is in the coming home, so it is with an intellectual or emotional excursion: have the courage to let your lover take such trips for the shared joy of the homecoming your well-founded trust makes possible time and time again.

Decide whether or not you have a solid marriage, excluding your own concern about the workplace relationship. Remember the secondary relationship isn't a cure for a failing marriage—and neither should it be made either partner's excuse for ending one.

When you sense a problem, tune in to it like you did when your relationship was new. If the work relationship concerns you, ask for more information so you can understand it. In the process, show interest in preserving your marriage. Communicate with your wife or husband, and monitor your behavior and that of your spouse (just like he or she monitors behavior and provides feedback in the more-than-friends-less-than-lovers relationship). Communication is the key to understanding.

In doing these things, there is every reason to believe that your spouse's secondary relationship will be a positive, rather than a dreaded, addition to your life together. Have the courage to see the possibility that the more-than-friends-less-than-lovers relationship will contribute much to your lives as your happy and professionally satisfied spouse comes home to you with new energy, new ideas, and renewed love.

DIFFERENT KINDS OF RELATIONSHIPS

Dr. Robert J. Sternberg, professor of psychology and education at Yale University, has a paradigm for representing loving human relationships that can be used to compare the more-than-friends-less-than-lovers relationship with marriage. His thinking provides us with more than a graphic picture of love;

his model explains how relationships evolve and is useful in explaining the more-than-friends relationship in a way that distinguishes it from simple friendship or romantic love. He suggests that we "picture love as a triangle . . . [with] one side representing *intimacy*, which includes support, communication, warmth, and sharing. This provides the emotional content to a relationship. Another side stands for *passion*, . . . a motivational force that leads to arousal, physical excitement and a desire to be united. . . . *Commitment* makes up the final side. This is where a decision to love another person and maintain that love is made." When you put the sides together in a perfectly balanced triangle with equal sides and angles, you have what Dr. Sternberg calls *consummate love*, or the perfect relationship, in which each of the components plays an equal role.

The length of each of the triangle's sides represents the relative amounts of passion, commitment, and intimacy in a relationship. The area of the triangle represents the amount of love. (Change *love* to *caring* for more than friends, less than lovers.) One of the basic principles of geometry tells us that the length of the sides can be quite different and the *area* remain the same; likewise, you can have equally caring relationships made up of entirely different measures of intimacy, passion, and commitment.

All three elements—intimacy, passion, and commitment—are essential components of a more-than-friends-less-than-lovers relationship. Just as romantic relationships have triangle sides of various lengths, so, too, does an intimate association between opposite-sex coworkers. But while the latter has a large measure of intimacy and commitment, it places a significant limitation on the passion component.

This is where you—the spouse or lover—are asked to remember that the basic ingredients of your marriage are combined in radically different proportions in a nonromantic work relationship. The latter has a lot of commitment, which is required if the relationship is going to be substantive and productive. It contains a healthy measure of intimacy; how could it be otherwise if there is to be depth and understanding enough to find significant, albeit nonromantic, meaning together? The passion is of a very different sort and consciously limited, but it also must be present to activate the relationship. As we have said throughout this book, sexual attraction is what drives and energizes the relationship, but it is sublimated and shared professionally—*not* romantically.

The Sternberg-inspired more-than-friends-less-than-lovers triangle must be balanced if it is to be stable. If you have only intimacy you end up with everyday friendship. Add passion to the intimacy but leave out disciplined and limited-purpose commitment and it becomes an old-fashioned love affair. But if a man and a woman put it all together, willingly clamping a lid on the passion at a point where the energy that only sexual chemistry can unleash drive them to work but not love, the end product is a motivated work team who love only their lovers. You, as a spouse, quite possibly feel the same kind of resistible attraction for a member of the opposite sex, manage it in this way, and find that your primary relationship does not suffer for it.

Your own or your spouse's sharing of particular interests with a work partner removes nothing from your marriage. In fact, it may lift a burden from you. You no longer have to either feign enthusiasm for things that don't interest you at all or disappoint your lover because he or she has no one with whom to enjoy them.

Intimacy is a legitimate part of a close working relationship. If you can develop the comfortable assurance that the co-worker is not a potential lover, you will find it natural enough that your spouse is happy and having fun at work, holding a colleague in high regard, counting on him or her, enjoying mutual understanding, communicating deeply, even deriving emotional support in the trying times of shared effort. You have room in your marriage for each of you to share outside interests with friends and relatives. Trust each other unless you have a definite reason not to. And bring home what you learn, exchange ideas and information, and keep your relationship fresh and growing.

As psychiatrist M. Scott Peck points out, we live in changing times where everything that happens in human relationships can't necessarily be measured against the standards of yesterday: "People are no longer accepting the answers they've been given; they want more. They realize the old program doesn't work. There's a larger and larger segment of the population that has made a decision to question the givens—things the culture takes for granted, things people's parents taught them. They are becoming enlightened." Dare to do the same. For your spouse and for yourself, open the door to the kind of trust and growth that you each can experience independently but still share in a long, loving relationship broad enough to embrace the changes in your lives.

8. *More Than Friends, Less Than Lovers, at Last!*

NO SINGLE SET of motivations applies to men and women involved in a more-than-friends-less-than-lovers relationship. For some, at the beginning, it seems almost like a love affair, and they spend the early stage of the relationship learning that it really isn't and never will be. Others don't experience these near-romantic feelings; they may feel twinges, but they have enough discipline not to let them come to the surface. Many are deeply attracted and acknowledge their feelings, but never directly deal with the issue because personal reasons prevent them from even considering this as a possibility. For the majority, perhaps, the sexual charge that fires them as a working team is not a true romantic attraction—just a natural biological magnetism that they feel and use professionally, but don't act on out of deference to a firm commitment to their existing personal and professional lives.

You need to think about into which camp you fall; expectations are important in determining your success and happiness as more than friends, less than lovers. Each of you views your relationship from the perspective of your own personal situation, limitations, and values. Nothing in the realm of human behavior is totally predictable—least of all your ability to foresee precisely how you will feel and be motivated in a caring relationship with another human being. But eventually most work couples develop the following view of their relationship relative to life and work. They grow confident that in an electrified but responsible way they can:

- share a controlled attraction without disrupting marriages and careers
- gain insights and satisfaction from a carefully managed second intimate relationship that makes them better workers and spouses. They do this by self-actualizing beyond the limits of their existing relationships, and by finding new sources of creativity and motivation
- appreciate more deeply the value of the careers and marriages that make this level of self-discovery and personal development possible. They do this by motivating themselves to respect the limits of their more-than-friends-less-than-lovers relationships, and by preserving and enhancing the jobs and marriages that anchor what they value as satisfying lives

You need a positive attitude as you stay conscious of the pitfalls but enthusiastic about the gains that result when, as a sexually attracted man and woman working together intimately, you figure out how to manage your relationship and bring the energy of your attraction out of the business closet but not into the personal bedroom. The Public Broadcasting System's *Smithsonian World* recently aired a documentary entitled, *Gender: The Enduring Paradox*, which concluded by saying that we, as humans, have a unique ability to draw up guidelines that let us rise above biological imprinting and enjoy our dissimilarities more broadly in our lives. Defining and implementing those guidelines for having a physically stimulating relationship without sex is the core of becoming more than friends and remaining less than lovers.

SELF-DISCOVERY

You are actually liberated in some ways by the restrictive boundaries of your more-than-friends-less-than-lovers relationship. You know you have no romantic objective to achieve, no conquest to make or endure, no lover's loyalties to impose or enforce. With neither the relentless expectations of loving, nor the simplicity of a friendship where there is no sexual charge, you create a hybrid relationship that allows you to slip beyond the bounds of being either friends or lovers and enjoy the freedom to chart a course together with expectations that suit your aspirations.

You discover parts of yourselves that remain unexplored in your other relationships—professional and personal interests outside the cherished but different ways you interact with your husbands, wives, lovers, or friends. You might discover that you're both avid Elvis fans, and on a business trip to Memphis decide to use your free time to visit Graceland simply because it's there—something your mates wouldn't do for a king's ransom. You become pathfinders for each other on trails you haven't explored with anyone else, appreciating your ability to turn on the thinking and command the respect of someone with no incentive to react to you with anything but candor.

In time, these intimate quests become intellectually fascinating. You find yourself thinking in new ways, adding positive dimensions to what you see in yourself and other people, your approaches to living and working. You confirm long-held suspicions and fervent hopes about everything from your moral underpinnings to your untapped genius and head down lines of intellectual and professional inquiry that have teased you for years, but that you have only now found the incentive to explore. You introduce each other to a realm of totally new experience that neither would have known without the other. The catalyst for your renewal is the challenging interest in and of your coworker. You realize that he or she plays a role in your life and that you want it to continue.

Continued Growth Becomes a Goal

Of course your relationship is not without conflict and discomfort at various points along the way. But, willingly embraced, this can contribute to your growth. Carl Rogers, the noted psychotherapist, said, "Self-actualization is not accomplished without struggle and pain but the person engages in the struggle and stands the pain because the creative urge to grow is so strong. The child learns to walk in spite of his initial tumbles, the adolescent learns to dance in spite of his awkwardness and embarrassment."

Contemporary psychotherapist M. Scott Peck says that "there are only two valid reasons to get married. . . . One is for the care and raising of children. The only other valid reason . . . is for the friction marriage provides." Just as your marriage partner supplies a source of growth through the loving dissonance the two of you create, so does your special work partner.

You come together looking for little because the basic boundaries of your lives are drawn (you have established career and love interests). You find much with each other (a safe work outlet for your sexuality, an inspiration for your work), but not everything (no love, no sex). What you discover will continue to amaze you as you go on—the way you learn to use sex and not have it, to hold on to each other without touching or possessing, to grow comfortable with the contradiction you live as an increasingly committed and interdependent couple deriving your creative energy from a sexual attraction you've chosen never to indulge physically.

Your relationship is woven comfortably into your life's overall tapestry. Each time you push the relationship's boundaries successfully, you increase your prospects of finding continuing success and growth together. Your relationship is always changing to accommodate your growth. The boundaries seem less restrictive because for each boundary that stands, two shift or crumble under the weight of trust grown so completely that they are no longer needed.

When Professionals Get Personal

One of the most dramatic aspects of the new office atmosphere is how men and women who are peers handle their attractions to one another. Some of them already have formed a *work marriage*—a marriage without sex. They are a couple within the office family, taking their identity as a highly successful professional team. They have chosen to draw specific boundaries around their association to preserve other valued relationships, or just to avoid a lifestyle that would be too densely packed with each other if it went on every day in every way. The following examples of people happily sharing their love and their work, taken from an article in *New York* magazine, echo the more-than-friends-less-than-lovers relationship.

- CBS News correspondents Betsy Aaron and Richard Threlkeld found they felt better about sharing dangerous assignments like Beirut together; they are also able to "supply each other with material, insights, and moral support."
- A pair of air-traffic controllers at La Guardia said, "Our work is so highly technical that it's really hard for an outsider to understand what goes on. . . . We both know the same people, the jargon, what the atmosphere is like. We understand the pressure."

In an article in *Newsweek* titled "Love in the Office," reasons were cited for happiness and increased success for those living and working together:
- The shared commitment to a profession or a cause can be a powerful bond.
- "We work well together. . . . We don't think about outdoing each other. We think about how to make each other look good."
- "We don't have to feel competitive and our victories are joint victories."

You place a great deal of value on your more-than-friends-less-than-lovers relationship. You have learned to cope successfully with a number of problems that a lot of men and women in the workplace are going to be facing, and you are able to enjoy the benefits that two caring but nonloving intimates working together can provide. The *Newsweek* piece ended with this look at the future:

> *It seems likely that employees will keep looking for love in the office next door. [Leslie Aldridge] Westoff [author of* Corporate Romance*] thinks both employers and employees will benefit in the long run. "I believe that when you are in love, you are happy and very creative," she says. And if the workplace changes to accommodate both the personal and professional needs of employees, the new refrain might well be: "Thank God it's Monday."*

These examples illustrate that as more than friends and less than lovers, you are walking onto a stage already crowded with look-alikes—men and women on the job dealing with a mutual attraction of a sexual nature. But you're different because you have resolved to find a way to deal with and use the attraction that lets you bring a personal dimension into your professional lives without making the complete conversion to life partners.

You have decided that you have good reasons to draw the line at the point of being more than friends, less than lovers. And, of course, working and living together can have its down side. When you're at your creative best, with both work and the personal side of your relationship going swimmingly, and you start to feel tempted by fantasies of how wonderful it might be to complete the relationship loop and become one in life and work, consider some of the following drawbacks:

Newsweek reported that "for ambitious careerists who want to be recognized for their work and not their love life, coupling [at work] can . . . be stressful. . . . Spouses [and lovers] have to work hard to establish separate identities in the office. They don't want to be seen as a unified front without individual opinions on work-related matters."

New York magazine listed a series of awkward situations reported by couples on the job:

- A woman editor left her position after marrying a senior person at the firm with the conviction that "professionally, it seemed to make sense. 'The situation was uncomfortable, rules or no.'"
- "There are disadvantages [to couples working together] as well. Peter Guzzardi, editorial director of Harmony Books, whose wife, Isabel Geffner, is associate publisher of Delacorte and Dell, says, 'Life can become monolithic. You lose a little of the variety of having someone come home and talk about a totally different industry.'"
- "'It's nice to speak the same professional language, but not constantly, and especially not on weekends,' says Cathy Squires, a Columbia University bacteriologist [who shares an office with her research-scientist husband]. 'I don't always like to wake up on Saturday morning and have a whole research situation laid out in front of me when Craig's already been up for two or three hours thinking about something.'"
- "In law . . . there's the tricky issue of partnership. . . . Although a partner may bow out of decisions regarding his or her mate, the discussion beforehand is likely to make colleagues uncomfortable. 'Partners are very open,' says one at a major firm. 'If you weren't at a meeting, I can't believe you wouldn't hear everything that was said. It's got to inhibit people.'"
- "The possibility of divorce is a double jeopardy when careers are at stake. Probably a worst-case scenario was that of Joni Evans, who just stepped aside as publisher at Random House, and Richard Snyder, . . . Evans's ex-boss, soon to be her ex-spouse. Working together may have made—and ruined—their marriage, friends agree."

As more than friends and less than lovers, you can avoid the pitfalls cited in these examples by limiting your personal attraction to the workplace, where you share professional interests and enjoy each other's company. Then at the end of the day you can go home to a fresh face and a different set of interests.

Satisfaction in the Workplace

We are part of a society that is becoming increasingly individualistic and more inner directed, according to Joseph T. Plummer, managing director of Paine Webber/Young and Rubicam Ventures in New York. He calls this process a *paradigm shift*, explaining that "a social paradigm is that constellation of values, beliefs, and experiences that—because they are shared by the majority of the members of society—enable people to work together and to communicate with one another with some degree of social success. When a culture undergoes a paradigm shift, the new paradigm does not immediately replace the old one as the dominant paradigm. Rather, the shift occurs in . . . phases."

Plummer cites Young and Rubicam research that shows outer-directed people in the United States declining from 67 percent in 1984 to 62 percent in 1990 while inner-directed people rose from 22 percent to 26 percent in the same time period. Here is what that means for the values that drive us, according to a table in Plummer's article "Changing Values: The New Emphasis on Self-Actualization, in *The Futurist*.

These trends will lead to work environments that favor "high levels of creativity, flexibility, and responsiveness by organizations rather than bigness and consistency." Higher ethical standards will be expected. A lot of value will be attached to lifelong education, growth in the arts, and maintaining good health. Plummer concludes that "research on changing values points to the need to rethink our old rules, recognize emerging new rules, and spend time understanding people as

TRADITIONAL VALUES	NEW VALUES
self-denial ethic	self-fulfillment ethic
higher standard of living	better quality of life
traditional sex roles	blurring of sex roles
accepted definition of success	individualized definition of success
traditional family life	alternative families
faith in industry, institutions	self-reliance
live to work	work to live
hero worship	love of ideas
expansionism	pluralism
patriotism	less nationalistic
unparalleled growth	information/service growth
receptivity to technology	technology orientation

human beings with the capacity for change. If our efforts to anticipate the future rely primarily on economics and technology, we could miss wonderful opportunities for a better world."

The more-than-friends-less-than-lovers relationship offers you a way to accommodate these trends while working in a large, complex organization. Together, you find a personal source of motivation and establish a smaller, more intimate work environment, conducive to increased productivity with a compatible member of the opposite sex who complements you professionally and adds a safe measure of personal pleasure to your work. As work partners who relate as working intimates, you can use your personal attraction as an important mechanism for achieving the paradigm shift in your own lives. Your higher level of satisfaction at work will lead to higher productivity for your employer.

Finding Pleasure in Your Relationship

We all seek pleasure in our lives and work. As George Leonard, author of *Ecstasy and Education*, writes:

Pleasure calls you to eat when you're hungry, drink when you're thirsty, sleep when you're weary; to care for others, to make love, and to do numerous other things that are good for you, for society, and for the species. . . . And our primitive ancestors, who lived closely with nature, probably had less trouble pursuing pleasurable impulses than we do; anthropological studies show that with every advance of technology, the societal demand for impulse control rises, even in primitive bands and tribes.

One of the most important challenges you and your partner will face as more-than-friends-less-than-lovers is developing the skills to manage the call of sexual pleasure so that it ends up safely doing what you want it to do—energizing your professional relationship.

Leonard offers a number of guidelines for managing our pleasure impulse that may prove valuable as you encounter difficulty struggling with this problem.

Avoid the quick-fix route to pleasure. *Learn to love the plateau. . . . The development of almost everything in life involves working diligently for extended periods of time without seeming to get anywhere. Now and then you enjoy a spurt of progress, of easy success—the occasion for celebration. But there's an inescapable rhythm of existence that demands that, for lasting success and satisfaction, you have to spend most of your time on a plateau.*

Think about this as you monitor each other's behavior and expectations, and you will fully enjoy the limited pleasures you bring each other. You won't have the dramatic consummation of an affair, but rather the sustained high of an attraction that brings you more pleasure than pain as long as your relationship lasts—and in the midst of existing commitments and satisfactions that aren't destroyed in the process.

Adopt the Zen strategy of finding joy in the commonplace. *. . . A visit to a Zen retreat quickly reveals that, po-*

tentially, everything *is meditation—building a stone wall, eating, walking from one place to another, sweeping a hallway. The secret is in the way you approach the matter of time. . . . Most of us have been taught to direct our attention to the past and to the future. Those are nice places to visit— necessary, in fact, for survival and success. But they are not where pleasure resides. If you're really interested in finding pleasure, start by directing your attention to the present. . . . In lovemaking, it's enough to say that the very essence of sex and sensuality lies in staying in the present moment. . . . But we have to keep reminding ourselves to cherish the moment, especially in a society that stokes our craving for objects and experiences out there in the future or back in the past.*

What could be a more logical place to find pleasure than in your everyday work? Who could be a more ordinary source of that pleasure than the colleague who shares the experience? The more-than-friends-less-than-lovers relationship is designed to exploit the simple pleasures of the present. You define no permanent future together, agreeing to work together only as long as it is mutually beneficial. You have no right or reason to dwell on each other's past; only those experiences that are shared voluntarily make it to the table for discussion.

Don't be a loner. Do things with and for people. If there's anything that studies on health show, it's that man is a social animal, that good health involves a loving, caring connection with other people. This doesn't deny the joys of solitude . . . a retreat to the fastness of your own room, a long, lonely walk. There's an old tradition that enlightenment requires a withdrawal from daily entanglements, a period of time in a literal or figurative desert. But even for a saint, there's the return to the family of humanity and a chance to do service for others. . . . It's not just giving pleasure; it's also receiving. In concert, these two essential human acts join in a circle of interaction that expands with use. When the circle is complete, the more you give, the more you get, and vice versa.

So it is in the more-than-friends–less-than-lovers relationship, where you share deliberately bounded but important
aspects of your being with another person. Learning to trust
and give, receive and care without unwanted strings, you find
true pleasure in your working interaction. You've always been
able to verbalize your personal and business ethics. Now
you've tested them, resisted the temptation to push them aside
to pursue fleeting pleasure, and deliberately established a fulfilling relationship that meets your ethical and moral standards. You take each other beyond normal colleague relationships and friendships and find a unique pleasure based on man/
woman intimacy without sex but not without desire.

> Honor your sexual desire. Stay sensual. . . . *Sexual
> arousal calls us to our most primal pleasure and offers us the
> latest news about creation itself. The act of love turns ugly only
> when it becomes an instrument for exploitation. If you can't
> bring love to it, you can at least bring a caring heart. The health
> of sex and sensuality lies in the personal, in that ancient, ever-
> new feeling of unselfish bonding that can create a new relation-
> ship, a new life, or a new society.*
>
> Yes, it's true that the senses can lead you astray and the
> pursuit of pleasure can get you in trouble. Sensual pleasure
> needs the guidance of practical and ethical judgment. But you
> won't gain . . . by repeatedly vetoing the vote of the senses and
> denigrating the wisdom of the body. Nature was neither ca-
> pricious nor perverted in making sure that, *other things being
> equal, what feels good is good for you.*

Sexuality plays a crucial role in our lives—far broader
than we often realize. Leonard puts it eloquently as he writes,
"Love is healthier than hate. Enthusiasm is healthier than
despair. Hope is healthier than cynicism. . . . Nothing else
speaks with the robust clarity of sensuality, which is not just
the spice of lust or the urge of love and creation, but also . . .
the pulsing caress of a song, the lure of speed, salt spray on

your lips . . . all those delightful sensory messages that call you to the present joys of this world and just possibly give you the zest to go beyond."

In a more-than-friends-less-than-lovers relationship, you recognize physical attraction as a motivator and responsibly enjoy the pleasure of sexual energy. You don't bring each other love, but you do bring deep caring as you use your sexual attraction to open the floodgates of boundless creativity and energy on the job.

As Leonard puts it:

> *There's no question that gratification must in many cases be delayed in order for you to enjoy long-term satisfaction. But it's really not pleasure itself that's at loggerheads with the world, but rather its misappropriation. There are many immediate delights that are good for you and for society. And there are ways of finding quite a bit of joy—spontaneous, sensuous joy—not through the achievement of material or symbolic goals, but through disciplined practice. Yes, pleasure can lead you astray, but properly harnessed, it remains an effective guide for good living and good health.*

THE PROMISE FULFILLED

You are two veterinarians in a rural partnership, two MBAs completing a Fortune 500 company's management-trainee program at a major business center, a pair of service technicians making the regional circuit together for a large retailer—you are any man or woman who ever went to work, became attracted to a member of the opposite sex, and decided you couldn't just do the simple thing and fall in love.

You had other personal obligations, strong business ethics, and limitations that spoke more loudly than your libido—or Cupid. There was an attraction that said, "Oops! I could have a problem here," and a mature strain of judgment somewhere deeper inside that responded, "No. I *won't* have a problem here!" but went on to say, "However, I *will* have what this promising person has to give me—and they will have me. We'll find a way to fit into each other's lives."

Your attraction lingered and changed with the seasons of your relationship to the point where you now share a fulfilling and productive man/woman association you never considered possible. The love never came and the sex didn't happen—but together you seem to know what it would have felt like if they had. And you went another direction. By choice.

You decided that your relationship would make a fine emotional adjunct to your work, but would never dominate it—or you. The benefits of being teamed with someone who stimulated your mind and body made life easier at work and the job more fulfilling and lucrative. Romance would have ruined it all, so you passed on the biologically obvious and set about the task of building the psychologically and emotionally unique structure of a more-than-friends-less-than-lovers relationship.

What you have created is amazingly satisfying and workable. You take time out from each other and go home to friends and family to recharge yourself for new work. You pursue your work with an abandon you never could afford if it was also necessary for the two of you to get along harmoniously, continuously in your broader lives.

You do genuinely inspired work together and honestly love it. You have friends, coworkers, and family who know you are special to each other but feel no threat to their own places in your lives. Your relationship, though different, rings true to these important people, and this is a source of unending satisfaction for you. And finally, you do have each other, after a fashion, the way you've chosen to be—as more than friends, less than lovers.

Notes

CHAPTER 1

Page 7   "Each person has to work out his or her own resolution . . ."
           David L. Bradford et al. The Executive Man and Woman: The
           Issue of Sexuality. In Dail Ann Neugarten and Jay M. Shafritz,
           eds., *Sexuality in Organizations: Romantic and Coercive Behaviors at
           Work*. Oak Park, IL: Moore Publishing Company, p. 27.

Page 8   "begin slugging through professional channels . . ." Patricia A.
           McBroom (1986). *The Third Sex*. New York: William Morrow
           and Company, p. 216.

Page 9   . . . work teams composed of men and women were more pro-
           ductive . . . Norma Peterson (1988, February 22). When a
           Friend Goes from Platonic to Passionate. *USA Today*, p. 5D.

Page 9   "a certain zest, a special excitement . . . a flirtatious qual-
           ity . . ." Lillian B. Rubin (1985). *Just Friends*. New York: Harper
           and Row, p. 157.

Page 9   "Sex, whether acted on or not, both gives the relationship . . ."
           Rubin, p. 149.

Page 13   "twenty years ago women with chemical engineering de-
           grees . . ." Janice Castro (1990 Fall). On the Job, Get Set: Here
           They Come! *Time* (Special Issue on Women), p. 50.

Page 13   "Nearly 18 percent of doctors are now women . . ." Castro, p. 50.

Page 13　"The demography of the American labor force . . ." James Martin and Sheila Murphy (1988, August 21). Romance at the Office. *Washington Post,* p. C4.

Page 13　"in medicine, law and management, [women] have increased . . ." Barbara Ehrenreich (1990, Fall). Sorry, Sisters, This Is Not the Revolution. *Time* (Special Issue on Women), p. 15.

Page 14　"Business travel, once . . . the domain of salespersons, sports . . ." Denise V. Lang (1988). *The Phantom Spouse.* New York: Dodd, Mead and Company, p. 5.

Page 16　"we become interested in people . . ." Peter Marsh (1988). *Eye to Eye.* Topsfield, MA: Salem House, p. 167.

Page 17　"People get involved in the workplace because . . ." Marilyn Moats Kennedy (1985). *Office Warfare.* New York: Ballentine Books, p. 263.

Page 18　"Shared work brings shared emotions . . ." Martin and Murphy, p. C4.

Page 18　"As people who have interesting careers . . ." Robert Seidenberg (1973). *Corporate Wives—Corporate Casualties.* New York: AMACOM, p. 129.

Page 18　"People in the same workplace tend to be . . ." Leslie Aldridge Westoff (1985). *Corporate Romance.* New York: Times Books, p. 14.

Page 19　"have months, even years, to learn about each other . . ." Kennedy, p. 263.

Page 19　"The time we spend with others . . ." Michael McGill (1985). *The McGill Report on Male Intimacy.* New York: Holt, Rinehart and Winston, p. 14.

Page 20　"vulnerable to double doses of trouble . . ." McBroom, p. 204.

Page 22　"Nearly every woman who befriends a man . . ." McGill, p. 106.

Page 29　"One of the most consistent findings of social psychological research. . ." Bradford et al., pp. 25–26.

Page 29　"Many recognized that there was a sexual undercurrent . . ." Peterson, p. 5D.

CHAPTER 2

Page 37   "For most of us, the sexual encounter taps layers of feeling . . ." Lillian B. Rubin (1985). *Just Friends.* New York: Harper and Row, p. 152.

Page 50   "The reality is that women experience life differently from men . . ." Anastasia Toufexis (1990, Fall). Coming from a Different Place. *Time* (Special Issue on Women), p. 64–65.

Page 56   "The accepted wisdom in the corporate world . . ." Maureen Dowd (1991, February). Everything but Sex: The New Office Affair. *Mademoiselle,* p. 121.

Page 56   "two persons of opposite sex considered together, . . ." *Webster's Encyclopedic Unabridged Dictionary of the English Language.* (1989). New York: Portland House, dilithium Press, p. 334.

Page 59   "our social history and the myths we have digested . . ." Leslie Aldridge Westoff (1985). *Corporate Romance.* New York: Times Books, pp. 165–66.

CHAPTER 3

Page 76   "sex, whether acted on or not, both gives the relationship . . ." Lillian B. Rubin, (1985). *Just Friends.* New York: Harper and Row, p. 149.

Page 80   "Being influenced and responding either consciously or unconsciously . . ." David L. Bradford et al. (1975). The Executive Man and Woman: The Issue of Sexuality. In Dail Ann Neugarten and Jay M. Shafritz, eds., *Sexuality in Organizations: Romantic and Coercive Behaviors at Work.* Oak Park, IL: Moore Publishing Company, p. 21.

Page 88   "between partners who share similar values, interests, and goals . . ." Robin Norwood (1985). *Women Who Love Too Much.* New York: Pocket Books, p. 273.

Page 92   "There is no more compelling chemistry than this feeling . . ." Norwood, p. 82.

Page 110   "Critical information about what is happening at the boundary . . ." Peter Rutter (1989). *Sex in the Forbidden Zone.* Los Angeles: Jeremy P. Tarcher, pp. 165–66.

CHAPTER 4

Page 116   "where creative struggle is possible between two people . . ."
Lillian B. Rubin (1985). *Just Friends.* New York: Harper and Row,
p. 183.

Page 128   "In our head, we remind ourselves that . . ." Rubin, p. 153.

Page 139   "The sexual boundary is very easy to see once one has accepted . . ." Peter Rutter (1989). *Sex in the Forbidden Zone.* Los
Angeles: Jeremy P. Tarcher, p. 164.

Page 153   "In order to express differentness, judgment must be removed . . ." Shirley Gehrke Luthman (1972). *Intimacy: The
Essence of Male and Female.* Tiburon, CA: Mehertable and Company, p. 31.

CHAPTER 5

Page 165   "needs are arranged along a hierarchy of priority . . ." Calvin S.
Hall and Gardner Lindsey (1957). *Theories of Personality.* New
York: John Wiley and Sons, p. 326.

CHAPTER 6

Page 220   "Not only are nonsexual love relationships common . . ."
Maureen Dowd (1991, February). Everything but Sex: The New
Office Affair. *Mademoiselle,* p. 121.

Page 220   "Office affairs used to mean behind the doors . . ." Amy Levin
Cooper (1991, February). Letter from the Editor. *Mademoiselle,*
p. 20.

Page 221   "letting the attraction work as an underlying charge . . ."
Dowd, p. 121.

Page 221   "people may be making more mature decisions about not . . ."
Ibid., p. 122.

Page 221   "The tension is not a bad thing—sometimes it makes you . . ."
Ibid.

Page 222   "not only makes you want to work longer; it also stirs . . ." Ibid.

Page 222   "The main thing about these relationships is that they psych . . ." Dowd, pp. 121–22.

Page 222   "The more subtle changes necessary to successfully manage . . ." Janice Castro (1990 Fall). On the Job, Get Set: Here They Come! *Time* (Special Issue on Women), p. .52.

Page 229   "Will business judgment be affected by the relationship . . ." Marilyn Moats Kennedy (1985). *Office Warfare.* New York: Ballentine Books, pp. 265–67.

CHAPTER 7

Page 232   "When we look to a spouse or a lover to meet all . . ." David Scheff (1991, March). Interview with M. Scott Peck. *Playboy,* p. 52.

Page 233   "one of our myths is that we should be completely . . ." Scheff, p. 62.

Page 233   "the couple who say, 'What's the problem?. . . ." Ibid.

Page 233   "celestial boot camp," Ibid.

Page 233   "the one most fiendishly designed is sex." Ibid.

Page 233   "someone for a day or two or even a year or two . . ." Ibid.

Page 234   "She responds to him . . . early on. She . . . moves close . . ." Morton H. Shaevitz (1987, April). His 'N Hers Fantasies. *Health,* p. 76.

Page 235   "the more trusting we are, the more likely we are to . . ." Ibid.

Page 235   "Although trust in a partner means different things to different . . ." Avery, p. 27.

Page 235   "how a couple demonstrates their dedication is . . . a personal . . ." Ibid., p. 31.

Page 236   "By identifying the immediate underlying hurt and . . ." Ibid.

Page 236   "Your inclination may be to trust less . . ." Caryl S. Avery (1989, May). How Do You Build Intimacy in an Age of Divorce? *Pyschology Today,* p. 29.

Page 236   "Instead of complaining, initiators [those troubled by their . . ."
Diane Vaughan (1987, July). The Long Goodbye. *Psychology Today*, p. 38.

Page 237   "The signals become increasingly bold, however, as initiators . . ." Ibid., p. 42.

Page 238   "True trust is felt, not willed . . . It must be developed over time . . ." Ibid.

Page 243   Heed Dr. Diane Vaughan's counsel on the tendency . . . Ibid., p. 38.

Page 246   "picture love as a triangle . . . [with] me side . . ." Mark Golin (1987, July). A Different Kind of Love Triangle. *Prevention*, p. 80.

Page 246   The length of each of the triangle's sides represents the relative amounts of passion . . . Ibid.

Page 248   "People are no longer accepting the answers they've been given; . . ." Scheff, p. 44.

CHAPTER 8

Page 250   we, as humans, have a unique ability to draw up . . . *Smithsonian World* (1991, January 23). *Gender: The Enduring Paradox*. Washington, D.C.: Public Broadcasting System, WETA Channel 26.

Page 252   "Self-actualization is not accomplished without struggle . . ." Calvin S. Hall and Gardner Lindsey (1957). *Theories of Personality*. New York: John Wiley and Sons, p. 481.

Page 252   "there are only two valid reasons to get married . . ." David Scheff (1991, March). Interview with M. Scott Peck. *Playboy*, p. .52.

Page 253   CBS News correspondents Betsy Aaron and Richard Threlkeld . . . Fran Schumer (1990, November 19). The New Nepotism: Married Couples Are Working Together All Over. *New York*, pp. 49, 51.

Page 253   A pair of air-traffic controllers at La Guardia said, "Our work is . . ." Ibid, p. 49.

Page 253   The shared commitment to a profession or a cause can be . . . Barbara Kantrowitz et al. (1988, February 15). Love in the Office: The Old Rules of Conduct Don't Seem to Work Anymore. *Newsweek*, pp. 50–51.

Page 254   "It seems likely that employees will keep looking for love . . ."
           Ibid., p. 52.

Page 254   "for ambitious careerists who want to be recognized for . . ."
           Ibid., pp. 51–51.

Page 255   "professionally, it seemed to make sense. 'The situation . . .'"
           Schumer, p. 48.

Page 255   "There are disadvantages [to couples working together] as . . ."
           Ibid., p. 49.

Page 255   "The possibility of divorce is a double jeopardy when ca-
           reers . . ." Ibid., p. 51.

Page 256   "a social paradigm is that constellation . . ." Joseph T. Plummer.
           (1989, January–February). Changing Values: The New Em-
           phasis on Self-Actualization. *Futurist,* p. 10.

Page 256   outer-directed people in the United States declining . . . Ibid.,
           p. 13.

Page 256   "high levels of creativity, flexibility, and responsiveness by . . ."
           Ibid., p. 13.

Page 256   "research on changing values point to the need to rethink . . ."
           Ibid.

Page 257   Table. Ibid., p. 10.

Page 258   "Pleasure calls you to eat when you're hungry, drink when . . ."
           George Leonard (1989, May). The Case for Pleasure. *Esquire,*
           p. 153.

Page 258   "Avoid the quick-fix route to pleasure. Learn to love the
           plateau . . ." Ibid.

Page 258   "Adopt the Zen strategy of finding joy in the common-
           place . . ." Leonard, p. 156.

Page 259   "Don't be a loner, Do things with and for people. If there's . . ."
           Ibid.

Page 260   "Honor your sexual desire. Stay sensual. . . . Sexual . . ." Ibid.

Page 260   "Love is healthier than hate. Enthusiasm is healthier . . ." Ibid.

Page 261   "There's no question that gratification must in many cases . . ."
           Ibid., p. 154.

Bibliography

Alger, Pat; Brooks, Garth; and Bastian, Larry (1990). "Unanswered Prayers." Bait and Beer Music/Forerunner Music/Major Bob Music/Mid-Summer Music.

Avery, Caryl S. (May 1989). How Do You Build Intimacy in an Age of Divorce? *Psychology Today*, pp. 27–31.

Bradford, David L.; Sargent, Alice G.; and Sprague, Melinda S. (1975). The Executive Man and Woman: The Issue of Sexuality. In *Sexuality in Organizations: Romantic and Coercive Behaviors at Work*, edited by Dail Ann Neugarten and Jay M. Shafritz. Oak Park, IL: Moore Publishing Company.

Castro, Janice (Fall 1990). On the Job, Get Set: Here They Come! *Time* (Special Issue, Women), pp. 50–52.

Cooper, Amy Levin (February 1991). Letter from the Editor. *Mademoiselle*, p. 20.

Denholtz, Elaine (1981). *Having It Both Ways*. New York: Stein and Day.

Dolesh, Daniel J., and Lehman, Sherelynn I. (1985). *Love Me Love Me Not*. New York: McGraw-Hill.

Dowd, Maureen (February 1991). Everything but Sex: The New Office Affair. *Mademoiselle*, pp. 121–23, 181.

Ehrenreich, Barbara (Fall 1990). Sorry, Sisters, This Is Not the Revolution. *Time* (Special Issue, Women), p. 15.

Engleman, Paul (February 1989). Something Happens: What We Know About the Chemistry of Desire. *Playboy*, pp. 84–85.

Fast, Julius (1970). *Body Language.* New York: M. Evans and Company.

Gibbs, Nancy (Fall 1990). The Dreams of Youth. *Time* (Special Issue, Women), pp. 10–14.

Glucksman, Mary S. (April 1991). The Constant Office: The Dark Side of the Boom. *Omni,* pp. 36, 78.

Golin, Mark (July 1987). A Different Kind of Love Triangle. *Prevention,* pp. 80–82, 116.

Gutek, Barbara A. (1985). *Sex and the Workplace.* San Francisco: Jossey Bass.

Guttman, Stephanie (February 1991). Sexual Harassment: When Does Policy Become Propaganda? *Playboy,* pp. 37–39.

Hall, Calvin S., and Lindsey, Gardner (1957). *Theories of Personality.* New York: John Wiley and Sons.

Hinson, Hal (December 12, 1990). The Golden Boy's Golden Years. *Washington Post,* pp. G1, G4.

Hutchinson, Michael (April 1990). Sex on the Brain. *Playboy,* pp. 77–78, 88, 152–54.

Jaffe, Dennis, and Scott, Cynthia (July 1988). Take This Job and Love It! Turn Your Work into Pleasure. *Prevention,* pp. 31–34, 96–97.

Kantrowitz, Barbara, et al. (February 15, 1988). Love in the Office: The Old Rules of Conduct Don't Seem to Work Anymore. *Newsweek,* pp. 48–52.

Keen, Sam, and Zur, Ofer (November 1989). Who Is the New Ideal Man? *Psychology Today,* pp. 54–60.

Kennedy, Marilyn Moats (1985). *Office Warfare.* New York: Ballentine Books.

Kinsey, A. C., et al. (1948). *Sexual Behavior in the Human Male.* Philadelphia: W. B. Saunders.

———. (1953). *Sexual Behavior in the Human Female.* Philadelphia: W. B. Saunders.

Lang, Denise V. (1988). *The Phantom Spouse.* New York: Dodd, Mead and Company.

Leonard, George (May 1989). The Case for Pleasure. *Esquire*, pp. 153–56.

Luthman, Shirley Gehrke (1972). *Intimacy: The Essence of Male and Female*. Tiburon, CA: Mehertable and Company.

Mainiero, Lisa A. (1989). *Office Romance: Love, Power and Sex in the Workplace*. New York: Rawson Associates, MacMillan Publishing Company.

Marsh, Peter (1988). *Eye to Eye*. Topsfield, MA: Salem House.

Martin, James, and Murphy, Sheila (August 21, 1988). Romance at the Office. *Washington Post*, pp. C3–C4.

Masters, William H., and Johnson, Virginia E. (1966). *Human Sexual Response*. Boston: Little, Brown and Company.

McBroom, Patricia A. (1986). *The Third Sex*. New York: William Morrow and Company.

McGill, Michael (1985). *The McGill Report on Male Intimacy*. New York: Holt, Rinehart and Winston.

Mead, Margaret (1978). A Proposal: We Need Taboos on Sex at Work. In *Sexuality in Organizations: Romantic and Coercive Behaviors at Work*, edited by Dail Ann Neugarten and Jay M. Shafritz. Oak Park, IL: Moore Publishing Company. (Reprinted from *Redbook*, April 1978, pp. 31, 33, 38).

Michaels, Leonard (December 1, 1990). This Space Is for Real. *New York Times*, p. 25.

Norwood, Robin (1985). *Women Who Love Too Much*. New York: Pocket Books.

Owen, David (February 1987). Reports and Comment: Work Marriage. *Atlantic*, p. 22.

Peck, M. Scott. *The Road Less Traveled, Part Two: Love*. New York: Simon and Schuster. Sound cassette.

Peterson, Norma (February 22, 1988). When a Friend Goes from Platonic to Passionate. *USA Today*, p. 5D.

Pietropinto, Anthony, and Simenauer, Jacqueline (1977). *Beyond the Male Myth*. New York: New York Times Book Company.

Playboy Advisor (December 1990). *Playboy*, p. 42.

———. (November 1990). *Playboy*, p. 47.

Plummer, Joseph T. (January–February 1989). Changing Values: The New Emphasis on Self-Actualization. *Futurist*, pp. 8, 10–13.

Rubin, Lillian B. (1985). *Just Friends*. New York: Harper and Row.

Rumreich, Judith M. (November 14, 1990). Personal interview.

Rutter, Peter (1989). *Sex in the Forbidden Zone*. Los Angeles: Jeremy P. Tarcher.

Sarnoff, Irving, and Sarnoff, Suzanne (October 1989). The Dialectic of Marriage. *Psychology Today*, pp. 54–56.

Scarf, Maggie (1987). *Intimate Partners*. New York: Random House.

Scheff, David (March 1991). Interview with M. Scott Peck. *Playboy*, pp. 43–44, 46, 48, 50–54, 56, 58–60.

Schumer, Fran (November 19, 1990). The New Nepotism: Married Couples Are Working Together All Over. *New York*, pp. 46–51.

Seidenberg, Robert (1973). *Corporate Wives—Corporate Casualties*. New York: AMACOM.

Shaevitz, Morton H. (April 1987). His 'N Her Fantasies. *Health*, pp. 74–76, 85.

Smith, Brian R., and Milani, Myrna M. (1989). *Beyond the Magic Circle: The Role of Intimacy in Business*. Unity, NH: Fainshaw Press.

Smithsonian World (January 23, 1991). *Gender: The Enduring Paradox*. Washington, D.C.: Public Broadcasting System, WETA Channel 26.

Tannen, Deborah (1990). *You Just Don't Understand*. New York: William Morrow and Company.

Tehan, Arline B. (November 1990). George Bernard Shaw, In Love and Out. *Smithsonian*, pp. 154–68.

Toufexis, Anastasia (Fall 1990). Coming from a Different Place. *Time* (Special Issue, Women), pp. 64–66.

Vaughan, Diane (July 1987). The Long Goodbye. *Psychology Today*, pp. 37–42.

Webster's Encyclopedic Unabridged Dictionary of the English Language. (1989). New York: Portland House, Dilithium Press.

Weinrich, James D. (1987). *Sexual Landscapes.* New York: Charles Scribner's Sons.

Welych, Maria T. (May 4, 1987). Companies Crack Down on Paying for Spouse Travel. *Business Travel News*, p. 16.

Westoff, Leslie Aldridge (1985). *Corporate Romance.* New York: Times Books.